the Unofficial Guide™ to Investing in Mutual Funds

Stacie Zoe Berg

D0681861

Macmillan • USA

Macmillan General Reference
A Pearson Education Macmillan Company
1633 Broadway
New York, New York 10019-6785

ISBN: 0-02-862920-5

Manufactured in the United States of America

10 9 8 7 6 5 4 3 2 1

First edition

To my wonderful husband, parents, sister, and brother

Acknowledgments

I want to thank my husband for all his support and enthusiasm; my parents for teaching me the value of a dollar and for all their support; my uncle for his support; Nancy Mikhail, senior editor, for allowing me to write this book and for her great sense of humor; Al McDermid, development editor, for all his hard work; Jennifer Perillo, managing editor; Amy Borrelli, copy editor; Mike Thomas, production editor; and the technical editors, Howard Yasgur, Craig Israelsen, Arnie Koonin, and Alaric Sang Hu; and all the other editors and support staff who worked behind the scenes to help make this book a useful tool for investors.

Contents

The *Unofficial Guide* Reader's Bill of Rights

We Give You More Than the Official Line

Welcome to the *Unofficial Guide* series of Lifestyles titles—books that deliver critical, unbiased information that other books can't or won't reveal—*the inside scoop*. Our goal is to provide you with the *most accessible, useful* information and advice possible. The recommendations we offer in these pages are not influenced by the corporate line of any organization or industry; we give you the hard facts, whether those institutions like them or not. If something is ill-advised or will cause a loss of time and/or money, we'll give you ample warning. and if it is a worthwhile option, we'll let you know that, too.

Armed and Ready

Our hand-picked authors confidently and critically report on a wide range of topics that matter to smart readers like you. Our authors are passionate about their subjects, but have distanced themselves enough from them to help you be armed and protected, and help you make educated decisions as you go through your process. It is our intent that, from having read this book, you will avoid the pitfalls everyone else falls into and get it right the first time.

Don't be fooled by cheap imitations; this is the *genuine article Unofficial Guide* series from Macmillan Publishing. You may be familiar with our proven track record of the travel *Unofficial Guides*, which have more than three million copies in print. Each year thousands of travelers—new and old—are armed with a brand new, fully updated edition of the flagship *Unofficial Guide to Walt Disney World*, by Bob Sehlinger. It is our intention here to provide you with the same level of objective authority that Mr. Sehlinger does in his brainchild.

The Unofficial Panel of Experts

Every work in the Lifestyle *Unofficial Guides* is intensively inspected by a team of three top professionals in their fields. These experts review the manuscript for factual accuracy, comprehensiveness, and an insider's determination as to whether the manuscript fulfills the credo in this Reader's Bill of Rights. In other words, our Panel ensures that you are, in fact, getting "the inside scoop."

Our Pledge

The authors, the editorial staff, and the Unofficial Panel of Experts assembled for *Unofficial Guides* are determined to lay out the most valuable alternatives available for our readers. This dictum means that our writers must be explicit, prescriptive, and above all, direct. We strive to be thorough and complete, but our goal is not necessarily to have the "most" or "all" of the information on a topic; this is not, after all, an encyclopedia. Our objective is to help you narrow down your options to the best of what is available, unbiased by affiliation with any industry or organization.

In each *Unofficial Guide* we give you:

- Comprehensive coverage of necessary and vital information

- Authoritative, rigidly fact-checked data

- The most up-to-date insights into trends

- Savvy, sophisticated writing that's also readable

- Sensible, applicable facts and secrets that only an insider knows

Special Features

Every book in our series offers the following six special sidebars in the margins that were devised to help you get things done cheaply, efficiently, and smartly.

1. "Timesaver"—tips and shortcuts that save you time.

2. "Moneysaver"—tips and shortcuts that save you money.

3. "Watch Out!"—more serious cautions and warnings.

4. "Bright Idea"—general tips and shortcuts to help you find an easier or smarter way to do something.

5. "Quote"—statements from real people that are intended to be prescriptive and valuable to you.

6. "Unofficially…"—an insider's fact or anecdote.

We also recognize your need to have quick information at your fingertips, and have thus provided the following comprehensive sections at the back of the book:

1. **Glossary:** Definitions of complicated terminology and jargon.

2. **Internet Resource Directory:** Lists of relevant agencies, associations, institutions, Web sites, etc.

3. **Recommended Reading List:** Suggested titles that can help you get more in-depth information on related topics.

4. **Index.**

Letters, Comments, and Questions from Readers

We strive to continually improve the *Unofficial* series, and input from our readers is a valuable way for us to do that. Many of those who have used the *Unofficial Guide* travel books write to the authors to ask questions, make comments, or share their own discoveries and lessons. For lifestyle *Unofficial Guides*, we would also appreciate all such correspondence, both positive and critical, and we will make best efforts to incorporate appropriate readers' feedback and comments in revised editions of this work.

How to write to us:

Unofficial Guides
Macmillan Lifestyle Guides
Macmillan Publishing
1633 Broadway
New York, NY 10019

Attention: Reader's Comments

The *Unofficial Guide* Panel of experts

The *Unofficial* editorial team recognizes that you've purchased this book with the expectation of getting the most authoritative, carefully inspected information currently available. toward that end, on each and every title in this series, we have selected a minimum of three "official" experts comprising the "Unofficial Panel" who painstakingly review the manuscripts to ensure: factual accuracy of all data; inclusion of the most up-to-date and relevant information; and that, from an insider's perspective, the authors have armed you with all the necessary facts you need—but the institutions don't want you to know.

For *The Unofficial Guide to Investing in Mutual Funds,* we are proud to introduce the following panel of experts:

Alaric Sang Hu Mr. Hu is an Investment Research Analyst covering the High Yield Debt market. He focuses primarily on the Media and Telecommunications industries, which represent approximately 40% of the entire High Yield market, and is part of a research group that has been named to Institutional Investor Magazine's All-America Fixed Income Research Team for the past three years. His previous work experience includes Fixed Income and Equity Derivatives Trading and Sales as well as Money Market Trading. Mr. Hu holds a Finance degree from The Wharton School of Business and a degree in English Literature from the University of Pennsylvania.

Howard Yasgur Howard Yasgur purchased his first stock at age 13. Ever since, he has been researching and investing in stocks, bonds, and mutual funds.

In 1992, his hobby became a career when he joined Gradison-McDonald Investments in Cincinnati, Ohio as an investment consultant. He is an NASD/NYSE Registered Representative and a Licensed Insurance Representative. He prides himself on helping his clients by involving them in the financial planning process.

Howard can be heard as a guest on several Cincinnati radio programs.

Craig L. Israelsen Craig L. Israelsen is an Associate Professor in the Department of Consumer and Family Economics at the University of Missouri-Columbia, where he teaches courses in Personal Finance, Investments, and Family Management. He holds a Ph.D. in Family Resource Management from Brigham Young University. He received a B.S. in Agribusiness and an M.S. in Agricultural Economics from Utah State University. Primary among his research interests is the analysis of

mutual funds and investment options for individuals and families. He is married to Tamara
Trimble Israelsen. They are the parents of six
children.

Introduction: Why Should You Invest in Mutual Funds?

Wouldn't it be great to have an extra income, something to put away for retirement or cover big expenses? One where you could just sit back and watch your money accumulate? Imagine starting out with only $2,000 at age 25 and watching it grow to nearly $100,000 by the time you turn 65 years old. Sound too good to be true?

You can put your money to work for you by investing in mutual funds. At an average market return of 10 percent annually, $2,000 can grow to nearly $100,000 in 40 years. Imagine the fortune you could accumulate if you added just $100 each month until retirement. You would have more than $700,000 by that same age, almost painlessly.

While investing in mutual funds has considerable potential for financial gains, it also poses risk. Staying out of the market, however, while less risky (at least in the short run), has a guaranteed negative impact. Inflation eats up your savings. In fact, by tucking your savings in a bank account, you're probably actually losing money. Why? Inflation at its current rate of about three percent eats up $30 out of each $1,000 annually of whatever you've socked away. Using that example, after a year, you'd only have $970. Plus, each year, inflation would eat up three percent more, and remember, inflation in the 1980s reached double digits, taking a much bigger chunk out of each dollar you saved. Meanwhile, prices continue to rise, taking another bite out of your buying power.

To find out more about inflation and the impact it has on your money, read Chapter 1, which will also tell you how you can counteract inflation's effects on your hard-earned dollars.

One strategy you can use to stay ahead of inflation is investing in the stock market using mutual funds. Rather than losing value each year, your money (again, based on historical market performance) builds upon itself. It's called compounded worth or compounded interest. Chapter 1 gives this example of the miracle of compounding:

> "Compounded growth has a snowball effect. If you take a set dollar amount, assuming an average 10 percent annual market gain, each year you'll have 10 percent more added to the pot. For example, if you had $500,000 invested, 10 percent of that would be $50,000. Add that to the principal, and you now have $550,000 invested. The next year, add in $55,000 (10 percent of the investment), and your investment for the following year becomes $605,000. By compounding your investments, in two years you've gained $105,000. That's making your money work for you."

Starting early is key. By investing $2,000 for eight years, and not one penny afterwards, you'll end up wealthier than someone who waited 8 years to get started but invested $2,000 a year for the next 32 years, assuming a 10 percent annual rate of return.

At the end of 40 years, despite having put in four times as much money, the second person's earnings will amount to $136,692 less than the person who started investing earlier. Whereas the first person with a total investment of $16,000 would end up with $515,188, the second person, who invested $64,000 would have only $378,496 at the end of 40 years. That's the power of compounded interest, letting your money earn money, as discussed in Chapter 2.

The miracle of compounded growth, as it's often called, can come in handy when you retire. However, many people spend more time planning their vacations than they do their retirement, leaving some financially strapped during their golden years. Read Chapter Two to find out more about why you need to save for retirement and how you can do it.

But it's not just saving for retirement that's important. The price of food, real estate, medicine, and other necessities has skyrocketed over the past several decades. Whereas 20 years ago it usually took just one breadwinner to buy a home and support a family, it now takes two incomes, and at that, money is often tight. And if you think making ends meet are tough now, what if you were to lose your job? Do you have enough saved up to pay your expenses for months, possibly a year? By investing enough and putting your money to work for you, if you fall on bad times in the future, it may be possible for you to live off the interest and dividends, and perhaps a bit of the principal, until you can pick yourself back up.

But why invest in mutual funds? Why not stocks, bonds, or money markets? Mutual funds have benefits that buying single stocks don't. By purchasing shares of even one fund, you're purchasing scores of stocks that have been thoroughly researched and handpicked by professional portfolio managers. You get instant diversification of your investment portfolio, and the more funds you buy into, the more diversified your portfolio becomes, reducing the risk of losing money.

Mutual funds offer:

- Growth potential
- Professional money management
- Record keeping for your account
- Diversification
- The possibility of purchasing securities that may not be available or affordable to you otherwise

Because mutual funds give you an instantly diversified portfolio and the purchasing power to get into stocks that may have exorbitantly high share prices, they provide an opportunity for financial success that was once available only to the country club set. They help level out the playing field, and, just like the stock portfolios of the wealthy, they're professionally managed by the biggest names in the business.

Chapter 3 explains all this and more, including how to develop your own financial plan.

Of course, the very rich don't have to worry as much about losing money during market fluctuations. But risk is an important consideration when it comes to investing; the stock market is not insured by the government or any other entity. A bad investment can be costly. So can market dips and bear markets.

Although there is some risk to investing in the market, over time, that risk is reduced (based on historical market performance). Looking back over the past 70 years, the stock market has outperformed other types of investments, such as bonds, certificates of deposits (CDs), and U.S. government securities. The market, which has historically averaged between 10 percent and 12 percent annually, has beat inflation, as well. Research also shows that if you lose money because of poor overall market performance, you'll probably come out ahead—way ahead—if you hold on to your investments rather than sell in a panic.

But it's tough to watch your hard-earned dollars disappear because of factors you can't control—factors such as the economy, politics, and market cycles, all of which are discussed in Chapter 6. That's why you must assess your risk tolerance and create a portfolio that matches it. For example, if you have a low tolerance for risk, that is, if you cling to every move the stock market makes and search Alan Greenspan's facial expressions for signs of future interest rate movements, you'll probably want to buy into funds that are conservative and don't fluctuate as much as aggressive funds when the market takes a dive. Chapter 6 will help you assess your risk tolerance level.

Once you know how much market volatility you can stomach, you need to pick funds that match your risk tolerance level and financial goals, which also must be determined. (Reaching your financial goals is covered in Chapters 4 and 5.) To pick funds to include in your portfolio, you must first do a little research and get answers to questions, such as:

- What type of fund is it?
- What are the fund manager's objectives?
- Who is the fund manager, and what is his track record?
- How does the fund rate?
- What do the analysts say about this fund and the stocks it holds?
- What are the characteristics of a winning mutual fund and does this fund have them?

These research strategies and more are discussed in Chapter 7.

Mutual funds pool money from thousands of investors and invest in a variety of securities, such as stocks, bonds, money markets, or a combination of these. Funds are categorized based on their investments. Chapters 8 and 9 review the different types of mutual funds. In general, there are three categories:

- Equity funds, which have mostly common stocks in their portfolio.
- Fixed income funds, which offer fixed rates of return by investing in government or corporate securities.
- Balanced funds, which invest in both stocks and bonds.

Those categories are broken down further by the characteristics of the securities they hold. As a general rule of thumb, those that go after higher returns carry more risk. Types of mutual funds include the following:

- Aggressive growth funds, which generally invest in stocks of small, lesser-known companies, seek rapid growth and capital appreciation.

- Growth funds, which generally invest in stocks of well-established companies, are considered more conservative investments than aggressive growth funds.

- International/foreign funds, which invest in securities outside of the United States, carry more risk than domestic investments but have the added benefit of investing in markets that often move in the opposite direction of domestic stock markets.

- Global funds, which invest in funds around the globe, carry a higher risk because of the foreign investments but have the added benefit of investing in a market that often moves in the opposite direction of domestic stock markets.

- Growth and income funds, which seek long-term growth of capital as well as current income through dividend distribution. In general, their risk factor falls somewhere between growth and fixed-income funds.

- Fixed-income funds, which provide a current fixed income. They often invest in government-backed bonds, and so are considered less risky.

These categories can be broken down even further. Chapters 8 and 9 discuss value funds, large caps, mid-caps, and small caps, specialty funds, index funds, money market funds, bond funds, and more.

The fund's objective and its portfolio of investments are important factors to keep in mind when designing your portfolio, since diversification is an important component of a successful investment portfolio. Because of market cycles and other factors, as discussed in Chapter 11, putting all your eggs in one basket, while exciting, isn't a wise investment strategy. Nor is trying to time the market. These and other investment strategies, primarily dollar cost averaging and the tried and true buy-and-hold strategy are also discussed in Chapter 11.

While investing can be lucrative, it is not free. There are costs associated with investing and earnings. You must pay commissions if you invest through a financial adviser or salesperson, and there are other fees. Plus, you must pay taxes, which take a big bite out of your earnings, especially if you let the IRS determine your tax strategies.

However, there are ways to reduce costs and taxes. Read about costs and get tips from industry experts in Chapter 13.

Another way to reduce costs, and a good way to research mutual funds and stocks, is by using the Internet. You can find a wealth of information on the Internet, from fund performance ratings to retirement calculators (which allow you to figure out how much you have to save, at what interest rates, and for how long in order to meet your financial goals). Read Chapter 14 to find out more about how you can use the Internet as an investment tool.

Yet another way to save money, or at least hold onto what you've got, is to avoid getting involved in scams. There are plenty of people out there who are willing to make a quick buck on your ignorance. They use strategies like the following to pique your interest and give you a sense of urgency so you'll act without due consideration:

- "Guaranteed return"
- "Limited offer"
- "Risk free"

- "High returns"
- Veil of secrecy
- High-pressured sales tactics

Experts consider these red flags. Read more about scams from the people who know—the Securities and Exchange Commission, a state security commissioner, and the North American Securities Administrators Association in Chapter 15.

And if it all is a bit overwhelming for you, return to Chapter 10. There you'll learn how to hire an investment adviser. But remember, having a basic knowledge of investing in mutual funds is still important. After all, it's your money.

The Benefits of Investing

GET THE SCOOP ON...
How exciting investing can be ▪ How you're
actually losing money by not investing ▪ How
your money can make you more money ▪ Why
you handle money the way you do ▪ What your
kids are learning from you

PART I

The Joys of Investing

Money can own you or you can own it. By owning it, you can experience true independence. If you invest your hard-earned dollars wisely, you won't have to worry so much about job stability because, even if you're fired, you'll still have money to pay your mortgage and other bills until you get a new one. You'll also have the financial ability to choose your own doctor, if the one you want is not on your health plan. Plus, you'll have the money to buy other services and products that would otherwise be unaffordable. That's what I mean by independence.

Investing in funds can be thrilling, if you pick the right funds in a bull market. It also can be satisfying, even in a volatile market, if you're patient. Sometimes you have to be patient for years. But if you are, it can really pay off.

For instance, once you accumulate, say, $250,000, dividends and increased mutual fund share prices can add up so much so that it's like having a second income, with relatively little work

3

involved. With a 10 percent annual return, you can increase your financial worth by a whopping $25,000. By reinvesting that $25,000 back into your portfolio, your investment will grow each year, even if the market bears the same interest rate. If the market drops slightly but you've increased your principal, you will still have a significant gain.

Of course, nothing is guaranteed in investing, so it's best to diversify your portfolio and commit to staying invested for the long run. History has demonstrated that the market has always come back, even from its deepest dips.

This chapter will focus on how you can make your money work for you rather than the other way around. It will explore how you handle your investments now, why you handle them as you do, and what your investment style teaches your children about handling money.

> **"**
> A billion here, a billion there, and pretty soon you're talking about real money.
> —Everett Dirksen
> **"**

The miracle of compounded growth

The whole idea of investing is to let your money make money. By leaving it in the stock market for many years and by reinvesting the dividends, your hard-earned dollars will work for you. That's the idea behind compounded growth.

Compounded growth has a snowball effect. If you take a set dollar amount, assuming an average 10 percent annual market gain, for example, each year you'll have 10 percent more added to the pot. For example, if you had $500,000 invested, 10 percent of that would be $50,000. Add that to the principal, and you now have $550,000 invested. The next year, add in $55,000 (10 percent of the investment), and your investment for the following year becomes $605,000. By compounding your investments, in 2 years you've gained $105,000. That's making your money work for you. While a 10 percent gain is not always a realistic expectation for returns, it is used here to show the effect of compounded growth.

Compounded growth is best illustrated by a story of a woman named Anne Scheiber. When she died in 1995, her story got a lot of press. Why? Because this poverty-stricken woman from an immigrant family scrimped and saved and invested almost every penny that she earned, lost everything, saved again, and made millions. In 1944 she invested $5,000 in the market, and by adding small amounts over the years, her investment grew to $20 million. How did it grow? She picked good stocks and left them alone. Even when the market dropped in 1987 and others rushed to save what they could of their investments, she left hers alone. Patience paid off for her.

Say, for example, you're 35 years old and you make just one investment of $2,000 in mutual funds. That's it. You reinvest all of your dividends back into the fund. Assuming the market returns an annual average of 10 percent on your investment, by the time you're 65 years old, you'll have accumulated $34,899. That's a gain of 1,645 percent—not bad for a one-time investment.

But what if you had made that same $2,000 investment when you were 25 years old? In that case, again with a 10 percent annual average rate of return, you would have amassed $90,519 by age 65. That's a 159 percent gain over that of waiting 10 years to invest at age 35.

And say, at age 15, you had decided to save your allowances, gift money, and anything you earned from babysitting or mowing lawns. That same $2,000 would have become $234,782 by age 65. That's a gain of 572 percent over starting at age 35

Watch Out!
Start investing as young as possible or you'll miss out on the miracle of compounded growth.

and a 159 percent gain over starting your investing when you are age 25.

But if you had waited until you were 45 years old to invest $2,000, your return would be only $13,455. And at age 55 that same $2,000 investment would reap only $5,187.

The stark contrast in these accumulations, as shown in Table 1.1, illustrates the miracle of compounded growth. The earlier you invest, the longer your investment has to grow and the longer it has to ride out market dips. You can also take advantage of these dips by reinvesting your dividends.

Note! ➡
You can end up with a lot of money for retirement by just making a one-time investment when you're young.

TABLE 1.1: VALUE OF A ONE-TIME INVESTMENT OF $2,000 AT A 10 PERCENT AVERAGE RATE OF RETURN AT AGE 65

Starting age	Investment return
15	$234,782
25	$90,519
35	$34,899
45	$13,455
55	$5,187

But what if you invested $2,000 every year until you reached age 65? How much more would you have as a result of compounded growth?

Investing more frequently over longer periods of time significantly impacts the return on your investment, as shown in Table 1.2. Moreover, if you invest at regular intervals, you will be taking advantage of buying during market dips, when shares are usually cheaper. This method is known as dollar cost averaging and will be discussed in more detail in Chapter 11.

So, if you start at age 15 and invest $2,000 per year at an annual average return of 10 percent, by the time you're 65 years old you will have invested a total of $100,000. However, your investment will be worth a whopping $2,327,817 because it has compounded for 50 years.

Likewise, if you start at age 55 and invest $2,000 a year for 10 years, again at a 10 percent average annual return, you'll have invested $20,000, which will have compounded to $31,875. Although $20,000 is a lot to invest, it did not have the time to compound into significant gains.

TABLE 1.2: ACCUMULATION OF WEALTH BY INVESTING $2,000 A YEAR, AT A 10 PERCENT ANNUAL RATE OF RETURN, UNTIL YOU REACH AGE 65

Starting age	Total invested	Total return
15	$100,000	$2,327,817
25	$80,000	$885,185
35	$60,000	$328,988
45	$40,000	$114,550
55	$20,000	$31,875

← **Note!**
You'll accumulate more wealth faster if you make investments regularly and give your investment time to compound.

How long will it take you to double your money if you reinvest your dividends? That depends on the rate of return. Use the Rule of Seventy-two to figure out different investment scenarios. (See Table 1.3.)

The Rule of Seventy-two is a simple math formula: seventy-two divided by the rate of return or interest rate equals the number of years it will take your money to double if earnings are reinvested.

Say you have $20,000 in the market and want to know how long it will take to double at a 10 percent rate of return.

$72 \div 10 = 7.2$ years

How long will it take to double at 8 percent?

$72 \div 8 = 9$ years

What if the market is performing exceptionally well and returning 15 percent over 10 years?

$72 \div 15 = 4.8$ years

Conversely, you can choose your investment risk by deciding how long you want to be in the market to double your investment.

Divide seventy-two by the number of years invested to figure out what interest rate will double your investment.

For example, if you have $10,000 and you want to double it in 10 years, the equation should look like this: $72 \div 10 = 7.2$ percent interest rate.

Note! ➡
Take a look at this table to see how many years it will take your investments to double at a given rate of return. Or you can use this chart to see what rate of return you'll need to double your money in a specified number of years.

TABLE 1.3: RULE OF SEVENTY-TWO

Rate of return	Number of years to double your investment	Rate of return	Number of years to double your investment
1%	72	14%	5.1
2%	36	15%	4.8
3%	24	16%	4.5
4%	18	17%	4.2
5%	14.4	18%	4
6%	12	19%	3.8
7%	10.3	20%	3.6
8%	9	21%	3.4
9%	8	22%	3.3
10%	7.2	23%	3.1
11%	6.5	24%	3
12%	6	25%	2.9
13%	5.5		

How inflation can eat up your (uninvested) savings

Some people are scared to put their money in the market because of the risk that they may lose some of it if the market falls. However, they are guaranteeing a loss by tucking that money safely away in a passbook account or hiding it in their mattress. How can that be? The reason is simple: inflation. Inflation eats up uninvested dollars.

Consider this: If you have $1,000 dollars today with a 5 percent inflation rate, your $1,000 is worth $950 one year later—that is, it buys 5 percent less. Everything essentially goes up in price 5 percent and you can afford less.

The Rule of Seventy-two can be used to see the impact inflation has on your money.

At 4 percent inflation, the prices of goods and services will double in 18 years: $4 \times 18 = 72$.

The current average annual inflation rate is 1.7 percent, according to the most recent available U.S. Department of Labor (DOL) statistics (June 1997–June 1998).

Inflation, however, is not steady among all industries. And inflation hasn't always been this low. Inflation in college tuition has skyrocketed in recent years, as it has in housing and communications.

Consider this: according to DOL statistics, college tuition and fees in the United States experienced an average annual inflation rate of 8.7 percent from 1978 to 1997. That's 3.8 percent more than the general average annual inflation rate of 4.9 percent during that same period.

Phone and cable rates from 1984 to 1997 had a 6.3 percent average annual inflation rate, 1.4 percent over the average annual inflation rate during those years.

Although the economics of medicine can't be easily compared to the general rate of inflation because of the many technological advances over the years that have done so much to improve medical services, nonetheless you still need to purchase services and commodities from this economic sector.

From 1978 to 1997, medical care services had a 7.4 percent average annual inflation rate while medical commodities, which include medication,

Moneysaver
Make sure you've invested your money so that it earns more than the annual average inflation rates and will cover taxes and the expenses associated with investments.

Watch Out!
When comparing inflation rates, numbers only tell part of the story. A low percent rise in inflation is still a high dollar amount. For example, 1% of $1 million equals $10,000.

experienced a 6.6 percent average annual inflation rate.

Although these percentages vary from the general average annual inflation rate by only a few points, when you're starting at a high dollar amount, even one percent is astronomical.

Another way to see the effect of inflation is to compare purchasing power, which measures the change in the number of goods you can purchase for a dollar at different times. For instance, a dollar in 1980 would buy 57 cents worth of goods in 1993. Likewise, you'd have had to spend $1.75 in 1993 to buy something that cost $1 in 1980.

Still another way to see the effects of inflation is through income. If you were earning $25,000 in 1980, in 1993 you would have had to earn $43,850 to maintain the same purchasing power. And that's not counting purchasing power in those industries that have exceeded the average annual inflation rates.

So, since salaries don't keep up with some inflationary factors, you will either afford less or need to invest your money to keep up with the highest inflationary rates or, better yet, exceed them and pocket a profit.

If you're in the 28 percent tax bracket, you must get approximately a 6 percent rate of return on your investment to break even with inflation and taxes.

Stock market history

The Dow Jones Industrial Average (DJIA) is the most-quoted market indicator in the media. The oldest index at 100-plus years, it has proven to be a reliable market trends indicator.

The DJIA started out in 1896 with 12 stocks, increasing to 20 in 1916, and climbing to the 30 U.S. "Blue Chip" stocks in 1928, where it remains today.

It's called an "average" because it originally was computed by adding up stock prices and dividing by the number of stocks.

The method for computing the average remains the same today, but the divisor has been changed in order to preserve historical continuity. Some adjustments reflect switches in the stocks that compose the DJIA. For example, if one stock in the DJIA was trading at $18.75 a share and was replaced by a stock trading at $114.875, the DJIA would appear to jump 284 points if there weren't a compensating adjustment in the divisor. Such distortions would make the industrial average useless to investors.

Adjustments in the divisor also are made when a company splits its stock. In a two-for-one split, for instance, each shareholder gets one additional share for every share held, so the total value of their holdings remains the same, despite the split. Generally, two-for-one splits cut the price per share in half. Without adjusting the divisor, this split would produce a distortion in the industrial average.

Consider this example, provided by Dow Jones Indexes: "Assume three stocks are selling at $5, $10 and $15. Their average price is $10. Now assume the $15 stock is split three-for-one, and the stock subsequently sells for $5. Nothing has happened to the value of an investment in these shares, but the average of their prices now is $6.67, not $10. An adjustment must be made to compensate so that the 'average' will remain at $10. This can be done in various ways mathematically, but at Dow Jones it is handled by changing the divisor, or the number that is divided into the total of the stock prices. In this example, the new divisor would be 2 instead of 3." (Current divisors for each of the Dow Jones averages

Bright Idea
When you get that first job out of college, invest your money rather than spending it on a nice car or expensive stereo equipment. Buy luxuries later, after your investments gain value and you can better afford them.

appear on page C3 of the *Wall Street Journal*
every day.)

The 30 stocks that make up the average are
picked by editors of the *Wall Street Journal.* It isn't a
"hot stock" index; the companies making up the
index are rarely changed, and it's this stability that
enhances the trust many people have in the DJIA.
(For a list of the companies that make up the DJIA,
see page C3 of the "Money and Investing" section in
the *Wall Street Journal* or visit the Dow Jones Indexes
Web site at http://indexes.dowjones.com.)

The DJIA differs from other indices in two ways:
It is small, with only 30 companies versus hundreds
or thousands in other indices; and it is unweighted
while almost all other indices weight their stocks by
market capitalization (price times shares outstanding). The DJIA is price-weighted, which means that
a 5 percent move in IBM when it is trading around
$100 a share affects the average twice as much as a 5
percent move in Goodyear when it is trading around
$50 a share. (However, a $1 move in IBM counts
exactly the same as a $1 move in Goodyear.) Even
with this fundamental difference, the popular
indexes generally tend to move together.

The first computed average price of industrial
stocks, on May 26, 1896, was 40.94; that number at
the beginning of 1999 hovered around 9,000.
Though noteworthy, the numbers, like 9,000, have
little significance except to where the market is and
where it's recently been. It's illustrative of a trend.
"The purpose and value of the industrial average is
to indicate the market's general trend; the numbers
are just marks on the measuring stick," according to
Dow Jones Indexes. Percentage change, on the
other hand, is more important than point change if
you're counting your money.

Historically, the DJIA has a near 10 percent annual rate of return (see Figure 1.1). Therefore, if you had invested $100 in the Dow industrial stocks in 1900, you would have more than $600,000 now, testimony to both the index's performance and the power of compounding over long periods.

**FIGURE 1.1: DOW JONES INDUSTRIAL AVERAGE
HISTORICAL PERFORMANCE**

← **Note!**
You can invest in the Dow Jones index through the Waterhouse Dow 30 Fund, a no-load, no-transaction-fee mutual fund offered through Waterhouse Securities [www.waterhouse.com/djif]).Dow Jones Industrial Average historical performance. Source: Dow Jones & Company

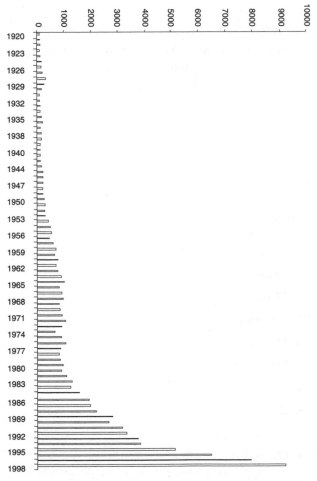

Source: Dow Jones & Company

What your investing style says about you

What do you do with the money you earn? Do you buy nice clothes, expensive cars, a big home (and in doing so, incur massive debt)? Do you go out for a lot of fancy meals? Hang out at bars? Essentially, are you buying status symbols to show your worth, or are you investing those dollars to gain a true net worth?

Many investors who end up with the biggest gains over the years tend to live more frugally. They view money as a means to independence.

But many people like to buy. Baby boomers are known for their lavish lifestyles. They're also known for having little saved compared with their incomes, and now they're scurrying to save for retirement, already having missed out on much of the miracle of compounded worth. Luckily, inflation is low and the market has had an exciting bull ride this decade.

Nonetheless, some people like to buy so much so that it inspired one psychoanalyst to divide people into spending and saving personalities.

Olivia Mellan, author of *Overcoming Overspending*, has defined eight money personalities. Each has a different investing philosophy.

- Money monks
- Spenders
- Hoarders
- Money avoiders
- Money amassers
- Risk takers
- Risk avoiders
- Overspenders

Moneysaver
The first thing that you should do after getting a paycheck is to put money into your investments as if paying a bill.

"Money monks"

Money monks tend to think that less is better because money corrupts. So if they do invest, it must be in harmony with their deeper values.

Craig Israelsen, associate professor of Consumer and Family Economics at the University of Missouri-Columbia, respects this kind of investing. These people aren't so much investing for returns but in companies that meet their social, philosophical, or religious objectives. Money isn't everything to these people, he says.

"Spenders"

Spenders want more liquidity. They tend to seek immediate gratification, so they want their investments to be easily accessible.

"Hoarders"

Hoarders use similar investment strategies, but for a different reason. They want their money close by, in a savings or checking account, for example. They think they're saving, but actually, they're not.

"Money avoiders"

Money avoiders just don't want to deal with investing. They want someone else to take care of it.

After meeting someone with this personality, Howard Yasgur, a financial adviser at Gradison-McDonald Investments, said to this client, "I will be happy to help you invest your money, but you must first commit to me that you will learn the investing basics....You're not going to get off that easy." It's important to me that my clients have enough knowledge so that they can ask the questions that will bring them into the investing process.

> 66
> A large income is the best recipe for happiness I ever heard of.
> —Jane Austen
> 99

"Money amassers"

Money amassers have the attitude that money is power. They want their money to grow. This is fine if kept in check, but some people with this personality can become "money worriers." They tend to check the status of their investments *too* often. Obsessing over the Dow can cause money amassers to transform into money avoiders in an effort to relieve their worries.

There is another concern with money amassers. Remember Anne Scheiber, the woman who turned $5,000 into $20 million? She was reportedly consumed with her investments, attending every single shareholder meeting. She also lived like a pauper. She reportedly wore the same hat and coat, summer and winter, every day. She died without friends and never married.

"Risk takers"

Risk takers, who tend to be men, like the thrill of the ride and tend not to think of the downside of risk.

"Risk avoiders"

Risk avoiders, who are more likely to be women, are afraid they'll make a mistake and lose it all. But risk is not synonymous with loss, Mellan points out.

"Overspenders"

Some try to fill the void they feel by wearing or driving all that they earn and more. However, Mellan, a recovering overspender, notes that filling one's life with material things doesn't fill the voids. Ultimately, shopping doesn't make overspenders feel loved, valued, or wanted. In fact, it leaves them wanting more.

Often, people who are wealthy—at least many of those who got their wealth by the sweat of their own

Bright Idea
To change your style, Mellan suggests practicing what you want to be once a week. A spender should do without once a week. A hoarder should spend once a week. A money monk should invest in something else, although it doesn't have to be in something that he or she deems unethical.

brow—live in modest homes and drive modest or used cars. It's knowing that they have the money that gives them self-esteem and the feeling of being in control of their lives.

Bill Stawski, a former Smith Barney broker, thinks that many people use their emotions rather than rational thought when making investment decisions. And, he says, some brokers will gladly take advantage of this.

One sales tactic some brokers use is to create an emotional situation rather than a rational scenario to sell a stock. For instance, they'll sell you in a company without a track record because you could hit it big if the company releases a successful product. Essentially, these brokers are selling pipe dreams.

Here's another example: Some mutual funds are segmented into certain industries that are socially responsible. These funds are created solely for their emotional appeal, Stawski says. They have nothing to do with earnings capabilities or future growth.

What your investing style teaches your children

Children's choices tend to reflect those of their parents. Election pollsters know they can just as easily find out about voting preferences from elementary school children as from their parents. So it should come as no surprise that your children are learning investment habits from you even if you're not aware that you're teaching them.

We deal with money all of the time. If your children see that you're comfortable investing, they will learn there's more to money than passbook savings, says Kathy Prochaska Cue, a family economist at the University of Nebraska-Lincoln.

Timesaver
Rather than teaching your children in abstract terms, show them how to invest. When you sit down to review your investments, make sure your kids are present and include them in on your thoughts.

Bright Idea
If you give a child a toy and he or she wants more, the toy will not magically multiply. But if you give a child a sum of money and invest it in mutual funds, it will multiply over time.

If you invest and speak positively about the experience even though the market is not going as you'd like, you'll teach your children that there are risks but they are not insurmountable. If you're scared or speak negatively about investing your money, your children will either refuse to get involved or they'll immerse themselves in the market, perhaps to the point of recklessness. It's better to teach them how to plan their investments.

Experts advise getting your kids started in investing at an early age. Purchase a few shares of a mutual fund in their name or let them use their savings to buy into the market. A small dividend check tends to get them interested, says Maurice Elvekrog, a licensed psychologist and chartered financial analyst in Bloomfield Hills, Mich.

People who have savings tend to look ahead to the future rather than to what's happening from day to day, he says. They also tend to have more self-esteem, particularly those people who come from families who don't invest.

Children from families without investments also feel that they're not plugged into the business world, that it has nothing to do with them, Elvekrog explains. But when they own funds, they realize that the business world does indeed affect them. Elvekrog says that young people who invest will feel like a part of the financial world, and will take an interest in it.

Elvekrog has firsthand experience with children from families who don't invest. Through the Rotary Club, he works with inner city kids, helping them open savings accounts. He sees that being involved in the world-at-large changes their outlook. In time, with Elvekrog's assistance, these children will form an investment club.

Nothing gets kids' attention more than asking them if they want to be millionaires. And they can be one with the tremendous power of compounded growth over the long term.

If you can get your kids interested in investing early in life, it's amazing how much they can earn. Save just $2,000 a year in an IRA invested in stock mutual funds with an average annual return of 10 percent and it will be worth more than $2 million in 40 years.

Having money will give your child (and you) an internal confidence. People with a lot of money saved don't pay a lot of attention to what other people think, which is a much more healthy approach than those who flash their money, or are totally obsessed with the opinion others have of them. (Those people will probably have a tougher row to hoe in later years.)

"What counts is who I am and what I know about myself," not can I make a big show for other people, Elvekrog says. People who have money put away carry themselves differently.

Unofficially... Albert Ellis, a noted psychologist, said the most pervasive neurosis is the obsession about what others think. What does that imply? Good investors don't spend all their time and energy trying to keep up with the Joneses.

Just the facts

- Investing money is often exciting, pleasurable, and profitable.
- Saving money is not the same as investing money.
- Inflation and taxes can reduce the value of your savings if your investment returns aren't high enough.

- History shows that if you reinvest your dividends and interest, your money will grow exponentially over time.

- Be aware that you're teaching your children about investing by your example.

GET THE SCOOP ON...
Why saving for retirement is so important ▪ Why
you should start saving when you're young ▪
Why you might have to work during your
golden years ▪ How moving after retiring may
affect your costs ▪ Teaching your kids the value
of investing

Investing in Your Future

Chapter 2

How much time have you spent deciding what to wear? What you'll make for dinner? Planning your wedding? Planning a family reunion? Planning your vacation? Now consider how much time you've spent planning your retirement. Which of these will affect you more if it doesn't get done right or done at all?

Some people think you don't have to plan for something that's supposed to be carefree and fun. Just leave your problems at the office on your last day of work and that's that. But things might not be so footloose and fancy free if you haven't planned for the decades ahead long in advance.

In this chapter, you will see why it is so important to plan ahead for retirement. You will learn what financial considerations factor into your retirement and how they may affect your income. You will see that the longer in advance you start planning, the more carefree your retirement will be because you will have less financial stress.

Who's investing for retirement

Nearly one-third of Americans are not saving for retirement, according to the results of the 1998 Retirement Confidence Survey (RCS) organized in part by the Employee Benefit Research Institute (EBRI). The reason they don't: They say they're stretched to the limit. "Almost 50 percent of non-savers cite too many current financial responsibilities as the most important reason they don't save, with 66 percent indicating that it is a major reason," says EBRI. Yet the same people admit they could save $20 a week.

With so few Americans saving, it should come as no surprise that only 20–25 percent of working Americans are confident that they will have enough money to live comfortably in retirement.

The good news is that increasing numbers of people (45 percent in 1998 versus 32 percent in 1996 and 36 percent in 1997) in all age groups are playing with the numbers, trying to figure out how much they need to save for retirement.

Timesaver
Take an invest-
ment planning
worksheet with
you when you go
out for dinner.
You'll have some-
thing construc-
tive to do while
waiting for your
meal.

But 30 percent of those surveyed think they won't have enough money to support themselves in retirement, and 20 percent of retirees said that their standard of living is worse than expected.

On the other hand, EBRI's Retirement Confidence Survey showed that learning how to save motivates people. "Eighty-one percent of those receiving employer information in the past year have money earmarked for retirement versus 67 percent of those who have not received information," according to EBRI.

The RCS revealed six distinct attitudes toward retirement. (See Table 2.1 to see how each personality type plans to fund their retirement and Figure 2.1 to see how content each personality type is that they will have enough money to live comfortably in retirement. Figure 2.2 illustrates the percent of each personality type that has actually saved for retirement).

1. Deniers (10 percent) feel that retirement is so far away that there is no reason to think about it. Six out of ten who fall into this category have saved nothing for retirement and plan to rely on Social Security benefits to foot the bill for their golden years.

2. Strugglers (9 percent) believe they have no money to save. They, too, are counting on Social Security, but 40 percent of them are saving for retirement. Both of these groups think planning for retirement is too time-consuming.

3. Impulsives (20 percent) know they should save but are weak when it comes to resisting purchases. They expect to work in retirement, although 51 percent are saving for retirement.

4. Cautious Savers (21 percent) put away a set amount into savings each month, although this money is not invested aggressively. They are saving more than those who fall into the previous categories. Sixty-one percent have saved for their retirement.

5. Planners (23 percent) believe that a comfortable retirement is achievable and are planning, saving, and investing to reach that goal. They are disciplined savers, and many are risk takers. This group has more men and more college graduates than the other groups. Eighty-one percent are saving for retirement.

6. Retiring Savers (17 percent) are enjoying their golden years because they have saved and

sacrificed for them. They've been disciplined but not aggressive investors and are debt-free. More than 84 percent of this group did not plan to rely solely on their pension plans, but saved for their retirement.

Note! ➜
Of all saving retirement personalities, only the planners believe a comfortable retirement is achievable and are taking action to ensure that their golden years are enjoyable.

TABLE 2.1: PERCENTAGE WHO SAY MAJOR SOURCE OF RETIREMENT INCOME IS OR WILL BE...

Deniers	Strugglers	Impulsives	Cautious Savers	Planners	Retiring Savers
Social Security					
58%	49%	29%	37%	22%	40%
Pension					
36%	36%	53%	43%	47%	46%
401(k)–Type Plan					
20%	30%	45%	36%	48%	38%
Other Personal Savings					
13%	14%	20%	25%	44%	35%

Note! ➜
Proportions confident they will have enough money to live comfortably in retirement. Source: EBRI

FIGURE 2.1: PROPORTIONS CONFIDENT THEY WILL HAVE ENOUGH MONEY TO LIVE COMFORTABLY IN RETIREMENT

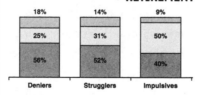

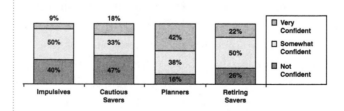

FIGURE 2.2: % WHO HAVE PERSONALLY SAVED FOR RETIREMENT

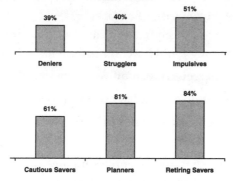

← Note!
Percent who have personally saved for retirement. Source: EBRI

Why you need to invest for retirement

Many picture retirement as cruise ships to balmy destinations, plane rides to exotic, faraway places, palm trees swaying in the salt-filled air, a comfortable front porch rocker and a lazy summer breeze, relaxing candlelight dinners in fine restaurants, and a comfortable car, not to mention grandchildren to ride in it and a big trunk for the toys they plan to buy them.

But the golden years require a golden nest egg to make those luxuries possible. If you invest your money right and you're young, you could have it all. But for those getting a late start, your golden years may not be so golden. Either way, you need to know what you can expect. If the reality of your retirement is no longer so picturesque, you can at least take steps to make it more comfortable.

Thanks to progress made in medicine and better nutrition, the average American today lives a much longer, more vibrant life than his or her grandparents and parents. Many Americans will live in retirement just about as long as they spent in the working world. In fact, there are more people than ever before over the age of 100 living in the United States today. So it's very important to prepare for those years when you won't be working.

There are three factors that affect the size of the pot of money you'll have at retirement:

1. The percent return on your investment

2. The number of dollars you've invested

3. The amount of time in which you leave your money invested

Timesaver
Place a quick call to the Social Security benefits office at (800) 772-1213 to find out how much you've paid in so far or to get an estimate on future benefits. This will eliminate guesswork and the time it takes to write a letter.

The truth is, most people's incomes are reduced in retirement even with Social Security benefits. And a dollar won't stretch much further, even with senior citizen's discounts.

Keep in mind that you may still have the same expenses you had before retirement, like car payments, rent or mortgage payments, electricity, water, gas, food, and other expenses. And, with the exception of a fixed rate mortgage, these expenses will probably increase over time.

Moreover, there are increased expenses as you age. Insurance premiums rise, both for health benefits and your car. As your home and its contents age, you may have added repair and replacement expenses. Roofs need to be replaced; washers, dryers, dishwashers, and refrigerators only last so long. Plumbing, air conditioning, and heating systems get old and fail. For that matter, so do cars. And, as you age, you'll probably make more doctors' visits and perhaps spend time hospitalized. These are all big expenses.

Not everyone will have the luxury of full retirement. The baby boomers, known for their lavish spending styles, are late in saving for their retirements, and, depending on how the market performs over the next decade and a half and on how much they invest, they may not have enough saved to retire. Plus, there are those who just didn't earn enough over the years to be able to invest in their retirement and those who lost their nest eggs through divorce. And, of course, there are those who by choice will continue to work, at least part-time.

But the baby boomers, like earlier generations, will have something to lean on. Social Security will be part of their retirement portfolio. But, for those who will continue to work, earning a paycheck can cut into that piece of their retirement pie.

In 1998, you could earn up to $9,120 and not lose benefits if you were under 65 years old. But every $2 you earn above that threshold will cut your Social Security check by a buck.

As you age you can earn more without losing benefits. In 1998, those between ages 65 and 69 can earn as much as $14,500. But after that, every $3 you earn drops $1 from your benefits.

To add salt to your wounds, the government will still take out FICA taxes from your paycheck. And you may have to pay additional income taxes if your paycheck (when added to your retirement income, capital gains, interest, dividends from your investments, and Social Security benefits) bumps you into a higher tax bracket. Being aware of these added taxes can help you better prepare for your financial future.

The good news is that these penalties end at age 70. And if you play your cards right, presuming there are no legal changes affecting Social Security benefits in the coming years, you can increase your Social Security benefits. Simply postpone taking them until you're over age 65.

But the forecast for Generation Xers and those following them into retirement 27 years from now

Bright Idea
Put as much of your income as you can in retirement plans to let it grow tax-deferred.

and beyond may be gloomier because the high number of baby boomers who will be eligible to collect Social Security benefits in the next decade is threatening to collapse the system.

In an effort to save the system, in May 1998 the National Commission on Retirement Policy recommended extending the age to receive full Social Security benefits to 70 by the year 2029. The NCRP legislation is enacted to start in the year 2000.

So even if members of Generation X and Generation Y get Social Security benefits, they will have to wait longer to receive them, which is another good reason to start investing early.

Theoretically, delaying retirement should help save the system for two reasons:

1. It lengthens the time period contributions are made into the system.

2. It defers the date at which benefits can be collected.

However, even delaying benefits may not save the system, according to Martin Greller, a University of Wyoming professor.

Beware of little expenses; a small leak will sink a great ship.
—Benjamin Franklin

The two factors listed above buy time for the system to replenish itself. But it makes faulty assumptions, according to Greller, who has studied careers of older workers and says that by age 58 half of the population is already out of the workforce.

This may come as a surprise considering the fact that people live longer, age discrimination laws are in place, and there is a concern about the stability of pensions and other retirement income sources.

Despite these concerns, Greller says that the trend, if anything, has been toward early retirement. He says this plan to delay benefits until age 70—that is, to have this group pay into the system an additional 5 years—won't be very effective if half the workforce retires at age 58.

Furthermore, those who do try to return to the workforce after retiring currently find it difficult to land a job, and those who do often take less skilled, less responsible positions for less pay.

On the other hand, some older workers are forced out of their jobs—because they do not have the technical skills necessary today, their positions are too physically demanding or they are ill—before they are old enough to qualify for their pensions or other retirement benefits. The possibility of being forced out of a job is another good reason to plan to have enough savings to tide you over into your retirement years.

Bottom line? Those of you born after 1959 will have to wait until you're 67 years old to retire and collect benefits. For those born after 1937, the age for collecting full Social Security benefits will increase from age 65 to 67 on a phased-in basis.

Howard Yasgur, investment consultant with Gradison-McDonald Investments, has younger clients that tell him not to bother figuring Social Security into their retirement plan. They're not going to take the risk of assuming it will still be there when they retire.

Even with Social Security to count on, those baby boomers who have lived high on the hog are now worrying about sending their kids to college and saving for retirement, Yasgur says. At that point, you can't make it on CDs. You must invest in the stock market, and clearly, good or bad, that is what they are doing.

Of course, as a result, Generation X and others can thank these investors for helping to propel the bull market of the 1990s.

Watch Out!
Don't let a financial adviser invest your money without having a solid understanding of the investments you're buying. Some funds pay heavy commissions and don't have good performance records.

Besides Social Security, other factors will affect how much you need to retire. Are you planning on moving to be close to your children or to a more tropical setting? What is the cost of living there compared with what you're used to in your town? To find out more, check out *Money* magazine's Web site. It has a cost-of-living comparison calculator that is based on data provided by The Salary Calculator, part of The Homebuyer's Fair, a Web site.

If you move from a place with a high cost of living, like Manhattan, to one with a lower cost of living, like West Palm Beach, your retirement burdens are eased. The cost of living in New York is a whopping 82.89 percent more than that in West Palm Beach. Plus, Florida has no state income taxes, in case you plan to go back to work.

But if your kids have taken high-powered jobs in Washington, D.C., and you want to move there from Pine Bluff, Ark., hold onto your hat and your wallet. Your purchasing power will be reduced significantly. The cost of living in the nation's capital is 40.20 percent higher than it is in Pine Bluff.

Watch Out! The cost of living differs among cities, states, and regions. Plan for your retirement according to the cost of living in the place where you plan to retire.

Then there's college tuition for your children, if you're planning on footing the bill for any part of it. By the time your newborn turns 18 you can expect to pay just over $100,000 for his or her college education, according to Strong Funds. You can plan your college expenses using the college cost forecaster calculator at Sallie Mae's Web site (http://www.salliemae.com).

Why you should take advantage of retirement investments

There is no better way to save for your future than by taking advantage of retirement investments. If you are eligible for a 401(k) plan, you could benefit threefold:

- By investing pretax dollars
- By lowering your taxable income by the amount you invest in the 401(k), or similar retirement plans in some cases
- By your employer matching, at least in part, the amount you invest
- By putting money into a retirement fund, you'll get compounded growth on the tax-deferred portion as well as the principal investment.

All of these "extra" savings will compound over time.

A common tool used by financial advisers to figure out how much you'll need to save for your retirement is the three-legged stool:

1. Social Security, at least for those who will retire in the next 15–20 years or so, will serve as the basic income.

2. Your pension from work (or your retirement plan) will make up the second leg, raising your income further.

3. Finally, your savings, those funds not in your retirement portfolio, makes up the balance.

According to Vanguard, a mutual fund company, Social Security will pay less than half of what the average American will need to live on in retirement. That means your investment portfolio must provide the rest, or you'll have to return to work or depend on your children for additional income. And if you're in a higher tax bracket, Social Security will make up even less of your retirement pie.

Furthermore, few employees will get gold watches. Businesses are no longer paternal. Few people spend their entire careers at one, or even two, companies; in fact, most young and middle-aged people tend to switch jobs every few years as a strategy to move up the ladder in both income and responsibility. Furthermore, according to news reports, some companies in recent years have had their pensions collapse from mismanagement, while others have disqualified long-time employees from their pension plans by forcing them to leave the company shortly before they were qualified to retire.

So, with traditional employer-provided pension plans being phased out and Social Security uncertain, at least in its current form, those in their 20s and 30s must plan for their own retirement. Experts agree that investing in tax-deferred savings plans like a 401(k) and an IRA is the best strategy.

The tax advantages these plans offer to someone in his or her 20s can't be recouped later on. (See Table 1.2., Chapter One.) The longer you wait to invest in retirement plans, the fewer benefits you'll reap through compounding the principal and tax deferment (that is, the tax you will eventually pay to the government will be earning income for you until you retire). Furthermore, the government limits the amount you can put in each year.

If you invest $2,000 a year for the first 8 years of a 40-year period with the annual interest compounding at 10 percent, you will earn more than someone who invests $2,000 a year from years 9 through 40. (See Table 2.2.)

At the end of 40 years, despite having put in four times as much capital, the second individual's earnings will amount to $378,503, less than 75 percent of that of the first individual, who started earlier.

The amount of wealth accumulated is also substantially affected by seemingly small differences in the annual rate of return. For example, a $10,000 initial investment, with nothing added to it other than the reinvestment of earnings, will grow to $46,610 over 20 years if the compounded annual rate of return is 8 percent. If the rate of return is 10 percent, however, that same initial investment of $10,000 will increase to $67,275, or 44 percent more.

The best strategy for making your retirement plan grow rapidly is to place as much money in it each year as the government will allow (see Chapter 5). If you can't afford to do that, save at least as much as your employer will match in your 401(k). If you put a dollar in and your employer matches it, that's a 100 percent gain on your investment even before you see the impact of market performance and compounded interest. Even 50¢ to your dollar is a hefty 50 percent immediate return.

Another benefit of saving for retirement using your 401(k) plan is that the money is subtracted before you get your paycheck.

Furthermore, every dollar you put into a 401(k) retirement plan reduces your taxable income by the same amount that year. If you're in the 28 percent tax bracket, that's 28 percent savings, or $2,800 saved on a $10,000 retirement investment.

According to Yasgur, there are a lot of ways to cut down on your tax bill these days, so you should take full advantage of all the tax-advantage retirement plans available, both from the government and your company.

But it's not enough to just save for retirement. Once you retire, you must keep a portion of your money invested. Consider this: At a relatively low inflation rate of 4 percent, your money will lose

> "If you can count your money, you don't have a billion dollars."
> —J. Paul Getty

Note! ➡
Just by investing
$2,000 for 8
years and not
one penny after-
wards, the power
of compounding
interest will
make you
wealthier than
someone who
waited 8 years to
get started but
invested $2,000
for the next
32 years.

TABLE 2.2: THE POWER OF COMPOUNDING

Year	Amount #1 $ Invested	Amount #1 $ Worth	Amount #2 $ Invested	Amount #2 $ Worth
1	2,000	2,200	0	0
2	2,000	4,620	0	0
3	2,000	7,282	0	0
4	2,000	10,210	0	0
5	2,000	13,431	0	0
6	2,000	16,974	0	0
7	2,000	20,872	0	0
8	2,000	25,159	0	0
9	0	27,675	2,000	2,200
10	0	30,442	2,000	4,620
11	0	33,487	2,000	7,282
12	0	36,835	2,000	10,210
13	0	40,519	2,000	13,431
14	0	44,571	2,000	16,974
15	0	49,028	2,000	20,872
16	0	53,930	2,000	25,159
17	0	59,323	2,000	29,875
18	0	65,256	2,000	35,062
19	0	71,781	2,000	40,769

20	0	78,960	2,000	47,045
21	0	86,856	2,000	53,950
22	0	95,541	2,000	61,645
23	0	105,095	2,000	69,899
24	0	115,605	2,000	79,089
25	0	127,165	2,000	89,198
26	0	139,882	2,000	100,318
27	0	153,870	2,000	112,550
28	0	169,257	2,000	126,005
29	0	186,183	2,000	140,805
30	0	204,801	2,000	157,086
31	0	225,281	2,000	174,995
32	0	247,809	2,000	194,694
33	0	272,590	2,000	216,364
34	0	299,849	2,000	240,200
35	0	329,834	2,000	266,420
36	0	362,817	2,000	295,262
37	0	399,099	2,000	326,988
38	0	439,009	2,000	361,887
39	0	482,910	2,000	400,276
40	0	531,201	2,000	442,503

Invested	Earnings	Invested	Earnings
$16,000	$515,201	$64,000	$378,503

about half its value in 18 years. What should change in retirement is your asset allocation.

Raising investment-savvy children

If you get your kids started investing when they're young, it will be much easier for them to get ahead. Saving just $5 a week ($260 a year) in a tax-deferred account starting at age 10, assuming a 10 percent rate of return, will build up to $302,616 at age 65.

You also can have a more selfish reason for getting them started early. If you get your children investing in mutual funds when they're young by opening up an account for them, chances are you won't have to worry about supporting them during your retirement years because:

1. If you start them with $1,200 at age 10, followed by investments of $260 per year, by the time they're 35 they will have accumulated an impressive sum of $38,572, assuming a 10 percent rate of return.

2. They will develop into good money managers because they will understand the value of saving and investing their money.

So, what might cost you $500–$1,000 now may end up saving you money later. Moreover, this is an investment in their education.

The actual number of children who invest is probably a minority, says Janet Bodner, a.k.a, Kipplinger's "Dr. Tightwad," who answers money questions for kids. But those who do, she says, are enthusiastic. They have parents and grandparents who have gotten them into it. Sometimes parents and grandparents don't know what to talk to the kids about and this is a good subject, she says.

"
Change is good, but dollars are better.
—Unknown
"

Bodner gives four tips:

1. Get kids interested in investing when they're young. Don't make the mistake of thinking that it's beyond their grasp, because it isn't.

2. Give them as a gift shares of mutual funds that they can follow.

3. If you can't afford a large chunk, or don't want to, have the children save up for the investment using a bank savings account.

4. Ask relatives for gifts to be sent to your kids' college funds.

When you do help your children select mutual funds in which to invest, buy them on performance, not simply on low minimum investments.

Bodner stresses that you should answer any questions your kids have about money directly. With money, adults are often secretive. But children need to be prepared to manage their own money when they go off to college. You don't want them moving back home because they can't manage money, she says.

On the other hand, you don't need to tell them how much you earn or how much you have in the bank. Younger children aren't really interested in the dollar amount, she says. If a child wants a bike and you say it's too expensive, they may ask you how much you make and compare that to the cost of the bike, and your argument, to them at least, loses its power.

What they're really looking for is comfort level, Bodner says. Instead of revealing your salary, you could say, "We make enough to pay the bills and have some left over." Or, they may want to know how

Bright Idea
Dr. Tightwad suggests giving your children an incentive to save by matching their investments.

much you earn compared with other people, which can lead into a productive conversation about how much different professions make.

So, Bodner says, if your child comes home and asks why you can't have a big-screen TV like the neighbors do, rather than telling him or her to go live with the neighbors, you can explain that you prefer to pay less for your TV and invest your money or that you simply can't afford luxuries like that.

Bill Stawski, founder of Cash University, a program in Grand Rapids, Mich., which offers tools to help parents teach their children about money skills, thinks the key is including your children in your investment activities. Make it family time, he says.

By including your children when reviewing your statements, you'll teach them how to read financial documents and what they mean, and the kids will pick up your style.

Your kids are watching what you're doing. They'll mimic your style, he says.

But be cautious what you teach them. You may have an aggressive investment style but have $500,000 in savings. You don't want your kids to start out investing aggressively when they get their first professional job if they have no safety net.

Include them in your investment decisions, Stawski suggests. Don't ask for their advice, but let them go through your thought process with you. Plus, by hearing yourself talk about your strategies out loud, it may help you be more rational, he says. That way you'll make better investment decisions.

Using money from gifts, allowances, and jobs such as mowing lawns or baby sitting, your kids can invest in a mutual fund. Many funds are waiving minimum investments to get people started,

Timesaver
Gear dinner conversations toward investing. That way you won't have to find "extra" time to sit down and talk with your children about money matters.

although you may have to make minimum monthly investments.

By getting your children invested, they will become more personally involved because it's their money. Furthermore, you and your children can open up statements together to compare and contrast, and talk. For children who are too young to understand the meaning of money, talk in terms of how many Beanie Babies™ it could buy, Stawski says.

Of course, if you have a large chunk of money invested and your child tends to broadcast information to neighbors and strangers, it might be prudent to show him or her only one statement for a small account. But this also presents a good opportunity to teach your kids not to talk in public about private family matters and why.

Investing side by side with your children provides a great learning opportunity. Be less concerned about letting them know how much you have and more concerned about teaching them the basics about investing, Stawski says.

The bottom line is to demonstrate the concept of earning money with money. But don't forget to teach your children about risk, says Kathy Prochaska Cue. Let them get used to seeing how the value of the fund goes up and down. Invest small, especially if your fund is volatile. You don't want your kids to lose interest in investing when the market takes a down turn.

Some parents let their kids keep track of their college investments to teach them, she says. It has a direct impact on them, even though you're providing the money.

Some kids will be interested in investing; others won't. The ones who are not interested are the ones who should get involved using their own money.

Bright Idea
Dr. Tightwad suggests opening a Roth IRA for your children once they start earning money.

Learning about money can be all fun and games at money camp. For the past 14 years, The Breakers Hotel in Palm Beach has been running an investment camp for kids. That program ceased recently, but Susan Bradley, the certified financial professional who ran the camp for the last 3 years, will begin investment camps in several cities. (For a list of locations go to http://www.moneycamps.com.)

Bright Idea
Let your children pick a stock they have an interest in, like Disney.

Kids are not long-term investors, says Bradley. They just don't think that way. Their intuitive approach is market timing, which doesn't work for most people. She teaches them to set short- and long-term financial goals, and they develop a financial plan from that.

Another great way to get kids of all ages interested in investing in mutual funds, get involved with them at the same time, and perhaps get a little investment stress relief is through the newly released board game "Mutual Fundz." This game has a humorous twist on investing, taking the stress out of Wall Street. But it piques interest and teaches fundamentals while bringing families together. "It does the opposite of what our investments are doing—which makes us serious and noncommunicative with kids," says inventor Norman Kay. This game is sold at upscale retail stores and catalogs, as well as through their internet site (www.mutualfundz.com). Or you can call 888/765-4263.

Just the facts

- Those who aren't saving for retirement suffer from anxiety about it and worry they will not have enough money to fund their golden years.
- Kids will become more interested in investing if they have hands-on experience at it.

- You need to invest for retirement because Social Security checks alone likely will not cover all of your expenses.

- If you plan to relocate after retirement, your expenses may increase or decrease, depending on the local cost of living.

Investment Strategies

PART II

GET THE SCOOP ON...
How mutual funds work ▪ How to get a diversified portfolio ▪ How you can cut back on
expenses to increase investments ▪ Why women
investors hold back ▪ How to develop an investment plan

Investing in Mutual Funds

S ince the mid-1930s, the stock market has
beaten all other types of investments in experiencing long-term financial growth. It has
outperformed bonds, CDs and U.S. Government
securities, all of which have stayed ahead of inflation.

Mutual funds make it easy for anyone to invest in
the market. Perhaps that's why they have become so
popular in the past decade and a half, with more
than $3 trillion dollars currently invested.

In a mutual fund, the shareholders' money is
pooled and invested in a variety of stocks, bonds,
and money market securities. The funds take care of
the record keeping for your investments.

By investing in mutual funds, you own shares in
many companies (20–1,000 or so), and with that
ownership you share in both the companies' profits,
through stock dividends and interest and through
rising share prices.

In this chapter, you will see that there are many
advantages to investing in mutual funds. You will

learn how to determine investment goals and objectives, how to find ways to tighten your belt to find more money to invest, and how to develop an investment plan. If you are a woman, you may find it comforting to learn that other women also struggle with investing. In this chapter you'll discover where you can go to get additional help investing, if necessary.

Bright Idea
Don't put all your assets in one basket. Build a diversified portfolio. That way, if one segment of the market plummets, you generally won't suffer as much as a consequence.

The advantages of investing in mutual funds

There are many advantages to investing in mutual funds, including professional management, affordability, diversification, and the availability of data on which to make your investment decisions.

Professional management

Each mutual fund has a team that is dedicated solely to the management of that fund. The managers are in charge of picking the stocks and/or bonds that go into the fund's portfolio. Generally, they are compensated on how well they manage the progress of that fund, so their incentives are similar to those of the investor—they want the fund to make money, says Cindy Bohlen, assistant vice president of the Marshall Funds and a securities analyst.

Most individuals don't have the resources or the background to invest as well as most investment professionals. Fund managers and analysts have access to more information than the average investor does. They also generally have the education and training to manage the fund. When you invest in a mutual fund, you're buying the expertise of a portfolio manager.

Each fund has an objective stated in its prospectus that discloses to the investor the mix of stocks and/or bonds and/or money markets, etc., that are included in its portfolio to meet the stated objective.

So when you buy a fund, buy a fund with objectives that match your own.

Bohlen says that if she's getting paid to beat the S&P 500, she has very little incentive to go out and get bonds. So even though there's a 35 percent leeway, fund managers don't want to take much risk. But it can happen, she says. Holdings are not published everyday, so you won't know on a daily basis what's in those funds. You can find out quarterly in publications like *Morningstar,* a mutual fund research company, or semiannually through the fund's report. However, most larger funds publish holdings quarterly, and you can always call and get the information sent to you, she says.

Affordability

Generally, mutual funds have relatively small minimums for investing. For $1,000, you can instantly have a professionally managed, diversified portfolio. It would be hard to buy enough individual stocks to diversify for this amount, and it would be an inefficient way to manage your money, Bohlen says. Plus, you can buy more shares with as little as $50 per month in some funds.

Diversification

Every mutual fund owns a collection of investments. Some own all stocks, some all bonds, and some all money markets. Many own a mix of these securities. Therefore by its very nature, mutual funds offer diversification. You can own an entire basket of investments without having to invest a great deal of money as you would if you were buying individual stocks. In bond funds, you'll own a variety of bonds, in stock funds, you'll own a variety of stocks.

By diversifying through a mutual fund, you're spreading the risk of your investment over many

Timesaver
By having a
mutual fund
company take
money directly
from your bank
account each
month, you will
save the time
needed to write
and mail a
check, thereby
ensuring that
you are investing
in your account.

companies and/or bond issuers. There are two types of risk:

- market risk
- company-specific risk

When the market is moving down, most stocks are doing the same. This is market risk. There's also company-specific risk—that is, risk that a company's stock will move down as a result of its own performance.

But investing in individual stocks alone presents a much greater risk than buying a mutual fund because you're putting all your eggs into one basket. If the one company you bet on didn't come through, you've lost it all, Bohlen points out. In Las Vegas, you wouldn't stake all your money on one bet. Why would you do that with your investments?

A mutual fund gives you diversification by offering a whole portfolio in one fund. If you invest in more than one category of funds, like domestic and international funds, you can double-diversify. You can further diversify by buying a variety of asset classes:

- domestic large-cap stocks
- domestic small-cap stocks
- international stocks

> A. Domestic large-cap stocks (stocks of companies whose market values is more than $5 billion) and the S&P 500. If you're like most people, it is unlikely you'll be able to pick stocks that will outperform the S&P 500 index (an index of 500 of the largest, most actively traded stocks on the New York Stock Exchange) over the long-term, says Kacy Gott of Kochis Fitz investment planners and

adjunct professor in the Personal Financial
Planning Program at the University of
California-Berkeley. In the large-cap arena,
with brand-name company stocks such as
Coca-Cola and Disney, it makes most sense to
buy the index through the use of mutual
funds, he says.

It is cumbersome and expensive to buy
enough stocks on the S&P 500 index to get a
diversified portfolio that mirrors the performance of the index. You'd have to have a
huge amount of money to buy all of the
stocks listed on the S&P 500 index and
weight them appropriately to mirror the
index, which itself is weighted. Furthermore,
individual stocks can be very expensive, Gott
says. Mutual funds are the only practical way
to get this type of exposure. And, as stated
above, index funds have a very low turnover
rate and very low transaction costs.

B. Domestic small-cap stocks. It is possible to
find small-cap stocks (stocks of companies
whose market value is less than $500 million)
that will outperform the S&P 500 index.
Because there are fewer analysts following
individual stocks and less information available on the companies, it's possible to find
gems, Gott says. But you must be able to
glean information that others can't, possibly
on a stock in an industry you know well.
Otherwise, you just have to be lucky. While
small-cap stocks can perform well, compared
with large-caps, they're volatile and have a
higher risk.

There are periods in time when large companies' stock outperform small companies'
stock prices, and vice-versa, says Howard
Yasgur, investment consultant with Gradison-
McDonald. Including both large-cap and
small-cap stock funds will give your portfolio a
better balance.

C. International stocks. It is very difficult for
an individual to assemble a diversified portfolio of overseas stocks, Gott says. Not all of
these stocks are readily available in the
United States, so possible problems with currency exchange, language differences, and
political issues could make it difficult to buy
individual stocks overseas. Therefore, in international asset classes, mutual funds make the
most sense. Good managers have access to
the information needed to buy stocks that
are expected to perform well, whereas that
information is hard for the individual investor
to get.

History has shown that there's a low correlation
between most foreign and domestic stock market
performance, says Yasgur. Sometimes when one
goes up, the other goes down. By having a mix of
domestic and international funds, you'll reduce
your portfolio's overall volatility, and thereby reduce
risk, he says. (Note, however, that there is a strong
correlation between the U.S., Canada, and U.K.
stock market performance.)

In addition to the different types of stock funds,
there are also different types of bond funds. (For
those in higher tax brackets, Yasgur suggests tax-free
municipal bonds.) There are also foreign and
domestic bonds, as well as high-yield (junk) bonds.

By developing a bond portfolio including high-yields, foreign bonds and treasuries, or corporate bonds, you can develop a balanced bond portfolio, he says.

However, keep in mind that long-term bonds are risky because the face value of the bonds stays constant. During a high inflationary period, which devalues the dollar and cuts your spending power, the bonds are worth less.

For example, if you buy a 30-year bond at 5 percent and you run into a 10 percent inflationary period, you'll only get half the face value of your bond if you sell it. However, if you hold onto the bond, you'll still receive the same interest payment, and over time, the value of the bond may return to its original value. Short-term bonds, though, are considered much safer because they come due at face value quickly, leaving little time for inflation to adversely affect their value.

There are also balanced or asset allocation funds, which are divided among stocks, bonds, and cash. Such funds give you immediate diversification in the major asset categories, but you have no control over the asset allocation. Some so-called "asset allocation funds" try to time the market by changing their mix of assets. Remember, you'll pay taxes every time they sell assets. Consider avoiding these.

Availability of data

Mutual fund managers have access to information about small and international companies that the individual investor does not. They have researchers who actually visit these companies. Even if the information was available to the individual investor, it is very time-consuming to go out and get it. It simply makes more sense to hire mutual fund managers to

Watch Out!
When investing internationally, check to make sure that the fund isn't concentrated too much in one area. If it is, it's likely it'll be more volatile. Also, check to see if the fund invests only overseas or in combination with U.S. companies.

Watch Out!
Warning: Even fund managers make mistakes.

do it, Gott says. They have the time, access, and the know-how to properly diversify the fund's holdings.

As an individual you can get access to large-cap company stock information, but so can everyone else, so how can you beat the fund managers? Gott asks. It is possible to beat them in the small caps, but how do you get the information? Again, Gott and Tim Kochis, a partner at Kochis Fitz, argue for mutual funds.

However, Kochis, who has been named top financial investor by *Worth* magazine every year since 1994, says that some investors express interest in selecting their own securities. He encourages his clients to limit their purchases to "gambling" money if they want to have an investing adventure. But he discourages large investments that would jeopardize their portfolio and objectives. It's just not likely they'll do well, he says.

But there are disadvantages to buying mutual funds, too. Howard Yasgur and Cindy Bohlen of the Marshall Funds noted the following drawbacks:

1. The price you pay to buy mutual fund shares or get for selling those shares—that is, the share price—is only figured at the day's end. Consequently, if the market is falling or rising, you will only be able to sell or buy at whatever the price is at the end of the day. (Of course, using funds to time the market makes little sense, since the point of investing in them is to diversify and gain balance. In highly volatile markets, funds can be hit by heavy redemptions by investors who become frightened or by those trying to make a profit. When investors in the fund sell shares, it causes the price of the fund to drop more than might be warranted, given

the market's performance. Often times, if you believe in your manager's ability, it's wise to ride out any short-term volatility.)

2. You have no control over what investments the fund's manager buys and sells. You have to trust the manager to stay in line with the objective stated in the prospectus. However, there's a 35 percent legal leeway which they may or may not use, Bohlen says, depending on how they expect the market to perform.

3. The manager realizes capital gains at his or her discretion, thus reducing your ability to control your tax liability. (The obvious response, Bohlen says, is to buy index funds, which haven't distributed capital gains in the last few years. Their net positive cash flow has been enough to allow them to realign their portfolio to match the index without having to sell stocks due to the bull market. However, she notes, if they had to sell they'd have huge gains. Or, if a large number of investors take their money out of the funds compared to what is being put in, the fund would have to sell off stocks to pay these investors. That means capital gains taxes for you.)

4. Mutual funds have expenses, even if you don't pay a load. You're paying for professional money management, Bohlen says. (But, there's also a fee for buying stocks through a broker.)

5. The fund's portfolio may include stocks, such as tobacco, which are socially or ethically controversial, unless you buy a so-called socially responsible fund. Shareholders have no control over the portfolio. On the flip side, Bohlen says,

everyone has their own social biases, so it's difficult to run a socially responsible fund.

But unless you are extremely wealthy—that is, unless you have a multimillion-dollar portfolio—the only way to get a well-diversified stock portfolio is through mutual funds.

Women investors need to get savvier

As a group, women tend to be more conservative, less knowledgeable investors than men. Part of the reason for investing conservatively is justified because most women earn less than men do.

Watch Out!
You can lose a lot of money by not asking the right questions. Learning about investing will lead you to ask good questions.

The effect snowballs, say many brokers, because women tend not to ask too many questions about investing—they worry that it will make them look bad.

A study conducted by the Dreyfus Corporation, in conjunction with the National Center for Women and Retirement Research (NCWRR), found that people who didn't own mutual funds but hold other investment tools worry more about finances and stock market fluctuations than those who do own funds. Sixty percent of those who didn't own funds were women.

The research, a gender investment comparison study, was conducted to determine differences in the levels of retirement preparedness between those who are invested in mutual funds and those who are not.

Only 36 percent of the women surveyed said they make retirement savings a top priority. That number was 46 percent for men. Women and non-fund owners preferred stable, easy-to-manage investments such as money market accounts and CDs, both of which are poor long-term investment tools.

Another study, this one co-organized by the Employee Benefit Research Institute, indicated that women show much less confidence in their ability to invest wisely and make investment decisions (38 percent were very confident about making investment decisions versus 52 percent of men).

Research by the American Association of Retired Persons (AARP) found that women were making financial decisions that weren't good for them. Financial planners were advising them to use their products regardless of whether these investments met the clients' investment objectives and risk tolerance. This study found that women didn't ask questions because they felt intimidated.

A more recent study by the AARP found that women are less aware of brokers' fees and the impact they have on total return.

Women need a nest egg and one of the ways to make sure it won't run out in their golden years is to have returns that reflect historical stock market averages of 10–12 percent. Moreover, women need to make investment decisions based on useful information.

There are several barriers women must overcome to gain investment savvy. For some women those barriers are being broken down.

In 1987, AARP debuted the Women's Financial Information Program, a low-cost, 7-week course held at university cooperative extensions, senior centers, Displaced Homemakers meeting places, religious centers, and the like to teach women (and men) of all ages about handling money and investing.

In Indiana, for example, they found that most participants were women in their mid-40s who wished they'd have had the information 20 years earlier.

Moneysaver
Take an invest-
ment course and
learn how to
handle your
money wisely.
Senior citizens
can often get
discounted
tuition rates
at community
colleges.

As a result of being in the program, some of these women either started an investment plan, or took a closer look at and revised their existing investment plan. They established record-keeping systems, set financial goals, and looked for ways to cut back on spending in order to invest more.

The women who take this AARP course feel more confident about managing their money and end up wanting to learn more. Many of them start investment clubs with their classmates.

Picking up on this gender gap, Susan Bradley has begun a Women's Money Camp. This 4-day program helps women turn life goals into financial goals, deals with the psychology of money, and conducts sessions on investing.

How much should you invest?

If you really want to get serious about investing, the answer is easy. Live beneath your means, and invest as much as you possibly can.

As a rule of thumb, some financial advisers suggest investing 10–16 percent of your income. The only caveat is to not dip into your emergency fund, which should be at least 3 months (and preferably 6 months) of your living expenses. (Without an emergency fund, should an unexpected expense arise, you may be forced into selling shares at a market low. By selling low, you'll have to sell more shares to receive the same dollar amount you would get from selling fewer shares at market highs. This method of selling is essentially the opposite of the dollar-cost-averaging investment strategy, which helps you buy more shares at market lows. With fewer shares you lose out on potential gains when the market turns upward. Plus, you'll have to sell off additional shares to cover any selling fees and capital gains. Selling a large percent of your shares can also throw off your portfolio balance. It's important to have an emergency fund.)

Another way to figure out how much to invest is to know how much money it will take to reach your objectives, Tim Kochis says. However, it's hard to put a price tag on those goals; how much should you pay for house or a car? There's no one answer.

You can come closer to putting a price tag on your objectives once you've developed lifestyle patterns, Kacy Gott says, and this usually happens in your 40s. If you're younger, he suggests taking advantage of pre-tax investments, whether or not your company matches what you invest. There are trade-offs, he notes. You might not be able to buy the car that you want when you want it, but that's the price of financial security.

One thing is certain: Unless you earn hundreds of thousands of dollars annually or receive a sizeable inheritance, if you don't invest, you will never accumulate wealth or even keep pace with inflation. After factoring in inflation and taxes, you lose spending power.

Finding more money to invest

Yasgur says he is always amazed at how big a nest egg a family earning $30,000 a year can accumulate, as compared to the small amount saved by a family earning double that.

How can people with average incomes find money to put away when the higher-income earners have trouble? Perhaps those in the latter category are living beyond their means, Yasgur says.

For those who wear their wealth or drive in it, it's easy to see how they could cut back their spending and invest more money. After all, clothes will wear

> **66**
> A young man with good health and a poor appetite can save up money.
> —James Montgomery Bailey
> **99**

out, eventually, and short of that, you can bet they'll be out of style next season, anyway.

How about the car? Most people can't afford to buy a nice sports car or sedan with cash. If you're like them, in addition to the price you negotiated, you're also paying thousands of dollars in interest over the life of the loan. The less expensive the car, the fewer dollars in interest you'll end up paying.

Moreover, some counties have a personal property tax based on the Blue Book value of the car. Again, the more expensive the car, the higher your personal property taxes.

Nobody's saying that you need to dress in rags or drive an old, beat-up car. Moderation is key.

There are many smaller ways to cut back on expenses. Cable television costs about $35 for just the basic service in some areas. There are plenty of shows on the major networks and PBS. Some people have cable in more than one room in their home; cutting back on the number of outlets will save money. Also, how often do you actually sit down and watch the extra movie channels that you are paying for? If you are only watching one movie a month, consider getting rid of those channels; go to the video rental store if you want to watch a movie.

You can save hundreds of dollars a year on your grocery bill simply by cutting out coupons for things you're going to be buying anyway. Go to a store that offers "double coupons" and you'll get twice as much off your bill. Find a store that has special promotions using a store card, and you'll save all the more.

Dining out is often much more expensive than eating at home or bringing your lunch to work. Consider cutting back here.

Moneysaver
Cut down on long-distance phone bills by shopping for the least expensive provider. Check often. Plans change, and the one that was least expensive last month may not be so cheap this month. Carriers will often cover the cost of switching, but you may need to ask.

Check out your home or rental insurance policy as well as that for your car and health. Plan prices vary for similar coverages. Note, however, that it is important to have comprehensive coverage on all your various types of insurance. One mishap could cost you a fortune.

If you're in the market for a new home, consider buying one that's less expensive than what you can afford. If you don't want to sacrifice size, consider moving farther away from the city or into a less pricey neighborhood. Downsize your home if your kids have flown the coop.

Most importantly, pay off all your credit card debt. With interests rates so high, leaving a balance is like buying things with price tags that have been raised 20 percent or more just for you.

Where does your willpower to cut back come from? Knowing that you have money should give you a sense of power and more self-esteem than any status symbol ever could.

Remember Anne Scheiber, the woman who turned $5,000 into $20 million? She scrimped and saved for 10 years to come up with an initial $5,000 investment, and then she lost everything. So she scrimped and saved again.

She did without new clothes, without much food, and without a nice home. She walked when she could have ridden a bus, all for the goal of saving to invest. If she could find the money when she was nearly destitute, then so can you.

Gott and Kochis see the equation of saving as having two other factors. In addition to decreasing your spending, you can get "extra" money to invest by increasing your income and reducing your taxes.

Most people don't want to stay at their current salary for more than a year and certainly do not

Watch Out!
It's easy to be tempted to buy all sorts of things. That's what advertising's all about.

want to take a salary cut. One way people move up the career ladder is through promotions. Another way is by changing jobs. Gott calls these offensive strategies and acknowledges that people take advantage of them to increase their earnings.

Many people make charitable deductions in the form of cash, Kochis says. But it would be more advantageous to donate appreciated assets like mutual funds. By doing so, you'll get the same income tax deduction (subject to limitations for some people), and you won't have to pay a capital gains tax on the funds that you sell to donate. Now you have the cash you otherwise would have donated to invest in the market.

Another way to reduce your tax burden is to take advantage of retirement plans and deferred compensation programs from employers. Many employers allow executive-level employees to delay receiving a certain portion of their income until a later time (such as retirement), Kochis says. By taking advantage of this, not only will you defer paying taxes on the sum, but the taxable amount is earning interest. However, the investment is not insured, but it's not considered risky, according to Kochis.

Bright Idea
If you get a bonus, invest it.

Making investing easier

Sometimes it's hard not to spend money and it's difficult to take the time to write out checks to the various fund accounts. But many funds make it possible for you to step aside from your administrative duties and have your monthly investments transferred automatically from your savings account or directly from your paycheck. By putting your investing on automatic pilot so you don't ever see that money, you'll eliminate having to make a new decision every week or every month, Kochis says.

Another way to find money to invest is to take advantage of increases in income by increasing the amount you contribute electronically to your funds, Gott says. Essentially, the temptation to spend that money is eliminated.

If you have a 401(k), the increased investment will be automatic, since your employer deducts a percentage of your salary rather than a specific amount.

Another way to make investing easier is to use a "supermarket" investment company like Schwab or Fidelity, Gott says, because you can buy different funds in different asset classes all on one account. You can do this through some full service brokers as well.

Developing a plan

After you've decided what your goals and objectives are and have identified where you can cut back to find more money to invest, you should develop an investment plan. You can do this either on your own or with the assistance of a financial adviser.

If you choose to use a financial adviser, be aware that some see their job as helping you attain your goals, like buying a new car or home.

Gott and Kochis say that there is no single right way to pursue financial opportunities. One person may place a high priority on getting an early start on retirement, whereas someone else may think buying a new home is important and retirement can wait. It's the investor's money, so he or she should determine how it's used. The planner should coach the investor on how to do attain their financial goals through a solid investment plan.

Other investment advisers view their jobs as looking out for your best financial interests, and will

> ❝
> You can't have everything. Where would you put it?
> —Stephen Wright
> ❞

therefore guide you first and foremost in investing for your future. You will be encouraged to take advantage of all tax-deferred investments you can qualify for, since, in the long run, that's where your money will make the most money for you. These advisers will not neglect your other goals, like buying a new car or home, but will tell you to save for those as a second priority unless absolutely necessary.

In order to establish your investment plan, you need to come up with some goals. These are goals like money for a down payment for a house in 3 years, to pay for college in 15 years, or to retire in 30 years.

After you've thought about what you would like to achieve, then you need to figure out how to invest for them. Ask yourself these questions:

- What type of funds should you invest in to reach your goals?

- What proportion of your investment should you put into each of the funds?

- Should you buy risky funds or less risky, conservative funds? Risky funds often have better returns over time and conservative funds are more likely to produce less profit.

- What types of returns are associated with each of the funds that you are thinking about investing in?

- Are there minimum amounts of money that must be invested in order to open an account?

- How much money do you have to invest?

This last question will determine, to some degree, which of the 9,500 mutual funds will be open to you because all funds have a minimum initial investment.

If you have only $50 per month to invest, you will have to find funds that will allow you to buy in amounts that small. (Some mutual funds will waive the minimum if you make monthly investments electronically until you reach a certain level.) Some have a $10,000 minimum, some a $10 million minimum. But their performance is not better than the others, says Craig Israelson, an associate professor of Consumer and Family Economics at the University of Missouri-Columbia.

Once you've narrowed the list of funds down to those you can afford, you must decide which ones will best help you to reach your goals. The more money you have to invest, the larger the number of funds you'll have from which to choose.

Or, you can take a different approach; rather than using minimum initial investment requirements as the first criteria for selecting funds, select funds that meet your investment strategy and save up to make that investment.

Be sure to pick funds you'll want to stick with because every time you shift funds you must pay taxes.

Kochis advises that after you've outlined your objectives, prioritize them. Then you'll know where your trade-offs are going to be.

Look at it this way, says Gott. If you're a kid saving for a special toy, it makes it easier for you to pass other toys over because you know what you're saving for. Most people find that goals help them save. It motivates rather than causes resistance.

Kochis gives these tips for formulating an investment plan:

- Prioritize your goals. You'll have more than one goal—think of them all, even if you're not certain you'll be able to accomplish everything.

Timesaver
Track your planned portfolio before you buy the funds to see how well they perform. Go to a Web site like *SmartMoney* magazine(www. smartmoney.com) which has a feature that allows you to track your portfolio online.

- Decide who will spend the money, for what purpose, and when. Financial planning for individuals is all about spending money. Kochis says this revelation provides motivation for his clients.

- Have measuring sticks in place. Measuring specific goals lets you know if you're reaching them or not. If you have vague goals like getting rich or getting a high rate of return, you'll never know when you've arrived.

- Invest in mutual funds. They are an appropriate tool to fund almost all of your objectives.

Watch Out!
Young people sometimes falsely believe they should seek greater risk in pursuit of returns. This is not always prudent.

Age plays a role, as well, in your investment choices. "The younger you are, the more time you have to recover from any investment losses," Yasgur says. Consequently, you can afford to have a higher percentage of your investments in stocks rather than bonds. If you're older, you don't have the luxury of time and may want to readjust your portfolio, he says.

Although conventional wisdom says you should shift into less volatile investments as you near retirement, as the average life-span gets longer that thinking is changing, Israelson says.

Consider this, according to Fidelity Investment calculations if you have $500,000 to foot the bill for your retirement you will only have $22,202 after taxes to live on if you take out equal installments during a 25-year period. Even if you had $1 million, you'd only receive $44,403 after taxes for 25 years. (These calculations are based on the following assumptions: a 6.00 percent growth/interest rate, a 3.50 percent inflation rate, and a 28 percent income tax bracket.)

It becomes apparent from these equations that even large sums of money at below average growth rates will not have high enough distributions to support a comfortable lifestyle during retirement.

Much has been said by financial planners about stating your investment goals in specifics rather than generalities; for example, saying you want to be "wealthy" is too vague. But for some, having enough money to know you can live off your investments is the goal.

Planning by this method is possible using the Rule of Seventy-two or retirement calculators found on the Internet, as long as you know how much money you want in a specified amount of time.

For example, if you already have $150,000 and you want to double it in six years, divide seventy-two by six to get the rate of return you need to achieve your goal: 72 ÷ 6 = 12 percent.

So, if you achieve a 12 percent rate of return, you will have $300,000 in 6 years.

Likewise, if you know what rate of return you expect to get, you can divide that into 72 to find our how long it will take to double your money: 72 ÷ 10 percent = 7.2 years.

In any investment plan, the major hurdles you must overcome are inflation and taxes. If you're in the 28 percent tax bracket, you must get close to a 6 percent rate of return before you break even, Yasgur says. If you invest in a retirement plan, the government will give you help with your tax burden. (See Chapter 2 and Chapter 5 for information on tax-deferred plans for retirement.)

No matter which way you approach your investment goals, there are four basic elements to consider when choosing funds:

Bright Idea
Use software like Quicken to track all of your expenditures. It's a real eye-opener. You will see how much you spent on everything from groceries to gifts, and learn where you might be able to cut back.

- Time horizon—how many years you have to add to your investment and how many years it has to grow
- Risk tolerance—how much loss you can take in a volatile or down market before you want to redeem shares
- Object/goal—what you're saving to buy—a house, car, financial independence
- Investment—how much you have to invest now and how much you can invest monthly

Keep in mind that no matter what strategy you choose, especially if you balance your portfolio with investments other than mutual funds, you should check to make sure your allotments are still within the goals of your plan as market returns and inflationary rates change.

Just the facts

- When you invest in mutual funds, you're not just buying securities, you're buying professional management.
- If you want to own brand-name stocks but don't have a lot of money, you can invest in mutual funds.
- By cutting back on unnecessary luxuries and by shopping smarter, you'll have more money to invest now and more to spend later.
- Knowing how much money you want by a certain time will help you choose your investments.
- Mutual funds with high minimum investments don't necessarily perform better than those with lower minimums.

GET THE SCOOP ON...
Why you should invest in your retirement first ▪
Why you shouldn't buy the most house you can
afford ▪ Why stock mutual funds should be part
of your portfolio at any age ▪ How allocating
your assets can help you reach your goals

Savvy Investment Strategies

O ne of the most difficult things about financial planning is figuring out how to take
generic advice and applying it to your own
situation. Generic advice does not address individual factors such as your current and future financial
obligations, nor does it take into consideration how
many family members you have or your current
income.

Therefore, in order to develop an investment
strategy, you must assess your situation and define
your goals. Are you saving to buy your first home? A
car? College tuition for your children? Retirement?
Or, do you have a less-defined goal of "saving for the
future"? You also must decide in what time frame
you'll need the money to reach these goals. Do you
need the money in the next couple of years or will
you need it in 15 to 20 years or more?

Saving for a car, home, college tuition, or retirement can be part of your plan at any age. What really
determines your investment strategy are your

Bright Idea
Don't count on Uncle Sam to take care of you in your added years. Social Security benefits may not be around when you retire.

objectives, how you prioritize them, and how much time you are allowing yourself to achieve your goals.

In this chapter, you will see how you can allocate your assets to reach your financial goals. Since every investor's income, family status, financial obligations, risk tolerance, and time horizons (length of time until they need the money) differ, no one scenario will likely meet all of your needs. The information provided in this chapter will show you how to reach your own financial objectives and goals.

Investment strategies by goals and time horizons

There are many different investment strategies you can use at different ages, depending on your financial goals. But, in general, the younger you are, the more heavily invested in aggressive funds you should be in order to build wealth. Of course, if you are starting late, you may feel that you need to be more aggressive. But be warned; this usually entails more risk, and as your time horizon shortens, losses become less tolerable.

As you age, conventional wisdom says that your portfolio should be weighted with more conservative funds to protect against market slumps. Once you retire, you will probably want some income-producing investments added in to your asset mix.

But keep in mind that there is no one strategy that is right for everyone. Some 70-year-olds want their entire portfolio in equity mutual funds, and some young investors can't tolerate risk and choose to fill their portfolio with more of a mix. Then there are those who get started late and must tolerate added risk to make up for lost time. (See Chapter 6 for a look at risk and how risk tolerant you are.)

Another rule of thumb is that the percentage of your investment in bonds should equal your age, says Howard Yasgur, investment consultant with Gradison-McDonald. However, in the earlier years that formula tends to be too conservative, he says. As you grow older, you may tend to become more conservative; consequently, your portfolio would have more bonds, CDs, Treasuries, and money market funds.

Yasgur adds that most of the money currently invested in stock mutual funds has been added since 1990. Consequently, these investors have not lived through the market crashes of 1987 or 1990, much less the gut-wrenching bear market of the early seventies. As a result, a lot of young investors want only stock mutual funds in their portfolios. They ignore the asset allocation principle and the potential risk from having their entire investment in stocks.

Another way to look at investment strategies is to consider the different securities offered. For example, stock mutual funds offer growth potential for younger investors and provide a way to keep pace with inflation for those already in retirement.

For these reasons, investment advisers think that investment strategies should be tied to your objectives rather than your stage of life.

There are three main objectives in financial planning. They are:

- Growth potential
- Preservation of capital
- Maximizing income

Each objective corresponds with a generic investment strategy. If you want growth potential, consider investing in a growth stock mutual fund.

Timesaver
Keep track of your portfolio on one of many Web sites. Many of them will track up to ten funds for you. Try http://www. moneymag.com, http://www. quicken.com, or almost any of the brokerage sites.

For preserving your capital, choose mutual funds that invest in stocks and bonds, or only in bonds. If your objective is to maximize your monthly income, financial planners advise investing in bonds, whether through mutual funds or single bonds.

Your investment can be broken down further for better diversification to reduce risks. For an aggressive growth portfolio (one with 100 percent of your investment in stock funds), you can reduce your portfolio risk and volatility somewhat by dividing your portfolio equally among domestic large-cap mutual funds, domestic small-cap mutual funds, and foreign mutual funds. And remember, because you're investing in mutual funds, by their very nature they're diversified, reducing your risk even more.

If you're interested in a growth portfolio but you're a little worried about risk, you can divide that balance of stocks from the aggressive portfolio just described into 80 percent of your portfolio and place 20 percent in bond mutual funds or money market mutual funds. You can also replace the foreign stock mutual funds with global stock mutual funds, which include domestic funds. (However, you have no control over how the managers of these funds allocate the assets.)

If you're nearing retirement, or just want added income in addition to growth, you can reduce the stock portion of your portfolio to 60 percent and fill it with equal numbers of domestic large-cap, equity income, bond, and global mutual funds, and put the remaining 40 percent into bonds.

Bond mutual funds as an asset class are good for all ages, says Scott Grittinger, an investment counselor at Strong Advisor. For those in retirement, bond mutual funds provide a means for a regular income. For younger investors, they provide a means for capital preservation for an emergency account (3–6 months of living expenses should be acquired before investing).

Grittinger says ultra short-term bond funds can be used as an alternative to a money market mutual fund for people with a 2–3 year goal or for an emergency account. Such funds offer the possibility of a slightly higher return than a bank savings account. However, bonds do come with a higher risk than money market mutual funds, CDs, and bank savings accounts.

To achieve intermediate goals (those with a time horizon of 4–10 years), investment strategies turn toward stock mutual funds with either a large mix of aggressive and conservative funds for balance or the balance can include bond funds or money market funds (about 20 percent), as well.

Generally speaking, short-term investments should be in something that's stable and easily accessible. Long-term investments can be placed in more aggressive securities because they will have time to ride out market dips and slumps.

No matter what your age, here are some cautionary notes:

- Don't underestimate the length of your retirement.
- Keep in mind that inflation deflates the value of your savings and income.
- Expect that there will be times when you must dip into your principal.
- Expect the market to take deep dips from time to time and decide beforehand how you're

Watch Out!
Bond funds, like others, can be loaded with derivatives, adding to their volatility.

going to ride it out. If not, decide at what point you will jump ship.

■ In retirement, don't spend more during the years the market peaks because you have more. Eventually it will dip and you will be left with less.

With any investment goals, there are no guarantees. So many factors play into market performance that it is impossible to predict. Investing is as much an art as a science, Grittinger says.

Throughout the time you're saving for retirement—or any long-term goal—there are several variables that could throw you off course. Therefore, you must re-evaluate your portfolio from time to time. Factors that can wreak havoc on your investment plan include the following:

■ Inflation

■ Changes in tax laws

■ Fluctuations in the stock market

■ Changes in principal

■ Changes in the amount you invest versus what you expected to invest

Having investment goals will help you determine where to invest your money. But rather than having material goals, such as buying a car or home, you may have wealth goals, such as, "By the time I'm 45, I want to have $500,000." Or, likewise, "Ten years from now, I want to double my investment."

By knowing how much money you're investing and how much you want by a certain age or time horizon (the amount of investment time you have to reach a particular goal), you can apply the Rule of Seventy-two to determine the overall rate of return you must achieve to meet your investment goal. (See Chapter 1 and Chapter 3.)

Age is an important factor when it comes to an investor's desire for growth, income, or capital preservation (or combinations thereof). For simplicity, I am covering investment strategies for age groups, and am assuming that at certain ages you will have certain goals. However, if you're buying your first home at age 40 and that's discussed in an earlier age bracket, look there for the best investment strategy. Each section ends with a case scenario. Some of the investment advice specifically in response to the case scenarios was provided by USAA's Larry Correa.

Investment strategies when you're under 20

Most people under the age of 20 don't have much money to invest. Even so, with the magic of compounded interest, even a small amount of money can grow to an enormous investment by the time you're ready to use it. In fact, you're better off investing small amounts now rather than relatively larger amounts when you're older simply because of compounded interest over time.

For instance, a one-time investment of $2,000 from years of babysitting or mowing lawns can become $13,455 in 20 years, assuming a 10 percent annual rate of return. (These numbers are in today's dollars. Results are not adjusted for inflation.) If the investor leaves it in the market until he's 65 years old, assuming a 10 percent rate of return, he would end up with $378,118. This is for a one-time investment for 55 years. (See Chapters 1 and 2 for more on compounded interest.)

Timesaver
Need a prospectus? Look on the Internet. More and more funds now have sites.

Since time is on your side when you're young, you'll probably want to be in an index fund, which mirrors the market performance, like the S&P 500. Historically, these types of funds average a 10–12 percent rate of return over the long haul.

Scenario 1: Tom is 10 years old and mows lawns each summer. He makes about $2,000 from this and another $250 a year in allowances. How should he invest this money?

Advice: Since Tom is only 10 years old, if he does not need part of the money until college or even further down the road, he could possibly invest the allowance in a savings account to purchase items as he desires. He could invest the $2,000 he earns from his lawn mowing service in a stock mutual fund designed for growth potential. He would have either an 8-year time horizon if he is investing for college, or longer if the intent is to use the money as a starter fund after college or as retirement supplement funds, in which case he could set it up as an IRA.

By socking money into an IRA when you're still a kid and letting it grow for at least 50 years, you can invest very aggressively without worrying about market performance. If the market slumps, there's plenty of time for it to make up for the losses and turn into a sizable profit.

> **"**
> [I]f you're saving for a long-term goal, fixating on short-term performance is like gazing worriedly at thunderclouds while walking headlong into an oncoming bus.
> —*Money* Magazine (Online)
> **"**

Investment strategies when you're 20–30

Once you're on your own, before you start investing, make sure you put away 3–6 months of savings in an easily accessible account in case of an emergency (for example, losing your job). Once you've accomplished this, it's time to start investing.

If you can't afford a large investment today, start with small amounts in a savings account or money market fund (for better returns) and save until you have enough to make the minimum investment in the mutual fund you've decided best meets your goals and fits into your risk comfort level, says Carol Nemec, a professor of accounting and finance at Southern Oregon University. Savings bonds take too long to mature and don't pay that much better, she says.

Many financial experts will tell you to start saving for intermediate goals first. Once you do accumulate enough to invest in the mutual funds you've picked, you'll likely want to buy a car or a home, Correa says. After that, you'll want to start investing for retirement or your children's college education, if there's money left over, he says. (See Figure 4.1 for general guidelines to asset allocations in this age range.)

FIGURE 4.1: 20-30 YEARS OLD

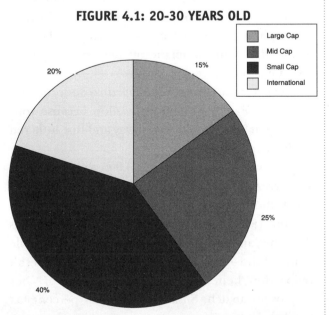

← Note!
General asset allocation guidelines for ages 20–30.

Assumes you have 3–6 months expenses in cash for emergency funds. These change according to world economics and developing markets.

Correa suggests looking at your time horizon over 3 years. That will guide you to the type of investment to consider, which he says in this case should be a short-term investment. Using the Rule of Seventy-two you can figure out if you can achieve your goal in that time allotment. It will depend upon how much money you're investing and the current and future rates of return on your investment tool.

But if you look at the numbers, it makes more investment sense to start saving for retirement first because of the tax advantages and how they play into compounded worth. If you are eligible for a 401(k) and your employer matches your investment, that's all the more advantageous. Why turn your back on money that's being handed to you by your employer and Uncle Sam? If your employer matches your investment dollar for dollar, that's an automatic 100 percent gain on your investment. If your employer matches fifty cents to every dollar you invest, that's an automatic 50 percent return on your investment.

Let's take a closer look at this option, even though it may be difficult to swallow because your retirement at this age is so far away and that little red car is so appealing.

Scenario 1: Susan makes $40,000 a year and puts 15 percent of her salary into a 401(k) ($6,000) of which the company matches 50 percent for up to 5 percent ($1,000) of her salary. She also contributes the same amount into the same fund as a taxable mutual fund—that is, with that account she doesn't reap the benefits of tax-deferment or her employer's match. Susan is in the 28 percent tax bracket. In this scenario we are assuming that each year the total return is 10 percent and there is 5 percent worth of dividends that are taxed as ordinary income in the regular mutual fund investment.

TABLE 4.1

Year	401k	Company	Mutual Fund	Taxes
1	$6,600	$1,100	$6,600	$92
2	$13,860	$2,310	$13,860	$194
3	$21,846	$3,641	$21,846	$306
4	$30,631	$5,105	$30,631	$429
5	$40,294	$6,716	$40,294	$564
6	$50,923	$8,487	$50,923	$713
7	$62,615	$10,436	$62,615	$877
8	$75,477	$12,579	$75,477	$1,057
9	$89,625	$14,937	$89,625	$1,255
10	$105,187	$17,531	$105,187	$1,473

Total: $122,718 vs. $98,227, a difference of 25 percent.

← **Note!**
Investing in your retirement is a savvy way to save your money. Investing equal amounts in a tax-deferred retirement account and in a taxable account has two starkly different outcomes.

After 10 years, the total amount in Susan's 401(k) is $122,718. The total amount in her regular mutual fund is $105,187. The taxes she paid on her regular mutual fund are $6,960, bringing the value of the taxable account down to $98,227. So, with the same dollar input, she has accumulated 25 percent more in her 401(k) account than in the same taxable account simply as a result of the extra money that her employer contributed in matching funds and the deferred taxes working for her in the market.

In addition to being able to make use of deferring payment of taxes through the 401(k), not only was Susan able to invest an extra $6,960 over those 10 years, but she also paid less in income taxes because the amount invested into the 401(k) was deducted before federal taxes were taken from her paycheck. Her taxable income was reduced from

$40,000 to $34,000, saving her $1,680 in taxes every year, which she could also invest. If she had invested the $1,680 that she saved in taxes every year (assuming she doesn't get a pay raise), she would have another $25,095 at the end of that 10-year period, bringing her total to $147,813, $49,586 over the taxable investment.

Furthermore, retirement plans offered from your employer deduct the funds from your paycheck before you even see it. If you plan your expenses based on your actual paycheck rather than on how much you make, you won't miss the money so much.

In the long run, it's better to invest for your retirement before you save for your children's education, say some financial experts. Your children will be better able to pay back loans on their education than foot the bill for your retirement.

It's the idea of trade-offs, says Tim Kochis of the investment firm Kochis Fitz. Most people don't have enough resources to fund all of their objectives immediately, though he says that any year you don't put in the maximum amount allowed by law into your retirement plan is a year lost. Therefore, he prefers not to advise someone not to put in the maximum. But, Kochis says, there is one exception: buying a home. If that goal is exceptionally important to you, then they advise saving for the down payment and other expenses associated with home buying, says his partner Kacy Gott.

If you do decide to buy a home, whether by saving additional funds or in lieu of investing as much as you can in a retirement plan, then make the smallest down payment possible. Twenty percent will eliminate PMI (an insurance on your mortgage) and still give you solid leverage on your investment. (Leveraging is achieved by investing the smallest

Moneysaver
Negotiate fees with your mortgage lender to reduce or eliminate extra costs like commissions and fees.

amount possible to reap the largest gains on that investment. For instance, if you invested $10,000 to buy a $100,000 home and it increased in value by 10 percent, to $110,000, your $10,000 investment would have a 100 percent return. Had you invested $20,000, your return would be reduced to 50 percent.) Ten percent or less will give you better leverage but the PMI expense should be considered when making that decision.

Some people think real estate is a good use of funds. But, especially during low inflationary periods, it's less attractive than equities, it's less liquid, and in the form of one lump sum, so it's not diversified. Property can go years without much appreciation and some properties lose value. Again, time plays a role.

Many people lose money by buying a home and moving before they can even recoup their initial investment. It costs roughly 10 percent of the purchase price to move. So, if you buy a $200,000 home, you'd have to turn around and sell it for $220,000 just to break even. Not many buyers are going to pay an extra $20,000 on a piece of property you just paid $200,000 for 2 years ago.

Gott and Kochis discourage clients from putting too much of their own money into their home. They give the following advice:

- Make the smallest down payment you can and still avoid PMI. Usually, that down payment is 20 percent. (You may want to consider a smaller down payment if your PMI rates are low in order to be better leveraged.)

- Don't pay down the mortgage rapidly. Get a 30- or 40-year mortgage rather than a 15-year mortgage. Gott even advises getting an interest-only

Bright Idea
Start putting money into a retirement plan when you start your first job. The investments of older first-time investors must be more aggressive, and aggressive investment tools are less safe.

loan if you invest the money that otherwise would have gone toward the principal.

▪ Don't make extra payments.

If you have a mortgage with an interest rate a few points lower than your investment returns, don't put money into your home that isn't necessary. Invest the extra cash in a portfolio that has a return that's greater than the cost of the interest on the mortgage. This investment strategy has nothing to do with the value of the house or appreciation. It has to do with your investment portfolio.

There is one important caveat to this strategy: The money that you would have used to pay down the mortgage must be used in market investments, not at a sale at Macy's. Furthermore, the rate of return on your investment must exceed the cost of that capital. If you don't think you can beat that rate of return, then pay down the mortgage.

For example, let's say you got a mortgage with an 8 percent interest rate. If you're in the 28 percent tax bracket, you'll be able to deduct about 30 percent of the interest from your federal and state taxes, so after tax you're paying 70 percent of the mortgage interest expense.

The after-tax cost of the mortgage is, therefore, 5.6 percent. (30 percent of 8 is 2.4 percent, the tax savings. Subtract the 2.4 percent from the 8 percent and you get the 5.6 percent rate.) If you can't do better than 5.6 percent after-tax on your investment then you should pay down your mortgage, Kochis says. But if you can do better, the last thing you want to do is pay down your mortgage, he says. Investors should find it pretty easy to get a return rate higher than 5.6 percent in mutual funds.

If you hold your investment for at least 12 months, you'll pay 20 percent on capital gains taxes.

If you get a 10 percent rate of return, your after-tax rate of return is close to 8 percent.

There's a solid spread between 5.6 percent and 8 percent, Kochis says, noting that after tax you'll earn close to 2.5 percent on your investment. That might not sound like much, but on $200,000 it's about $5,000 a year—every year—if you never pay off the mortgage. But as you pay off the mortgage, that advantage begins to diminish.

Many people just want to pay off the mortgage to be free of that monthly expense and use it for investing. But, Gott and Kochis point out, you'll be better off investing it, at least early on. On the other hand, Gott says, paying down the mortgage is better than just spending your money.

This strategy makes a lot of sense during low inflationary periods. But in a high inflationary period, such as the situation that existed from the late 1960s into the early 1980s, buying the most house you can afford makes sense. For example, say you bought a house for $100,000 when inflation was at 5 percent. If you borrowed 80 percent of the money and put $20,000 down with 5 percent inflation, the house would go up $5,000 in value. So, the house is now worth $105,000. You've made 25 percent on your $20,000 investment.

To continue our look at examples of investing for each age group, if you start putting money into your retirement plan, Gott suggests investing 100 percent in equities. A key point to remember when planning your retirement is not to target the year you retire, but the rest of your life, he says.

Scenario 2—Mary, at age 22, just landed her first full-time job as a teacher. She'll be earning $25,000 a year and is eligible to put funds into a retirement plan. She'll be living in an apartment. Her share of

Timesaver
Review and rebalance your portfolio in April when you're figuring your income taxes. That way, the information will be readily handy.

the rent will be $300, plus an estimated $50 for utilities.

Advice: Mary should consider setting short-term, intermediate, and long-term financial goals. She should start with an emergency fund and look at investments with greater return potential as her time horizon increases. She should also look into her employer's retirement plan and contribute as much as possible. It may have a matching feature, so she should contribute at least up to the maximum matching percentage, if possible.

At her age, Mary should consider investments with growth potential suitable to her risk tolerance as underlying vehicles. She may also consider a house purchase as an intermediate financial goal. The funding vehicle should take into consideration her time horizon, for risk purposes.

Investment strategies when you're 30–40

At this age, people are beginning to get more serious about investing for their retirement, says Kochis. But they also tend to focus on investing for their children's education. Kochis and Gott have a rather complicated investment strategy for people in this age group. It has been simplified in the following example:

Say your child is 15 years old. You expect her post-secondary education to span 5–6 years. So you have quite some time—about 8 years—to let at least some of your investments grow since you want to keep every dollar invested until the last bill is paid. Presuming you're starting with $10,000, Kochis and Gott advise putting $2,000 into equities for her master's degree. It will have 8 years to grow and ride out market downturns.

For her senior year of college, which is now 6 years away, they advise putting $2,000 into an S&P 500 index fund. The junior year is 5 years away so Kochis and Gott suggest putting $2,000 in a balanced fund, one which has 60 percent equities and 40 percent funds to reduce the risk somewhat. Her sophomore year is 4 years away. For that year, they suggest placing $2,000 in an intermediate term bond fund for added safety. For her freshman year, which is only 3 years away, they advise putting $2,000 in a CD that matures close to that date.

Gott says the key to planning is putting your objectives in terms of spending. The real benefit of doing this is to provide real motivation, Kochis says. Planning this way, he says, makes it possible for you to spend what you want to spend at certain ages. It gives people motivation to save, he says.

As a general guideline, Yasgur says you can invest 100 percent in equities if you'll be in the market for 10 years or longer. But it depends on the pool of money, he says. If it's for retirement, and you can tolerate the volatility, then invest 100 percent in equities. If it's your entire portfolio, then you'll need more of a balance because you'll have other expenses coming up. You don't want to put short-term money at risk in case the market slumps before you need it, he says. Guidelines depend heavily on time horizons—that is, the amount of time you can leave your money in the market.

To be conservative, Yasgur suggests putting 30–40 percent of your portfolio in bonds, with the exception of your retirement portfolio.

See Figure 4.2 for general guidelines to asset allocations in this age range.

66
I'm opposed to millionaires, but it would be dangerous to offer me the position.
—Mark Twain
99

Note! ➜
General asset
allocation guide-
lines for ages
30–40.

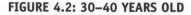

FIGURE 4.2: 30–40 YEARS OLD

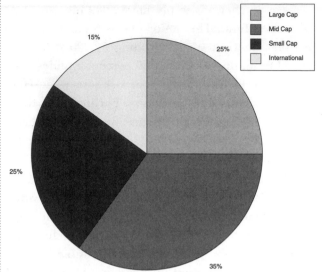

Assumes you have 3–6 months expenses in cash for emergency
funds. These change according to world economics and developing
markets.

Scenario 3—Jasmine is 30 years old and works as
an engineer. She earns $45,000 a year and is mar-
ried to Harold, who earns $50,000 as a computer
programmer in a small company. They own a home,
and their mortgage is $1,300 a month. Their utilities
run about $200 a month. They have two young chil-
dren, ages 2 and 4.

Advice: Jasmine and Harold should consider the
following:

- Establish short-term, intermediate, and long-
  term financial goals. First and foremost, make
  sure they have sufficient short-term emergency
  funds.

- Maximize company retirement plans. At their
  ages, Jasmine and Harold should consider
  investments with long-term growth potential,

relative to their risk tolerance, as funding vehicles. Their time horizon is over 25 years, at least. This would allow a retirement nest egg to build up and provide some current tax relief at their tax bracket, since contributions would probably be pre-tax.

■ Establish college funds for the two children. They should consider the pros and cons of making outright gifts under the children's names with Jasmine or Harold as custodian, as opposed to having the accounts under their names. Since the time horizons are approximately 12–15 years, they should consider investments with growth potential.

Investment strategies when you're 40–50

There's an assumption that you should have more discretionary funds and assets in this age group, says USAA's Correa. He suggests moving a portion of your investment into world funds for better diversification. It will increase the asset mix and theoretically reduce overall portfolio risk by balancing domestic with international holdings. (However, considering recent world events, you may want to take into account your tolerance for risk.) Be sure to keep funding your retirement. You will also want to keep some stock funds to hedge against inflation.

See Figure 4.3 for general guidelines to asset allocations in this age range.

Scenario 5—Eleanor is 45 years old and earns $65,000 a year as an attorney. Her husband, Tyler, earns $70,000 as a manager. They have two children, ages 15 and 17. They've saved $40,000 for college tuition.

Bright Idea
Protect your assets with health, auto, and homeowner's insurance. One uninsured mishap could wipe out your entire savings.

Note! ➡
General asset
allocation guide-
lines for ages
40–50.

FIGURE 4.3: 40–50 YEARS OLD

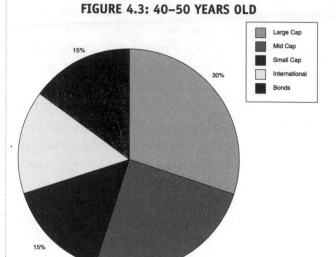

Assumes you have 3–6 months expenses in cash for emergency funds. These change according to world economics and developing markets.

Advice: Eleanor and Tyler should consider the following:

- Consider taking a more conservative, low-risk approach with the college funds since the time horizon is only 1–2 years. The time horizon should take precedent in this instance rather than the potential for higher returns. If these are the only funds for college, their focus should be more on maximizing the yield as opposed to growth potential. They should also consider scholarships, especially for the 15-year-old.

- Eleanor and Tyler should also establish a sufficient emergency fund cushion for the short term and set intermediate and long-term financial goals. For the long term, they should look at maximizing their company retirement plan contributions with an emphasis on investments with long-term growth potential, relative to their risk tolerance. At their income levels they are in a higher tax bracket, so the retirement plan would provide a nest egg and some immediate tax relief since their incomes, for tax purposes, would be lowered.

Investment strategies when you're 50–60

At this age you've probably met most of your financial goals, leaving only retirement. This also tends to be the decade when most people are in their highest earning years.

Appropriate investments are heavily oriented toward equities, Kochis says. At this point, you're still far enough away from the time at which you'll be spending the money. The total spending time horizon could range from being 20–40 years away with the midpoint at about 15–20 years away.

See Figure 4.4 for general guidelines to asset allocations in this age range.

Scenario 6—Tiffany is 50 years old and single. She earns $45,000 a year as a graphic designer in a mid-size city. She rents an apartment for $700 per month and pays about $150 monthly in utilities.

Advice: Tiffany should consider the following:

▪ Set short-term, intermediate, and long-term goals. Being single, she should especially focus on building up an emergency fund, preferably with 3–6 months of disposable income.

▪ Maximize her company retirement plan. This would provide her a retirement nest egg for the long term and provide some current tax relief since contributions would be pre-tax. At a

$45,000 annual income with a single status, she is in a higher tax bracket. Her time horizon is approximately 10 or more years, so she has sufficient time to consider adding some investments with growth potential to her asset mix, relative to her risk tolerance. She may also want to consider some income-oriented investments to diversify relative to her time horizon.

■ She may also consider purchasing a house as an investment.

Note! ➡
General asset
allocation guide-
lines for ages
50–60.

FIGURE 4.4: 50–60 YEARS OLD

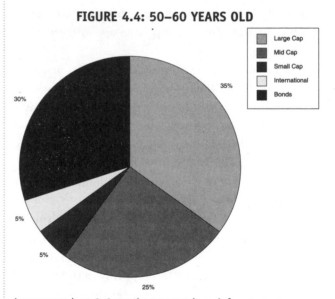

Assumes you have 3–6 months expenses in cash for emergency funds. These change according to world economics and developing markets.

Investment strategies when you're 60 and over

USAA's Correa suggests using common stock in your retirement portfolio as an inflationary hedge. But for the most part, your investment objective should be investments that provide income. So, look into investments that maximize monthly income, but still include some international funds, which provide asset and risk diversification.

Gott fine-tunes this investment strategy. When you're within 5 years of retirement, he says, the most recent money you've earned should be the first money you spend. This is referred to as LIFO—last in, first out. The money you've saved previously can still be in equities.

See Figure 4.5 for general guidelines to asset allocations in this age range.

FIGURE 4.5: OVER 60 YEARS OLD

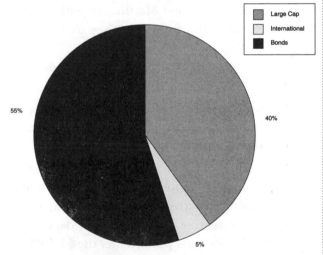

← **Note!** General asset allocation guidelines for ages 60 and over.

Assumes you have 3–6 months expenses in cash for emergency funds. These change according to world economics and developing markets.

To figure out what you'll need after you retire, add your pensions and Social Security and see what the shortfall will be. Set up "pots" for the next 5 years. For the first year place the shortfall amount in a money market account, he says. Get bonds that mature for the next 4 years. Once those are set up, go back into equities. The implication is it keeps rolling over——after the first year you use your equity portfolio and make a fifth-year pot, another bond. And then convert the bond that's maturing into a money market fund to spend it.

Many financial advisers these days stress the importance of having your money invested in the market during your retirement years. Just make sure you spend consistently to ride out the market downturns and don't spend any more than you've allotted for if the market produces well. Market returns will fluctuate.

Scenario 7—Rich and Martha are both 65 and have just retired with $400,000. They own a home worth $250,000, which is paid off.

Advice: Rich and Martha should consider the following:

- Setting aside sufficient liquid cash for emergencies and short-term use for enjoying their retirement.

- Invest some of the funds in income-generating investments to supplement their other retirement income sources. They could look at either taxable or tax-free income sources, depending on their tax bracket and whether the $400,000 is comprised of tax-deferred retirement and/or non-retirement income. They should also consider allocating some of the funds to investments with growth potential, relative to their risk, as a hedge against inflation and to build an estate investment plan.

Just the facts

- Saving for retirement first allows you to take advantage of investing deferred taxes.

- Starting your investments when you're young gives you plenty of time to ride out market swings.

- The makeup of your portfolio depends on both your goals and your time horizons.

- The balance of funds in your portfolio will depend on your risk tolerance level.

- Investing for your retirement doesn't stop the day you receive your gold watch.

GET THE SCOOP ON...
Which retirement plan(s) you qualify for ▪
Whether you should invest in a Roth IRA ▪ Why
investing in a 401(k) makes so much sense ▪
Which is better: investing tax-deferred or taking
advantage of the long-term capital gains tax

Retirement

Many people have to change their lifestyles dramatically when they retire (usually at age 65). They are forced to sell their homes or take out a reverse mortgage, move to a less expensive area (often far away from their children and grandchildren), and cut back on food and entertainment expenses.

But it doesn't necessarily have to be that way for you. Even if you've reached or are just about to reach retirement age, you still must consider investing for retirement, because on average, many people will live well past the age of 65.

In this chapter, you'll learn about different types of retirement plans and their eligibility requirements, benefits, and drawbacks.

Why invest for retirement?

As noted in Chapter 2, there are many factors that play a role in how much money you'll need in retirement. While many of you will have finished paying off your mortgage, you'll still have all the other routine expenses, such as transportation, utilities, and

insurance (with increasing premiums due to age).
Plus, you'll have added expenses like increased medical bills. And you must consider inflation and the
tax impact of post-retirement employment. (See
Chapter 2 for more detailed information on why
you need to invest for retirement.)

On the other hand, you'll probably have Social
Security benefits and possibly a pension, but that
won't be enough if you want to have a comfortable
lifestyle now that you'll have the time to enjoy it.

The bottom line? Invest in your future now or
tarnish your golden years.

Roth IRAs, traditional IRAs, and SEP IRAs

All forms of retirement savings have tax advantages.
But only the Roth IRA allows you to withdraw money
tax-free during your retirement (after age $59^1/2$).
The others are tax-deferred. None is tax-exempt. It's
just a matter of when you pay the taxes and what
income bracket you'll be in once you reach retirement (except for the Roth because you've already
paid taxes on it).

You can use your retirement plan to invest in
mutual funds as part or all of your individual retirement arrangement, or IRA. If you're self-employed,
you can have a Simplified Employee Pension, or
SEP, a Savings Incentive Match Plan, or SIMPLE, or
a Keogh plan (all discussed later in this chapter).

Increases in value of the mutual fund shares and
earnings distributions grow tax-free until you begin
making withdrawals (except for the Roth IRA, for
which distributions are not taxable).

Investing for retirement is important because, as
baby boomers nearing retirement have found out,
they will not be able to continue living in the style to

which they have become accustomed if they haven't invested or saved large sums of money. Nor will they be able to depend on company pensions as their parents did to fund their retirements. Generation X and Generation Y seem to have no such fantasies and are starting to save at younger ages.

As a result, boomers will have to have more aggressive funds in their retirement portfolios in order to build up a nest egg quickly. Hence, they must take on more risk. While their parents invested in bonds, boomers must be, at least in part, invested in the market. Even during retirement, they will have to continue investing. Retirement plans are good investment tools because of the tax advantages they offer.

Roth IRA

Last year Uncle Sam gave us another retirement savings plan option. With traditional IRAs, you receive a tax deduction up front (if you qualify). While your earnings grow tax-free, you'll have to pay taxes at ordinary income tax rates when you take money out at retirement.

With the Roth IRA, you can't deduct contributions from your income taxes, but the dividend income does grow tax-free if you wait until age $59^1/2$ to make withdrawals (or if you have a severe disability, or you want to buy your first home or contribute to your child's first home purchase, up to $10,000). Withdrawals on principal are tax-free, unless you have taxes due, in which case you'll pay a 10 percent penalty.

Figuring out which retirement investment strategy—the traditional IRA or Roth IRA—is best for you involves a present value calculation to measure the benefits of paying the tax now versus later. To do

Watch Out!
Although it's highly touted, the Roth IRA may not be the best retirement plan for you.

this, you must predict what tax bracket you might be in at the time you'll be taking distributions. Income level and the length of your investment horizon also play a role in determining which IRA is best.

Tax experts say that for many investors it makes sense to contribute to the Roth IRA because very few people qualify for deductible IRAs anyway. But even the Roth IRA has a phase-out (for deducting your contribution from your earnings) between $150,000 and $160,000 adjusted gross income for married couples.

But if you've accumulated substantial wealth, it may not make sense to convert a traditional IRA to a Roth IRA because you won't have the opportunity to benefit taxwise later. For instance, if you didn't earn much in your investments, it may make sense to roll it over because the taxes due wouldn't be enormous. But if you have substantial returns, even over a short period of time, it might not be worth it to pay the tax now.

There are calculators on the Internet (mostly at mutual fund family sites) that take into account the time period that your wealth has accumulated and the rate of return to help you determine whether or not to make the move. The calculators look at a substantial number of variables to come up with a projection of the cost of both methods of saving for retirement.

Since calculators differ, try going to several Web sites and seeing if their calculators include the variables fitting your circumstances. (See Chapter 14 for a list of Web sites.) Also, check to see if there is a significant difference in results;. don't rely completely on the results of any one program. Have a good knowledge base so that you understand the calculation, and consult a tax adviser to review your decision.

Advantages and disadvantages of Roth IRAs

There are several advantages to having a Roth IRA:

- When you reach retirement, you won't have to pay taxes on the withdrawals, so what you take out is all yours.

- There is no mandatory withdrawal requirement for the Roth IRA. With traditional IRAs, you must start taking distributions at age $70^1/2$.

- Your earnings grow tax-free (as opposed to tax-deferred).

- If you retire in a higher tax bracket, you will have substantial tax savings.

But Roth IRAs have disadvantages, too, such as:

- Because you pay the tax on your contribution up front, your principal investment is less than it would be for a traditional IRA, and so its earning power is weakened. (But your withdrawals are tax-free, so you can withdraw less, allowing your funds to continue earning interest and/or dividends and it will last longer.)

- If you retire to a lower tax bracket, you will lose some of the tax benefits you sought to gain.

Who qualifies? Married couples of any age whose adjusted gross income is below $160,000 and singles whose adjusted gross income is below $110,000. However, the amount you're allowed to contribute begins to phase out at $150,000 for couples filing jointly and at $95,000 for individuals. (Traditional IRAs don't have an earned income limitation for contributions, but there is an income limitation for deductibility if either spouse is an active

> "
> Train up a fig tree in the way it should go, and when you are old sit under the shade of it.
> —Charles Dickens
> "

participant in a company plan. There is also an age limit of $70^1/_2$ for making contributions.)

Contributions to Roth IRAs are capped at \$2,000 annually and are not tax deductible.

You can convert your traditional IRA to a Roth IRA if your adjusted growth income (AGI) is \$100,000 or less, but you have to pay tax on the amount converted. (Note: If you're married and filing separately, you can't convert your traditional IRA to a Roth IRA.)

Tax rules do change, though. "There will come a day when Congress will realize what a wonderful benefit they have given us, so they will take it away," says Kay R. Shirley, a registered investment adviser.

Traditional deductible IRA

You can contribute to a traditional IRA if you are under the age of $70^1/_2$ and work for a company without a retirement plan. The same is true for your spouse. If you're single, you can't earn more than \$40,000 to participate. If you're married, you must be earning less than \$60,000. Or, if only one of you has a retirement plan at work, your joint income must be under \$160,000 to get the deduction. You'll benefit from this type of retirement plan if you retire in a lower tax bracket than you're in now.

You can convert a traditional IRA to a Roth IRA if your adjusted gross income is under \$100,000. If you withdraw funds before the age of $59^1/_2$, you'll be hit with a 10 percent penalty.

Early withdrawals are permitted if made under the following conditions:

- if they're made by your beneficiaries after your death.
- if you become severely disabled.

- to pay medical expenses in excess of 7.5 percent of your gross income.

- to pay health insurance premiums if you become unemployed.

- if you take out equal installments intended to last the rest of your life.

- to pay for higher education for your immediate family or your grandchildren.

- to buy your first home or a first home for a family member.

You can contribute up to $10,000 total for real estate from this plan during your lifetime.

You must have taken your first required minimum distribution by April 1 the year after you turn $70^1/2$. The minimum payout is based on your life expectancy (as determined by the IRS and in IRS Publication 590) or that of you and your beneficiary.

Nondeductible IRA

If you're working, earning income, under age $70^1/2$, and don't qualify for a traditional IRA or Roth IRA, you can qualify for this plan. All you have to do is set up the account and make contributions by April 15 for the previous tax year. You can contribute up to $2,000 annually if you're single or $4,000, split equally under each spouse's name, if you're married and filing jointly. But the contributions are not tax-deductible; that is, you can't deduct them from your gross earnings on your income taxes. However, withdrawals (except for rollovers) of the principal investment are tax-free. Earnings are taxed at your ordinary income tax rate at the time of withdrawal. Distributions are penalty free but not income tax free.

Bright Idea
Consider the ramifications of borrowing from your retirement.

Withdrawals are a combination of earnings and principal in this plan. Therefore, you must keep meticulous records of earnings, which are taxable, and principal, which is not taxable, since you've already paid taxes on it. (Note: you can also convert this plan into a Roth IRA.)

Heed this warning, though: Take money out before you're $59^{1}/_{2}$ and you'll incur a 10 percent penalty on the amount distributed.

Early withdrawal rules are the same as those for the traditional deductible IRAs, as are the minimum distribution rules.

SIMPLE IRA

The Savings Incentive Match Plan (SIMPLE) is a salary reduction arrangement that allows small businesses to make contributions on behalf of each eligible employee. You can set up a SIMPLE using IRAs (SIMPLE IRA plans) or as part of a 401(k) plan.

If you're self-employed and own an S-corporation or a C-corporation, you can set up this type of a plan, but you must do so by October 31 and contribute to it by December 31. You must make matching contributions by your business tax deadline. But you may not be able to use this plan if you have a 401(k) at your primary job if you have one aside from your business.

With this retirement plan, you can contribute up to $6,000 and make dollar-for-dollar matching contributions of up to 3 percent of your income. These contributions grow tax-deferred. You can roll funds from this plan over to other SIMPLE IRAs and, after 2 years, other traditional IRAs. Except for rollovers, all withdrawals are taxed at your ordinary income tax rate. But if you withdraw money within the first 2 years after making the first contribution, you'll be hit with a hefty 25 percent penalty. That penalty's reduced to 10 percent on anything withdrawn after the first 2 years and before age $59^{1}/_{2}$. The exceptions for early withdrawal are the same as those for the SEP, traditional, and nondeductible IRAs.

Keogh

You can set up a Keogh if you're self-employed or have a partnership business. If the Keogh is set up as a profit-sharing plan, you can contribute up to 15 percent of your qualified compensation after reduction for the contribution, or $24,000, whichever is less. If you set it up as a money purchase pension plan, you can contribute up to 25 percent of your qualified compensation after reduction for the contribution, or $30,000, whichever is less. Contributions are tax-deferred.

As an employer, you don't have to make contributions out of net profits to have a profit-sharing plan, nor does the plan have to provide a formula for figuring the profits to be shared. But there are numerous caveats. (See IRS Publication 560 for a complete description.) If you use the money purchase pension plan, your contributions are fixed and are not based on profits. Contributions for the profit-sharing plan are used to share profits and are not necessarily distributed at a fixed rate.

With the Keogh profit-sharing plan, you can benefit from tax-deferred investing even if you have another retirement plan. But if you have employees, it will cost you; you must make contributions for them, as well. The same holds true if you have a Keogh money purchase pension plan, except that once you set up that plan, you must fund it.

You must set up the plan by the end of the calendar or fiscal year (for the plan) and contribute to

When buying and selling are controlled by legislation, the first things to be bought and sold are legislators.
—P. J. O'Rourke

it by your tax-filing deadline, including extensions. If you decide to close the plan, rollovers into IRAs and other qualified plans are permitted.

Withdrawals from this retirement plan are taxed at ordinary income tax rates. But if you make withdrawals before age $59^1/_2$ you'll pay a 10 percent penalty. Exceptions to these penalties are the same as those for the 401(k) as will be described later, as are the minimum distribution rules.

SEP-IRA

A Simplified Employee Pension, or SEP for short, is simpler than the Keogh plan, although it doesn't have all the advantages of a Keogh. This plan allows you to make contributions to your own plan if you're self-employed, and to your employees' plan. You can make contributions if you're the boss of an S-corporation or a C-corporation, as well.

By setting up this type of IRA, you can make contributions of up to 15 percent of your net income or $24,000, whichever is less. You must set it up and contribute to it by your business tax-filing deadline.

You may roll over your SEP-IRA investment to a traditional IRA. Except for the rollover, all withdrawals are taxed at your income tax rate at the time of withdrawal.

There are exceptions to the early withdrawal rules. They are the same as for the SIMPLE, traditional, and nondeductible IRAs.

With this plan, you must begin withdrawing money by April 1 one year after you turn $70^1/_2$. The minimum payout is based on your life expectancy or that of you and your beneficiary.

Your contributions grow tax-deferred and you may contribute to other retirement plans. But if you have employees, you must contribute on their behalf as well.

401(k) plan

By enrolling in this employer-sponsored retirement plan, you can save up to $10,000 (maximum for 1998 and 1999) tax deferred or the maximum permitted by your plan. These plans often have an added benefit: The employer makes matching contributions or contributes a percent of what you contribute. However, you may have to stay with the company a certain number of years in order to become fully vested in your employer's contributions.

Contributions are made from pre-tax dollars and earnings grow tax-deferred.

You can roll over funds from a 401(k) into IRAs and other qualified investment plans. Withdrawals of tax-deferred contributions and earnings are taxed at your ordinary income tax rate. There is no tax on withdrawals on after-tax contributions, loans from your account, or rollovers to an IRA or new employer's 401(k).

However, there are penalties for early withdrawals—an additional 10 percent tax on withdrawals made before age $59^1/2$, except under the following circumstances:

- if the withdrawal is made by your beneficiaries after your death.
- if you become severely disabled.
- to pay medical expenses in excess of 7.5 percent of your gross income.
- if you leave your job after you reach age 55.
- in equal installments intended to last the rest of your life.

Moneysaver
Invest in a retirement plan and let your earnings grow tax-deferred.

If you continue to work, you can continue contributing to the plan. If you retire, you must begin withdrawals by April 1 the year after you turn $70^1/_2$.

Minimum withdrawals depend upon your life expectancy or the life expectancies of you and your beneficiary, as determined by IRS calculations. (See IRS Publication 590.)

This plan is especially enticing if your employer matches all or part of your investment. Plus, you can borrow against your account if your employer offers loans. However, this is not always such a good idea. While you pay yourself interest on the loan rather than paying a bank, you miss out on investment earnings. Furthermore, if you lose your job or change jobs before you've paid back your loan, you must repay the loan within 30–90 days. This can put you in a tough situation because, if you don't repay it within that time, you'll owe tax on the amount withdrawn and a 10 percent penalty for early withdrawal.

To contribute to a company's 401(k), you typically must be at least 21 years old and have worked for the company for a year, but some employers are making employees immediately eligible.

Taxes and retirement

Saving for your retirement using one of the methods described above gives you a significant tax advantage in terms of allowing your earnings to grow tax-free (in the case of the traditional IRAs) and getting tax relief in retirement (in the case of the Roth IRA).

But the traditional IRAs, depending on your circumstances, may have another tax advantage. You can deduct your contribution from your gross earnings, reducing your taxable income by the amount

Timesaver
Invest in a 401(k). The contributions come out of your pretax pay automatically.

you contribute each year you make a contribution. Then, at retirement, when you make a withdrawal, you pay taxes on the entire amount of the distribution.

Now with the new tax rules cutting long-term capital gains to 20 percent at most, there is some debate on where you should place your aggressive funds—in your tax-deferred retirement portfolio where the dividends can grow tax-free but taxes due at retirement can be as high as 39.6 percent or your taxable account where long-term gains are taxed at 20 percent.

In the taxable account, dividends and short-term capital gains are taxed at your income tax bracket, which can be as high as 39.6 percent. Most people, though, are in the 28 percent tax bracket. That's still a considerable tax bite.

But if you keep these funds in your tax-deferred retirement account (save for the Roth IRA, where you pay the taxes upfront), when you make withdrawals after age $59^1/2$, you'll pay tax at your income tax rate for ordinary income at that time.

The problem is, you don't know what tax rules will exist in the future. John Roberts, director of investment counseling services at Denver Investment Advisors LLC, a money management firm in Denver, finds investors spend a lot of time projecting what the returns on their investment will be and what their taxes will look like at retirement.

A lot of people say they will need X amount of dollars that will be taxed at X percent, he says. They use retirement calculators at fund sites to determine their projected financial needs. But you never know what the tax rate will be in the future, he says, and these investors spend too much time trying to figure that out in futility.

Watch Out!
In some cases,
you currently
may be better off
investing in tax-
able versus tax-
deferred
accounts.

Roberts notes that, historically, taxes have ranged from 15 percent to as high as 70 percent. He says it's better to spend time picking a good portfolio with long-term returns rather than trying to project what your taxes will be when you retire. While tax implications shouldn't be ignored, they shouldn't drive your investment decisions.

One factor that makes the Roth IRA more attractive is that it takes the guesswork out of the equation. You can withdraw accumulated earnings in a Roth IRA tax-free after age $59^1/_2$, as long as you've had the account for at least 5 years.

But if you can only afford to sock away 10 percent or less of your income, and if the company your work for has a 401(k) plan, your decision should be easy. Not only do you get to make your contributions with pre-tax dollars, increasing your potential earning power and decreasing your taxable income, but many companies match your investment dollar for dollar or 50¢ to the dollar up to a certain percent of your income.

The math is simple yet tells a dramatic investment tale. If you put a dollar in and your employer matches it, that's an immediate 100 percent return—risk-free—on your investment. You can't get much better than that, not even when you compare it to the 20 percent long-term capital gains rate.

A T. Rowe Price analysis indicates that tax-deferred compounding overcomes higher taxes. For long-term investors, the opportunity to compound earnings on a tax-deferred basis will probably outweigh the possibility that those earnings could be taxed at a relatively higher rate in retirement. (See Table 5.1.)

TABLE 5.1: IMPACT OF 20% CAPITAL GAINS RATE ON TAXABLE VS. TAX-DEFERRED INVESTING (AFTER-TAX VALUES OF A $10,000 GROWTH FUND INVESTMENT*)

	Taxable Account	Tax-Deferred Account
5 Years	$18,025	$17,510
10 Years	$33,071	$32,853
15 Years	$61,279	$64,199
20 Years	$114,162	$128,240

* Results are based on the actual average annual performance of growth funds from 1/1/77 to 12/31/96. Values assume the accounts are liquidated at the end of each period. Annual fund distributions in the taxable account are taxed each year at a 28% income tax rate and a 20% capital gains rate, and capital gains realized upon liquidation are taxed at 20%. All earnings in the tax-deferred account are taxed at 28% upon liquidation. To reflect the impact of differences in tax rates, values at the periods of less than 20 years assume that the average annual return for the full 20-year period was earned uniformly each year. Therefore, they do not reflect the actual investment results or market fluctuations during those periods. The advantage of the tax-deferred account would increase if withdrawals were made over a longer period of time, which is usually the case. Results also assume investments in the taxable account are held in the same fund for the entire period. Switching of funds further enhances the advantage of using the tax-deferred account. Source: T. Rowe Price

← Note!
Based on actual performance for growth funds over the past 20 years, using an initial investment of $10,000, a tax-deferred account provided a higher after-tax amount than a taxable account, even though all of the earnings were taxed at a 28 percent income tax rate upon withdrawal while the taxable investor benefited from the lower 20 percent rate on capital gains. Source: T. Rowe Price

If both investors had emptied their accounts at the end of 20 years, the one who had placed his or her money in the tax-deferred account would have netted $14,000 more than the one who invested in the taxable account to take advantage of the 20 percent long-term capital gains tax rate.

But use caution when considering entering this race. It took the tax-deferred investor 11 years to pull ahead of the taxable investor when you look at the net on an after-tax basis. If you don't have a long-term investment horizon, you may want to consider other investment strategies.

The T. Rowe Price analysis demonstrates that, based on actual fund performance over the past 20

Bright Idea
If you're tempted to spend your money, invest in a retirement plan. The penalties will help you keep you hands in your pockets.

years, holding the equity fund in the tax-deferred account and the bond fund in the taxable account proved more beneficial.

"Assuming an initial $10,000 investment in both a growth fund and a bond fund, a 28 percent income tax rate and 20 percent capital gains rate, and liquidation of both accounts at the end of 20 years, the investor who held the stock fund in the tax-deferred account and the bond fund in the taxable account netted $161,000, compared with $155,000 with the opposite strategy," says Steve Norwitz, vice president of T. Rowe Price. "In the long run, compounding the gains of the higher-earning growth fund on a tax-deferred basis proved more significant than the difference in tax rates."

Norwitz notes that stock funds had an unusually high pretax average annual return of 15.3 percent during this period and significantly outperformed bond funds.

"If returns in the future are lower, and stocks do not outperform bonds by as great a margin, it may be more beneficial to hold the bond fund in the tax-deferred account, assuming the long-term capital gains rate remains at 20 percent," Norwitz says.

Norwitz says that it's that investors in tax-deferred accounts normally don't take a single, lump-sum distribution from their accounts after 20 years of investing, as in their example. "They usually take systematic withdrawals over time to fund their retirement," he says.

"Taking that into consideration, the advantage of the tax-deferred account is even greater since the money left in the account continues to compound on a tax-deferred basis during retirement," Norwitz says. "And the investor is unlikely to hold the same stock fund for 20 years, possibly generating taxes on the sale of shares in the taxable account."

Just the facts

- If you have a Roth IRA, you can withdraw your earnings and principal tax-free.

- If you have a 20-year or more investment horizon, it's more advantageous to invest in a tax-deferred retirement plan.

- If you have less than a 20-year investment horizon, you'd probably fare better taking advantage of the long-term capital gains tax rate and investing in taxable accounts.

- With a traditional IRA, you can deduct your contribution from your gross earnings, reducing your taxable income.

All About Mutual Funds

GET THE SCOOP ON...
What risk means to you ▪ Why the stock market
fluctuates ▪ How you can figure out your risk
tolerance ▪ Why it's worth taking some risk ▪
How you can reduce your risks

PART III

Taking Risks

No doubt about it, investing is risky, especially if you invest all your money in just one stock and that stock happens to be in a small company that goes under. There's no way to predict how the market will perform, let alone individual companies.

If you're someone who reads the financial pages every day and worries when the market doesn't do well, take comfort. There are ways to reduce your exposure to risk in the stock market.

But in order to do that, you must first understand risk. What is risk? What are the different types of risk? What makes people so adverse to risk? What investment strategies are likely to reduce risk? These questions and more will be addressed in this chapter.

What is risk?

Risk and regret go hand in hand for the individual investor. Regret is the emotion you feel when you've made a decision that turns out badly, says Meir Statman, a researcher at the Leavey School of

113

Finance at Santa Clara University. It's not just the loss of money but the sense of, "Stupid me. If only I had waited another day," he explains. Risk really involves loss of ego and self-esteem as well as money.

So people come up with excuses to soothe the pain of regret, Statman says. When the market goes up, investors take full credit for their investment decisions, proudly declaring, "I bought that stock." However, when they lose money, they say, "My broker sold me that stock," using brokers as scapegoats, he says.

One strategy investors use to reduce their risk in the market is dollar cost averaging, which is investing the same amount of money in the market on a routine basis, so that they buy at market highs as well as lows.

But, Statman contends, the dollar cost averaging investment strategy has nothing to do with risk. It is, however, a good example of the issue of regret.

Statman uses this example to illustrate what really motivates the investor: If you have a $100,000 inheritance in the form of a stock portfolio, but you're a conservative—that is, risk-adverse— investor, you'd want to convert it into cash.

But people usually don't do that, Statman says. Instead, they dollar cost average out of stocks. They don't sell their inherited stocks all at once because the market could go up and they don't want to feel stupid and kick themselves later. Clearly, the motivation is regret rather than reducing risk.

It's the same for buying into the market. People don't want to invest lump sums because if the market falls they'll feel foolish, Statman says. They use dollar cost averaging to help reduce the feeling of regret.

The reality is that you just can't predict the market. No doubt, people like to speculate. They'd like to believe they know where the market will go next. But they don't know. It's like a football game, the Bears versus the Bulls, and the commentators can really only offer evidence of similar historical patterns. They can't predict the final score.

That people think they can predict the market is almost the definition of being human, Statman says. Many people believe there are patterns in the stock market that show them which way the market will go, or they'll listen to someone who claims to be able to predict market movements.

"It's the equivalent of an optical illusion," Statman says. "We are designed by evolution to figure out patterns."

The pattern of the market is like candy for the brain. "It's so tempting," Statman says. "Finding patterns is a useful trait, but the stock market presents patterns that look like they are decipherable when, in fact, they are not."

To assess your risk tolerance, see Table 6.1.

After deciding on your goals and time horizons, check the box that most appropriately describes your risk tolerance for each goal.

Types of risk

All investments involve some form of risk. Even a federally insured bank account is subject to the possibility that inflation will rise faster than your earnings, leaving you with less real purchasing power than when you started.

There are several types of risk with which investors must contend. Some risks, like market risk, are always present to one degree or another because

Watch Out!
Don't let your emotions get the best of you during market swings. Stick to your investment plan.

Note! ➜
After developing
your financial
plan, use this
chart by T. Rowe
Price to assess
your risk
tolerance.

TABLE 6.1: RISK TOLERANCE WORKSHEET

Short-Term Goals (3–5 Years)

low risk	I'm comfortable with price volatility, and I'm willing to give up the possibility of higher returns in order to keep most of my principal intact. I am satisfied with an investment that stays ahead of inflation.
moderate risk	I expect the value of my investment to fluctuate, but not drastically. I could potentially suffer a 5% loss or more in a single year, but I'm willing to assume this risk for the opportunity to earn higher returns.
high risk	Capital growth is my goal. During this short investment period, I hope to earn superior returns. However, I could experience a loss from 5% to 15% or more in a single year from which I might not fully recover.

Intermediate-Term Goals (6–10 Years)

low risk	I'm willing to accept fluctuations in the value of my investment to earn the returns that should protect my money from the effects of inflation.
moderate risk	Although my investment might suffer a 5% to 15% decline or more in a single year, my intermediate time horizon may give my money time to recover losses and potentially earn moderate returns.
high risk	I'm willing to take the risk of a double-digit drop in my investment for the opportunity to achieve superior growth. I plan to hold my investment for 6 to 10 years, which may allow me time to recover a loss.

Long-Term Goals (11+ Years)

low risk	It's important that my investment provide healthy returns over time to stay ahead of inflation. Therefore, I'm willing to accept moderate fluctuations in the value of my investment, which may allow me to achieve modest growth.
moderate risk	I'm investing for the long term and can withstand considerable fluctuation in the value of my investment. I may suffer a loss of up to 20% or more in a single year, but as a long-term investor, I may recover from these temporary setbacks over time.
high risk	I have the conviction necessary to hold on to my investment during those years when it could drop in value by 25% or more. My goal is to earn superior returns, so I'm willing to assume a high degree of risk.

the market fluctuates all day, every day. Other types, like inflation risk, are more predictable and less volatile in the short run. Consider the following common types of risk, and evaluate them against potential rewards when you select an investment. Nine types of risk are:

- Market risk
- Inflation risk
- Interest rate risk
- Credit risk
- Currency fluctuation risk
- Political turmoil
- Portfolio risk
- Impulsive selling
- Mattress risk

Market risk

The market reacts to many outside forces, such as predictions about or actual changes in inflation, a move in interest rates, company earnings, U.S. politics, world politics, unemployment rates and other economic factors, and the like. The market may move up or down as a result of changes in any of these factors, and that move may be drastic or minimal. There is really no way to predict market fluctuations, though analysts do try very hard.

Factors that play a role in market performance have a domino-like effect. For instance, take the competing levels of perceived financial returns for stocks versus bonds. If interest rates for treasuries are low, investors will want to move into equity investments, says Peter F. Mackie, president of the management group that has investment responsibility for the Commerce Funds Family. The higher the

> 66
> Courage is not the absence of fear, but rather the judgment that something else is more important than fear.
> —Ambrose Redmoon
> 99

fixed returns, the more likely it is that investors will come back to that safety and leave the volatility of the market behind.

At this point you can see why it's so important to have an investment plan. If you're not one of the investors who checked out of the market to go into bonds, you'd feel as though you're left with a devalued portfolio, at least for the short term.

Watch Out!
Think twice before selling your funds when the market tumbles. Besides losing money from the decrease of the fund's price, most likely you'll owe capital gains taxes, which will cost you even more.

That is why you must decide in advance that you will dig in your heels and stay until the market turns around, which could be years. If you pull up stakes, you'll be selling your funds low, possibly losing much of your investment. On the other hand, if you stay and continue to buy funds, you'll be getting them at what may turn out to be bargain basement prices.

Now, a low rate of inflation will lead to a low rate of fixed income returns. That will support higher equity prices, Mackie says. New investors will enter the market and old investors will invest more, supporting these prices.

The perception that the rate of inflation is declining is a positive environment for equity investing, Mackie says. The reverse is also true. Higher inflation leads to higher fixed-income yields. That will motivate those invested in stocks and mutual funds to sell, triggering a fall in market prices.

The Federal Reserve Board (commonly known as the Fed) plays a large role in determining short-term interest rates. In setting monetary policy, the Fed adjusts the interest rate at which banks can borrow.

If the Fed thinks short-term interest rates should be lower, it will look at economic activity and the level of inflation, Mackie says. By lowering the cost of borrowing money, the Fed can encourage economic activity, although there is a 6- to 9-month lag before that effect becomes apparent, he says.

However, if the Fed sees the economy is overheating and inflationary forces are heating, they will raise the cost of borrowing money to slow down economic growth, thereby controlling inflation.

Another important factor that affects stock market performance, and hence risk, is how the federal government is balancing the budget and the laws being enacted that will affect taxes. You can determine, at least in part, how the market will play in the current economic environment by asking yourself questions such as, "Are there economic incentives like lower capital gains encouraging investments?"

Inflation risk

As mentioned above, inflation plays an important role in market performance. No inflation would essentially mean that the dollar you earn today will be worth a dollar tomorrow. Your purchasing power remains the same. But as inflation rises, you lose purchasing power. The trick is to make sure your annual salary raises are equal to or above the rate of inflation and that your investment earnings keep up with or exceed the pace of inflation. Otherwise, you will experience a loss of purchasing power. Inflation risk occurs when inflation outpaces the earnings on your investments and when prices for goods and services exceed your annual salary increases.

Many people turn to fixed-income investments during high inflationary periods to protect their investments. But a high level of investment in fixed-income assets may lead to serious underperformance in regards to purchasing power.

For example, a 30-year bond at maturity will be worth close to what you paid for it because of inflation, Mackie says.

Timesaver
Want to double-check your risk tolerance? Many investment Web sites have interactive tests you can take.

Though bonds, particularly government-sponsored bonds, do offer more safety in terms of preserving capital, equities, at least during periods of low inflation, can provide a shield against inflation because corporate management can raise prices for their products and services, thereby increasing earnings over time. Corporations also can increase the number of dividends shareholders receive. Increasing dividends gives their stocks a higher valuation.

Besides playing a vital role in market performance, inflation presents another risk to investors. In an effort to reduce risks associated with stocks, bonds, and mutual funds, some people simply stay out of the market and tuck their savings "safely" away in a bank account, money market account, or certificate of deposit (CD). However, over time, inflation can eat up the purchasing power of those dollars. For instance, at a 7 percent rate of inflation, in 10 years your money will be worth about half of what it's worth today.

Interest rate risk

Changing interest rates affect both stock (mutual funds) and fixed-income investments such as bonds. The interest rates are related to the Federal Reserve Board's movement on short-term rates.

This is a risk associated with bonds or bond funds that most people forget about or don't pay attention to, says Kacy Gott of Kochis Fitz investment planners. When considering bonds, most investors look at default risks, he says. Really, the bigger risk is the interest rate risk.

The only way to minimize this risk is to purchase individual bonds with maturities matching your expenditure needs. For instance, if you want to invest your money but know you'll need some in one year and another lump sum in two years, you can get bonds with one-year and two-year maturity dates. This technique is called laddering because you're investing and redeeming your investments a rung at a time.

Credit risk

This type of risk has to do with the level of financial stability of a company for stocks and the company or municipality for bonds. When you buy a house, the mortgage lender goes to great lengths to check your credit record and assess your credit worthiness. Similarly, when you buy bonds or bond funds, you are the lender, so you must assess the credit worthiness of those companies or municipalities to which you are making loans. Will they be able to pay back your principal or pay you the interest rate promised?

Note, too, that mortgage lenders charge higher interest rates to borrowers with blemished credit because of the risk of foreclosure, which can cost the lender plenty. So, too, will you get a higher interest rate from companies whose track records are questionable. However, you'll also be taking on the risk that they won't repay your loans or the interest.

In addition to financial stability, Mackie says that marketplace perception plays a role in this type of risk. The supply and demand of bonds in the bond market is driven by pessimists who are trying to protect their purchasing power against inflation, he says. Any hint of increasing inflation will drive these bond buyers to sell their bonds, Mackie says.

On the equity side, you tend to have more optimists, Mackie says. These investors think companies

Moneysaver
Loan officers at banks carefully scrutinize potential buyers before they hand over the bank's money. You should scrutinize your investments just as carefully.

are growing and therefore are more growth-oriented in their investment style.

Credit risk comes into play in this instance if your bond is not perceived as high quality. It will then sell at a lower price. You want to make sure the municipality or company can sell off the bonds at face value, he says.

Currency fluctuation risk

We live in a global economy. The value of a U.S. dollar varies from country to country and from day to day. When the value of a dollar rises overseas, you can buy less with it; when it falls, its purchasing power rises, allowing you to buy more.

That's because there's an inverse relationship with the value of a U.S. dollar and overseas investments. As the value of the dollar rises, the amount of money invested overseas declines because investors get more bang for their buck in the domestic market.

The converse is true when the value of the dollar drops overseas. Then domestic investments decline, and investments in foreign markets rise in order to take advantage of the stronger economy and, subsequently, a stronger market performance.

66

The only thing we have to fear is fear itself. —Franklin D. Roosevelt

99

However, your decision to hold foreign investments will most likely still be affected by currency movements, because many American companies have foreign subsidiaries or hold joint assets with foreign companies. Therefore, their earnings are influenced by these fluctuations.

Currency fluctuation risk has to do with point of view. U.S. investors look to the dollar. Foreign investors look to their own currencies for comparison.

Currency fluctuations come into play when companies announce their quarterly earnings. Those that have invested in other companies or that have subsidiaries or joint ventures in assets in other currencies are repriced in accordance with exchange rates. Earnings are repriced as well.

If an international subsidiary is experiencing growth, those earnings become more important for the company, Mackie says. If the dollar is weak, that diversification outside the United States has a positive impact on earnings outside this country.

Conversely, major diversification to non-dollar assets brings risks if the dollar is strong because the foreign investment will lose value relative to the dollar.

If the dollar is stable over decades, then there will be no noticeable effect from a currency adjustment point of view, Mackie says. Economic conditions are more likely to be stable when the dollar is stable or when inflation or interests rates are stable, assuming those rates are not unusually high, he says.

Note, however, if the dollar is weak abroad and you are investing and spending here, for the most part, you will not be so affected.

Watch Out!
There are many types of risks involved in investing in mutual funds and other investment tools. Understand them before investing.

Political turmoil

Real or perceived problems outside U.S. borders can affect the economy. Uncertainty leads to depressed share prices. Often during times of war or skirmishes, or even just the threat of fighting, many investors sell their shares, putting their money into fixed-income investments like short-term government bond funds or money market mutual funds, which offer investors a safer haven.

Portfolio risk

This type of risk is, in part, defined by your investment strategy. Are you a long-term investor or short-term trader? The same should be asked of each of your mutual fund portfolio managers—that is, you should be aware of the turnover of the portfolio. (Of course, first you should be aware of the makeup of the portfolio. Those portfolios with higher risk securities, like small-cap stocks vs. large-cap stocks, and junk bonds vs. investment grade bonds, are going to be more risky.)

Secondly, if the managers' style is to buy and sell rather than buy and hold, you'll be dependent on the short-term investment trading skills of that team, and you'll be exposed to the short-term changes of the market. Hence, the funds will be more volatile.

The converse is also true. If there is a low turnover rate in the fund due to the manager's buy-and-hold strategy, he or she is betting on a group of companies doing well over the long term.

Thirdly, there will be tax consequences. The higher the turnover, the less likely the portfolio will be tax-efficient, leading to more capital gains.

Impulsive selling

Sometimes emotions will get the best of you; when it comes to investing, it's important to keep them in line. If you let your emotions rule, you risk letting them drive you out of a market midway through your investment plan. If that happens, you can end up with less money than what you invested initially. Keep your investment time horizon in mind before making emotional decisions during market downturns.

Keep in mind that there's a difference between volatility and risk, Howard Yasgur, a financial adviser at Gradison-McDonald Investments, points out.

Volatility is how bumpy the road is, Yasgur says. If the road is smoother you'll get to your destination with less of an upset stomach, he notes.

Timesaver
If you don't have access to the Internet, use toll-free 800, 888, or 877 numbers to get information about various mutual funds.

You can smooth out the ride by having a less aggressive asset allocation, Yasgur says. A hand-tailored allocation—that is, one based on your own risk tolerance—will increase the likelihood that you'll stay in the market, even during down markets.

Mattress risk

Remember that although there are many types of risk inherent in investing, there's also risk in not investing. Inflation and taxes can reduce your spending power if your money is tucked away between your mattresses or in a bank account.

Figuring your risk tolerance

When it comes to investing, most people tend to be either gamblers or very conservative. More fall into the conservative group. A gambler will have big ups but will also have big downs, and in the long run, gamblers don't make much more than what a conservative investor would make. But you may not think of yourself as either a gambler or a squirrel who stashes money away in safe hiding places. To see what your tolerance for risk is, answer the following questions about yourself. You can also use the worksheet in Table 6.1.

1. Do you enjoy going to Las Vegas or Atlantic City? If you gamble in casinos, do you place a few big bets or lots of smaller bets? If you place a few big bets, you're much more of a gambler, and therefore much more comfortable with risk. In fact, you probably get a thrill from risk similar to that of riding a roller coaster. It gets your adrenaline going and makes you feel vibrant.

   If you place smaller bets, you're obviously more conservative but you're still comfortable

Moneysaver
If you can toler-
ate the risk,
invest in lump
sums. Over time,
this style of
investing has
historically
shown better
gains. This style
in betting will
likely backfire
over time,
though, because
the odds are in
favor of the
house.

taking some amount of risk. The key to assessing
how much risk in this instance depends upon
the amount of your bets.

Either way, most people leave casinos with
less in their pockets than when they arrived.
The question here is how does that leave you
feeling? If you just brush it off as the expense of
a vacation, your risk tolerance is much higher
than if you leave contemplating getting a second job to pay yourself back a hundred dollars.
Of course, these scenarios are based on the
assumption that you gambled well within your
financial means.

2. Do you listen to financial news reports all day
   and let market performance determine your
   mood? Perhaps your tolerance isn't so high.

3. Do you check in on market performance daily,
   weekly, or monthly just to see how it's doing, or
   do you check annually to see if you need to
   readjust your portfolio? Checking infrequently
   shows a higher tolerance to risk (and a portfolio
   you're comfortable with).

4. When the market takes a dive, do you immediately think of 1929 and envision men jumping
   out of buildings and years of a depressed market
   and economy on the horizon? Or do you think
   of 1987 and see an opportunity to buy low and
   recover your losses quickly?

5. When you walk down the streets of a city and
   you see a bag lady, do you think that could be
   you if you invest in the stock market rather than
   just leaving your money in a bank savings
   account? Or, do you notice the wealthy-looking
   people and think with a few good investments
   and a lot of time, that that could be you?

6. When you buy a car, do you take the loan offered by the dealership or do you spend hours on the phone and Internet searching for another lending institution with the best deal on interest rates and loan terms? If you didn't shop around, it shows you either want immediate gratification or you're simply not aware that other options exist. Either way, it will make you more prone to risk whether or not you can tolerate it. Researching big ticket items—and that includes mutual funds and other investment tools—is essential to reducing risk.

Timesaver
Let a fund manager save you a lot of legwork. By investing in a mutual fund, you don't have to research hundreds of stock picks.

What you can do to reduce risks

Your goal is to protect your principal investment and increase your after-inflation and after-tax return on your investment. The question you must ask yourself is: How much risk can you afford to achieve this goal?

You can never eliminate risk in investing. But you can take actions to match the level of risk inherent in your portfolio to your personal comfort level with risk.

"Studies say up to 93 percent of your investment return will be determined by the asset classes that you pick," Peter Mackie says. Asset allocation determines the level of opportunity as well as the level of risk.

So, first determine which types of risk you're willing to take, and that will drive you into the different asset classes. For instance, the lowest risk class is cash. The highest risk class is an aggressive equity. Your age and knowledge of the financial market will also play a role in your selections.

(When determining the amount of risk you can tolerate in your portfolio, Mackie, like Yasgur, warns not to take on so much risk that when the market falls, you are forced into a sell position when you meant to take a long-term view.)

A well-diversified portfolio across different asset classes and within those diversified sectors of the market has the effect of protecting your investments during market declines. And, over time, the general effects of increasing earnings through well-managed funds will positively effect investment outcomes, Mackie says.

By investing in mutual funds, you're reducing your risks because by their very nature these funds are diversified. Each fund usually invests in somewhere between 30 and 100 stocks. You can further diversify by buying more than one fund and even further reduce your risk by investing in funds in different classes. Finally, you can balance your portfolio with other holdings, such as treasuries, money markets, CDs, cash, and bonds.

If you're not in the market for the long term, or if you know you have a low tolerance for risk, don't discover the stress when it's too late, after other investors have already sold their equities further reducing prices, Mackie says. (The other option, of course, is to ride out the volatility.)

Mackie suggests aligning your portfolio with your comfort level so you don't put yourself into a situation where you're forced to sell at a low. It's hard to get back into the market again, he says, because you've been embarrassed by the loss. But that's not really a good reason to stop investing.

"There are really only two people that know if you've taken a loss," Mackie says. "One is your spouse, and the other is the IRS. And nobody else cares."

But it's important not to take too many ego shots because it will make you more conservative in your investing. You may want to hire a financial adviser so you won't bear that entire burden on your back. If you're worried about investing, it may help to hire someone who has a neutral point of view to help protect your ego and aid you in making decisions. You can also do this by investing in mutual funds.

Bright Idea
If you can take the stress, buy at market lows as opposed to selling at market lows.

Keep your time horizon in mind when considering your risk tolerance. Maurice Elvekrog, a licensed psychologist and chartered financial analyst, invests mostly for seniors. The biggest discussions they have are over asset allocation.

Seniors are especially fearful about investing, since often, besides Social Security and perhaps a pension, they have no other form of income. It therefore should come as no surprise that they want to avoid risk and lean toward bond funds.

But, Elvekrog says, for the longer term, they should take a different view. Life expectancies are rising. At age 65, you might have 20 more years in which to invest, he says. Long-term investments are considered those invested for more than a 10-year horizon. These seniors, he says, should be in more aggressive funds.

Those who worry about the market going down are acting like short-term investors, Elvekrog says, although he certainly understands their desire not to lose money. But market fluctuations tend to be short term, less than a decade. When it goes down like a rock, as it did in 1987, he says, it often comes back quickly. Even in the '20s, the worst of all market drops and longest bear market, most losses were recovered within a few years.

Investing in long-term bonds carries risk, too. If interest rates rise, you'll lose a portion of the face

Moneysaver
If you can't afford to take large risks, possibly resulting in losses of large sums of money, stick to conservative mutual funds.

value of the bond if you decide to sell it. A portfolio of bond funds can carry derivatives (financial instruments whose value depends on changes in the value of another security), to hedge risk, but sometimes this strategy backfires. Furthermore, whereas a bond matures, bond funds don't. Because you have to get out at the "right time," market timing doesn't often work for investors.

You need to be invested in something that has returns in order to get gains, Elvekrog says. To determine this on any investment, subtract taxes and inflation and note the return. One percent won't do much for you, he says.

For example, take a long-term treasury bond at an interest rate of 5.65 percent (the rate in August 1998). For someone in the 28 percent tax bracket (plus state taxes), that 5.65 interest rate will be brought down to 4 percent. With an inflation rate of 3 percent, that leaves you with a 1 percent annual return. At that rate, it would take 72 years to double your buying power.

The short-term bond fund is a good hedge but not a good way to achieve any profits, Elvekrog says. He makes a distinction between investing and savings. He thinks short-term bonds are more like savings, noting that you need some savings for living expenses. Investments, he says, are for the future.

With mutual funds you can expect an average 10 percent gain yearly. That will keep you ahead of taxes and inflation, he says, adding that capital gains taxes at 20 percent (after being in the fund for 12 months) for most investors are less expensive than bond fund (income) taxes. (Note that there can be capital gains from bonds, too.)

Over time, investing in stocks and stock mutual funds is less risky because the probability of a loss is reduced.

Benefiting from risk

Everyone remembers it as Black Monday. On October 19, 1987, the stock market plummeted a record 554.26 points, which was a 22 percent drop.

While market downturns can be devastating to your portfolio, especially if you're a short-term investor in aggressive equities, these drops can present great opportunities to buy stocks, and therefore equity funds, "on sale." Those investors who saw this downswing as an opportunity rather than a crisis made a quick buck or two. (Note: This will not always be the case since you cannot predict market direction.)

Bright Idea
You need to invest to preserve your purchasing power over time.

Within 24 hours, the market rebounded 337.17 points, setting another record. As the days went by the market had more swings, but within a week, the market peaked just 41 points shy of where it had started.

"If you don't take any risk, most likely you won't have the opportunity to earn higher than the risk-free rate of return," Mackie says. Measuring from the 1920s, fixed assets returned about 3–4 percent and equities returned between 9–10 percent, he says, noting that the overall inflation rate averaged about 2.5 percent.

Just the facts

- Investing your money is not a guarantee for profit, especially for the short term.
- You can lose money investing.

- Figuring out your risk tolerance will help you invest so you can emotionally withstand market dips.

- There are many different types of risk involved in investing.

- Understanding risks and planning for and around them will probably help you profit in the long run.

GET THE SCOOP ON...

What you should research before investing in a mutual fund ▪ What you should know about "if you had invested $X" tables ▪ What funds with high turnover rates mean for your portfolio ▪ Why different publications rate the same funds differently ▪ Why analysts are overly optimistic ▪ What characteristics are associated with winning mutual funds

Starting Your Portfolio—Picking Funds

Chapter 7

There are more than 10,000 mutual funds in existence today. Your portfolio will probably only consist of between one and ten funds. How do you figure out which funds are managed well? How do you know which fund managers' styles match your style? And how do you decide which funds will best meet your investment objectives?

Regardless of whether you choose to hire a financial analyst or money manager, you will benefit by having an understanding of how to select funds. If you do hire an adviser, you'll be able to ask the adviser the right questions. If you decide to invest on your own, that's all the more reason to have a solid understanding of the factors that go into making good investment decisions.

This chapter covers how to pick a mutual fund and examines what role managers' styles, track records, ratings, and analysts' predictions should play in your selection of funds.

What you should research

Before investing in any mutual fund, you must first decide if that fund's objective, style, portfolio of securities, and other criteria match your investment objectives. You must also determine which portion of your portfolio the fund will fill. For instance, if your investment plan includes 60 percent aggressive growth funds, you must decide which fund or funds will match your goals and how many shares you'll buy. Will you fill the entire 60 percent with one fund or several funds?

The number of mutual funds has grown significantly over the past 80 years. (See Table 7.1.) You must establish some criteria for weeding out the vast majority. Perhaps you want only those funds that don't carry extra fees. True no-load funds make up only one-third of the mutual fund universe, according to Craig Israelsen, associate professor of Consumer and Family Economics at the University of Missouri-Columbia.

TABLE 7.1: ALL FUNDS (EXCEPT MONEY MARKET FUNDS)

Decade	Number of New Funds	Cumulative Total
pre 1930	10	10
1930s	42	52
1940s	26	78
1950s	55	133
1960s	111	244
1970s	169	413
1980s	1,388	1,801
1990 to Sept. 1998	8,299	10,100

Source: Craig L. Israelsen

Note! ➡
The number of mutual funds has grown significantly since the 1920s.

Although there were about 10,000 mutual funds by September 30, 1998, some of those are duplicate portfolios with the same managers, according to Israelsen. Funds are sold in different classes such as a, b, and z, and one fund can be listed in several classes. These class structures are used for marketing purposes. So a fund may have a specific portfolio that's listed as a front load (class a), and again with a back load (class b). So the fund shows up three or four times in Morningstar, but it's really the same fund, according to Israelsen.

Of the 10,000+ mutual funds, about 75 percent are redundant, Israelsen says, leaving about 2,500 unique mutual funds.

Israelsen is certainly not opposed to investors considering loaded funds. Load funds are marketed by sales representatives who can give personal attention, he says, and that has some value.

But in terms of earnings, no-load funds, according to his study, perform slightly better than loaded funds because they didn't start off handicapped— that is, all of the money went into the investment rather than part being skimmed off the top to pay for the commission.

Good research is necessary for selecting the mutual funds that will help you reach your financial goals. Otherwise your choices, should you decide to handle your own investments, will be based on opinions or whimsy.

Joan Payden, president and chief executive officer of Payden & Rygel Mutual Funds, suggests approaching mutual fund investing as you would approach shopping. Good shoppers compare similar products in terms of unit prices, figuring out which box of cereal or can of soup is least expensive.

Bright Idea
When shopping for a mutual fund, look at the companies that make up the portfolio. What are the companies' revenues? Do any of them have new product lines that make them appealing?

Timesaver
Want to buy more books on investing, but don't have time to go to the store? Head over to http://www.amazon.com. Not only will you get a discount on the price, but you will find books with the same keyword as this one and a list of books other readers bought when they bought this one.

But good shoppers don't make their financial decisions based simply on money. They look at the product's ingredients and check the percentages of fat, sodium, and other ingredients to see what goes into the product and if it matches their dietary goals.

Most people don't look at annual reports to see what's in the mutual fund, Payden says, but they should. Take note whether the fund has only domestic stocks or if it includes stocks in emerging markets, small caps, bonds, or other securities that might alter the performance of the fund or where it fits into your portfolio. Although the listing of investments is only a snapshot in time, it will give you an idea of the types of securities the manager invests in.

Payden suggests running down the list of securities noted in the report to see if you recognize any of the company names. If you don't, that should tell you something, she says. It's probably made up of companies that are either small or based in other countries.

Then she suggests looking at the size of the mutual fund. If a mutual fund is under $5 million, the manager has more flexibility. Payden notes that small funds, however, can be very volatile.

Payden shared several more interesting tidbits:

- In order to have a fund listed in *Morningstar,* it must have at least $25 million invested and 1,000 shareholders.

- The name of the fund only has to identify 65 percent of its investments.

- The distribution yield is what the fund wants to distribute. (Payden finds that people are confused about the difference between return and yield. Mutual funds can distribute more than the yield. Look at the fund on a total return basis. Total returns reflects both dividend and share price changes.)

Payden suggests reading the prospectus and seeing if expenses are capped. If a fund's expenses increase, that could cost you plenty.

Also, any marketing piece that uses the word "guarantee" should raise a red flag. Nothing is guaranteed in investing. Sales people use this term and investors don't question this because they like guaranteed profits, Payden says.

Regulations preclude financial advisors from using the term "guaranteed," except when it pertains to those investments carrying some sort of government guarantee.

There are many more things an investor should research before buying into a mutual fund.

Fund performance

Mutual fund performance is measured by the average annual return or the annualized percentage return over a single- or multi-year period, according to Israelsen. Sometimes, he points out, a mutual fund will report its total cumulative return (the total percentage growth on its investment over a multi-year period).

The average annual return has three components:

- Capital gains or losses declared by the fund
- Dividends distributed by the fund
- Change in share price of the fund

Many investors turn to popular financial magazines and newspapers to determine returns.

Moneysaver
Use a credit card that gives you cash back on your purchases. Invest that cash in mutual funds. Or, use one with no annual fee, pay off the balance each month, and invest your extra cash.

Israelsen notes that mutual fund returns reported in the popular press assume the investor made a lump sum deposit rather than dollar cost averaging the investment. These return rates also assume that all dividends were reinvested into the fund, and that the investor made no withdrawals from the fund.

Israelsen says these assumptions are not always accurate. He gives this example: If you had invested a lump sum of $3,000 into T. Rowe Price's Equity Index Fund on May 1, 1992, it would have been worth $6,488.06 five years later. The average annual return would be calculated to be 16.68 percent.

However, if you had invested $50 each month over that same five-year period (investing a total of $3,000), you would have ended up with $5,010.92 and the average annual return would then be calculated as 19.45 percent. Israelsen says that how you invest—lump sum versus dollar cost average versus sporadic deposits—affects the average annualized return.

So, when you consider reported return figures for mutual funds, Israelsen says they will be accurate only if:

- You were invested during the entire period being reviewed.

- You had invested a lump sum only—that is, you didn't make additional investments.

- You had all your dividends reinvested back into the fund.

- You didn't make any withdrawals during the time frame being evaluated.

Note that dollar cost averaging had higher average annual returns and the lump sum investment had a lower return percentage but a higher dollar gain.

Turnover rate

When considering a fund for your portfolio, pay attention to the turnover ratio. A 100 percent turnover rate could mean that every stock was sold in one year and the fund has a totally new portfolio, or it could mean that some of the stock got turned over twice while some remained in the fund, Israelsen says.

The turnover rate measures how active the manager is in buying and selling; this rate has tax implications. "Dividends and capital gains in regular accounts are taxable even if you have them reinvested into the fund," Israelsen says, and therefore funds with low turnover rates are better from a tax perspective.

In an article titled, "Low Turnover, High Return," in *Financial Planning*'s September 1998 issue, Israelsen wrote that "lower turnover ratios are linked to some fundamental mutual fund characteristics…such as size of fund, equity style, expense ratio, manager tenure, and potential capital gain exposure."

Israelsen cites the following characteristics of equity funds with low turnover ratios:

- Those classified as large-cap funds within *Morningstar*'s style box
- Those with a higher percentage of portfolio assets concentrated in the top 10 largest holdings
- Larger funds, in terms of assets
- Those with lower portfolio price-to-earnings ratios
- Those with lower annual expense ratios
- Those funds that invest in larger companies

- Those funds with a higher 12-month return as of May 31, 1998

- Funds run by managers with more tenure

- Funds with twice as much potential capital gain exposure compared against funds with high turnover ratios

Bright Idea
In general, use stocks for growth, money-market mutual funds for liquidity, and bonds for steady interest.

Israelsen also studied 1,223 funds for the article "Characteristics of Winning Mutual Funds" in the April 1998 issue of *Journal of Financial Planning*. Those funds with a turnover ratio higher than 60 percent generally had a "lower return, a lower current Morningstar rating, lower net assets, higher expense ratios, less manager tenure, lower yield, and a smaller front-end sales load."

In most cases, higher turnover rates are associated with lower returns. From mid-1996 to mid-1997, "funds with a turnover rate of less than 20 percent gained an average of 12.7 percent, while funds with turnover rates from 50 percent to 100 percent—close to the industry average—gained 8.7 percent," with diversified stock funds reportedly averaging a 78 percent turnover rate, according to the June 9, 1997, edition of *U.S. News & World Report*.

Israelsen notes that you might be concerned about the potential capital gain exposure with funds that have low turnover ratios. (Funds must realize their capital gains, on which you must pay taxes, when they sell stocks that have appreciated.) Israelsen says this concern is warranted only if the fund suddenly liquidates its portfolio and realizes all of the potential capital gains.

"However," he says, "if the fund's turnover ratio is low, it is less likely that such a realization of capital gains will occur," while "funds with high turnover ratios have high actual capital gain exposure (that is, greater taxable distributions)."

Israelsen also notes that funds that hold onto stocks that have appreciated have higher amounts of potential capital gain exposure—in contrast, funds with high turnover rates have actual capital gain distributions.

If all things are equal, Israelsen advises using the high turnover ratio funds in tax-deferred accounts and low turnover ratio funds in the non-tax-deferred portion of your portfolio to save on capital gains taxes.

Fund managers

Is the fund you are considering actively or passively managed? Is it managed by one person or a team? What are his or her plans and track record for meeting fund objectives? (Note, however, index fund managers must simply try to match the index.) These are just a couple of the questions you should get answered before taking the plunge.

Information about the fund manager's views can be gleaned from the fund's annual reports, profile, marketing literature, shareholders' newsletters, and perhaps in the prospectus.

Interviews with fund managers about their style are often published in popular financial publications such as *Forbes, Fortune,* and *Barron's*. Also, some mutual fund Web sites contain question-and-answer style articles with their fund managers.

The American Association of Individual Investors (AAII) suggests using the following strategies for uncovering information about a fund's manager:

1. Start with the overall philosophy. For instance, if it is a growth fund, what parameters are used

Moneysaver
Earn frequent flier miles with long-distance phone calls, credit card purchases, and more. Buy mutual funds with the money you would have spent on airline tickets.

to define growth? Is the portfolio composed of small-cap stocks or large-cap stocks? Do the stocks have a history of paying out capital gains—that is, do they have a high turnover rate?

2. Next, are the stocks selected from a specific market segment, like technology stocks? Or are stocks hand-picked on the assumption that their individual performance will match the fund's objectives? Does the manager stick with a certain index when selecting the stock? Is this index the one used as his or her measuring stick? If so, is this the index you want your fund's performance to be measured by?

66

Money is a good servant but a bad master.
—Francis Bacon

99

3. Finally, you want to know about risk. Does the manager "time" the market? This rarely works. What criteria are used to decide to sell the stock? How much of the portfolio is kept in cash? What other types of securities are in the portfolio (bonds or derivatives, e.g.), and what is the ratio of stocks to other securities? How much does that ratio vary over time? What strategies are used to reduce risk?

The problem with this last question is that risk is defined differently among managers, and hence their strategies to keep it low will differ. You must determine if their definition of risk matches yours.

Liz Davidson, CEO of Davidson Andrade, an investment firm in San Francisco, says more and more managers are reducing the size of their portfolios—that is, they are becoming less diversified in an attempt to beat the market. They are holding 30–40 stocks instead of 100 or more, she says.

Holding 500 stocks is not reducing risk as much as it is reducing your return, Davidson says.

Managers who are this diversified aren't able to concentrate on the winners, she says, and the goal of an active manager is to beat the applicable index.

Furthermore, Davidson says, it's hard to find good stocks. And, she asks, how can you track hundreds of stocks? If one stock makes up only .5 percent of the 200 stocks in the portfolio, there's not much incentive for the manager to take time to really research that company.

"Managers have come to realize that high levels of diversification achieve only a marginal improvement in the risk of a portfolio, yet upside potential is effectively capped when a manager owns hundreds of stocks," Davidson says.

A concentrated portfolio gives the managers flexibility, she says. But remember, flexibility in terms of buying and selling stocks can be costly in terms of taxes. It also can be volatile.

In a recent study, Israelsen found that large funds do not, on average, lag behind smaller funds' performances.

Manager tenure also plays a role in fund performance, Israelsen found. In his article, "Characteristics of Winning Mutual Funds," published in the April 1998 edition of the *Journal of Financial Planning*, Israelsen writes, "Funds with manager tenure equal to or greater than 6 years...had higher returns, higher current and average Morningstar ratings, higher net assets, lower turnover ratios, more years in operation, higher yields, and higher front-end loads."

Israelsen was intrigued by the relationship in turnover ratio and manager tenure. It is possible, he said, that managers with more time at the helm are able to develop a portfolio strategy that leads to less turnover. Or, he says, it may be that managers with

Bright Idea
If you don't want to get advice from a financial adviser, talk to a university finance professor or take a class on investing at a community college.

more tenure feel more secure in their jobs and are encouraged to think and act over longer investment horizons, and that reduces turnover.

Fund ratings and rankings

Consider the fund's performance relative to others with the same investment objectives.

Making use of ratings and rankings is difficult, yet many investors throw down their money when they see a fund rated "A" by Lipper in the *Wall Street Journal* or five stars by *Morningstar.*

Yet, an A-rated fund in the *Wall Street Journal* may not be a five-star rated fund by *Morningstar* because they use different benchmarks to compare funds and different methodologies for ranking them. The result is disagreements on which funds are top performers.

Watch Out!
This month's best fund pick may be next year's dud! Why? Best fund picks attract more capital, causing them to have to buy more stocks, which leads to over-diversification.

In an article entitled, "Mutual Fund Performance: What Goes into the Rankings?" John Markese, president of AAII, states that "the *Wall Street Journal* ranks the return of a fund against the performance of all other similar funds for the period; in contrast, *Kiplinger's* magazine uses broad fund categories—such as all equity funds—as a benchmark." Markese goes on to note, "*Worth* magazine, while also apparently doing no-risk adjustment, uses fund expenses and eight other variables...to rank funds."

Nor are the letter rankings the same among some popular finance magazines, according to Markese. "Both *Forbes* and *Kiplinger's* give A to F rankings for bull and bear markets. Put aside the issue that these two magazines are unlikely to agree on the bull and bear market dates and just examine the assignment of rankings: *Kiplinger's* gives the top 20 percent, by risk-adjusted return, of all funds in a broad category an A for the bull or bear periods, the next 20 percent get B's, and so on. Forbes uses essentially the same technique, but curves the rankings. A curve means fewer A's and F's and more B's and D's, with the largest number of funds for any category getting a C ranking."

The result? Same funds, different rankings. "With all the differences in time periods, risk measures, weighting, benchmarks and treatment of loads, it is perhaps surprising that there is anything close to agreement on rankings," Markese says.

What the analysts say

In a December 22, 1997, *SmartMoney Interactive* article, "Can Analysts Be Trusted?" reporter Pablo Galarza writes, "Some of Wall Street's most highly touted investment picks have turned into the fourth quarter's biggest bombs. Where were the analysts? Most of them had 'buy' recommendations on the stocks up until the bitter end."

Analysts' stock predictions are often wrong. In fact, according to Michelle Clayman, managing partner for New Amsterdam Partners, during the first month of each fiscal year earnings estimates were typically 57.1 percent higher than actual earnings in the 10 years ending in 1992. Estimates declined over the year. Earnings estimates for the full year made in the final month of the fiscal year overestimated actual earnings by 11.9 percent.

Analysts tend to overestimate earnings for at least three reasons, according to Clayman:

1. "Analysts have a tendency to fall in love with their stocks, which means they have an overestimation bias," Clayman says. It's like following a sports team—you want to root for it, she says.

2. Analysts who work for investment firms that engage in banking activity are under pressure to produce positive predictions.

3. The lines of communications from public companies may be cut for analysts who say negative things about their earnings potential.

Even though analysts shave their estimates during the course of the year, "there's [still] a surprising amount of over-optimism," Clayman says. You hope mutual fund managers recognize this problem and adjust for it. "When companies disappoint, the stocks get punished tremendously," she says.

"There are some growth mutual funds that are momentum buyers," Clayman says. Some look at price, some look at earnings. These funds are susceptible to nasty drops if the stocks disappoint, she says.

Characteristics of winning mutual funds

In his article on winning mutual funds, Israelsen writes, "Load funds had, on average, a higher turnover ratio, larger expense ratio and more years in operation. The premise that loaded funds have lower expense ratios is not supported by this particular analysis."

Using only those funds in existence over a 5-year period (1992–1996) Israelsen found that, at least in recent years, "true no-load funds have, on average, produced returns that exceed those of comparable load funds." Several other factors also play a role in how well the fund performs.

1. Net assets. From the study it appears that larger funds (those with assets of at least $235 million) "have a higher mean return, higher current and average Morningstar ratings, lower expense

ratios, longer manager tenure, more years in operation, higher yield, higher front load and a higher deferred load." Israelsen concludes that large funds do not, on average, become performance laggards, and that larger funds typically have lower expense ratios.

2. Fund objectives. Israelsen analyzed the 5-year annualized return between no-load and load funds by fund objective and by Morningstar category. He found that "there were no fund objectives that produce higher mean returns among load funds." Note that sector funds were excluded from this study. Israelsen also found that "five true no-load fund objectives—balanced, foreign stock, growth, growth and income, and world stock—had higher mean returns than their load-fund counterparts."

3. Fund styles. Israelsen found that the differences among large-cap value, large-cap blend, large-cap growth, mid-cap value, mid-cap blend, mid-cap growth, small-cap value, small-cap blend, and small-cap growth funds were negligible for no-load funds. He did find more pronounced differences among load funds. Large-cap growth funds had the lowest mean return for both load and no-load funds. "The highest mean return among no-loads was in (the) mid-cap value category. For load funds, the highest mean return was in the small-cap blend category."

Combining both no-load and load funds, the overall mean return for small-cap funds was higher than mid-cap funds and large-cap funds, according to the study. "The difference between means for mid-cap and large-cap funds was not significant," Israelsen says.

Watch Out!
If the market has significant moves, your asset allocation may change in your portfolio.

He concluded from this study that the following fund characteristics produced, on average, higher returns. These characteristics can be used as screening criteria when you select a mutual fund:

- No loads

- An annual expense ratio less than or equal to 1.22 percent

- Net assets greater than or equal to $235 million

- Management tenure equal to or greater than 6 years

- Annual turnover ratio less than or equal to 60 percent

Markese's article on mutual fund winners gives the following selection criteria to consider:

1. Long-term relative performance. How did it perform relative to those with similar objectives in the same sector? What is its total return?

2. Risk taking. How much risk is the manager taking compared with other funds?

3. Expenses. What are the overhead costs compared to similar funds?

4. Portfolio turnover. How actively is the fund manager buying and selling securities? "Higher portfolio turnovers translate to increased transaction costs and lower returns," Markese says. "Transaction costs are not included in the expense ratio."

5. Total assets. "The total assets of a mutual fund can be significant for two reasons," Markese says. "First, a larger asset base usually translates into lower expenses. Second, for funds such as those in the aggressive growth category that have a small capitalization stock bias, size may

be a hindrance. Moving large blocks of money around in the small cap–area is difficult and reduces flexibility."

6. Diversification. "The number of different securities held gives some indication of whether or not a fund is broadly diversified," he says.

7. Special risks. "A reading of the prospectus and the statement of additional information (available from the fund upon request) will mention these special risks," Markese says. "The ability to borrow, use derivatives to speculate rather than hedge portfolio risks, invest in liquid securities or invest in lower-quality debt (junk bonds) adds to potential risk." He adds that "derivatives, options, and futures…can be used to increase or reduce risk. The ability of a fund to use derivatives is not the issue; how those derivatives can be used [is]."

How to read a prospectus

Where do you get all of that information? Start with the prospectus. This brochure is often tossed aside, but it contains a treasure trove of information, if you can get through its legalese language.

Buried in its depths you will find important information about the fund, its management style, its objectives, the types of stocks it owns, and more. You will also find information about expenses, including those you might not have thought about.

For instance, some funds waive fees for index funds. Sounds good to the investors, but if you read the prospectus you may find that the waiver expires.

Before investing in any mutual fund, you should sit down and read the prospectus. The prospectus is basically an agreement or contract between you and

Watch Out!
Don't pay much attention to analysts' predictions. They're usually overly optimistic.

the fund company, detailing all the important facts of your investment. Some of the items that it shows are:

- Expenses
- Financial highlights
- How to buy and sell shares
- Management
- Investment policies and practices
- Investment objectives

Expenses

Expenses are usually the first item that many of you will be worried about, and rightly so. If they are high, they can virtually eat up your profit in an under-performing market. Luckily, this is usually the first item that is listed in the prospectus. The most common fees are:

- Sales load: A load is an up-front charge that is added to your fund purchase. For example, if a fund charges a 4 percent load, then you pay 4 percent up front, and the value of your account is always going to be 4 percent less than it would be if the fund did not have a load. If you invest $1,000, then only $960 would go into the mutual fund. No-load funds do not have this charge, so the entire amount you invest is placed into your account. The load is used to pay an advisor for his or her services.

- Redemption fees: These are fees that are charged to a shareholder when he or she decides to redeem shares. They also are referred to as back loads. Often they are phased out if you hold onto your investment long enough. Most back loads are completely phased out by the end of the fifth year. For most no-load funds, these fees do not exist. (For true no-load funds they don't exist at all.)

- Exchange fees: These are the fees that are charged to a shareholder for exchanging shares among various funds at the mutual fund company. For most no-load or load funds, these fees do not exist.

- Management fees: This is the percentage of fund assets paid to the fund's investment manager. You can't get around this fee, but some funds, like index funds, charge less because they are not actively managed.

- Marketing fees (12b–1): This is an annual charge to existing shareholders to defray the cost of selling shares to new shareholders—in other words, marketing fees. Many funds do not charge these fees to their shareholders.

- Total other fees: These fees are generally used to cover the servicing of shareholder accounts; for example, providing statements and reports and disbursing dividends.

Moneysaver
If you buy funds with a low turnover rate, you'll save on taxes.

The prospectus usually has a table that shows how much you would have paid in expenses for 1, 3, 5, and 10 years. When considering the fees, generally you should be more concerned with the total expense ratio than the breakdown of the separate expenses.

Financial highlights

This section contains information in terms of one share and how it fared each fiscal year. Information includes the beginning and ending net asset value, distributions made, fund profit, fund net assets, and the portfolio turnover rate.

Buying and selling shares

This section reveals the minimum investment, gives you directions on how to buy or redeem shares, gives phone numbers to call for service, and tells you how to transfer money by wire to and from the fund.

Management

This section tells how the fund is organized and names the fund manager. Knowing when this person started managing the fund will help you determine if his or her investment views match yours. For instance, if the manager has only been running the fund for six months, then when you look at the performance of the fund for the last 10 years you'll know that it was based on someone else's management style. The new manager may have different investment strategies.

Investment policies and practices

This is a very important section because it tells what the fund manager can and cannot do. For example, even though you are investing in what you think is a fund that buys domestic stocks, the manager may be permitted to invest some money into foreign stocks.

In this section, you will find the maximum percentage of the fund that is allowed to be invested in the stocks and bonds, and what percentage is left in cash.

This can have a significant impact on your investment decision. In general, most funds, "under normal conditions," must invest at least 65 percent of assets in the types of securities implied by their objective and name. But that leaves a lot of wiggle room.

Investment objective

The fund's investment objective is the most important fact disclosed in the prospectus. It talks about the fund's goals and the types of investments that the fund will be acquiring. You should weigh your personal objectives and goals against the fund's objective.

While the prospectus is all you legally need to see before buying a mutual fund, it does not contain all the information you're likely to need to make a good investment decision. The fund's annual and semi-annual reports list the stocks and bonds the fund is actually holding (at the time the report is printed).

Many funds also print a brief letter by the fund manager. There you can read about the manager's strategies, thoughts on the recent performance of the fund, and what he or she sees as the outlook for the market in the future.

Just the facts

- If a fund's expenses are too high, it can eat up your profit.

- Analysts' over-optimism is often a result of "falling in love" with a stock.

- Funds with high turnover rates generally have lower rates of return.

- By reading a prospectus, you'll find out about the funds' expenses, investment objectives, investment policies and practices, and more.

Timesaver
Want to read more about mutual funds but don't have the time to go to the library and look through the shelves? Ask a librarian to pick a few good books and place them on hold for you to pick up.

Types of Mutual Funds

GET THE SCOOP ON...
Different types of mutual funds ▪ Which fund
types perform best ▪ Which is better: value or
growth investing ▪ Why index funds are so
popular ▪ When to invest in small or large
companies

PART IV

Stock Funds

Chapter 8

S tock mutual funds, also called equity mutual funds, are those funds in which the bulk of assets are invested in shares of stocks offered by public companies. Since companies vary in size, these stocks have been subdivided. There are large-cap, mid-cap, and small-cap stocks offered by large, mid-size, and small companies, respectively.

Companies differ in how they use the invested monies. Some businesses will invest much of it back into the company to make the company grow, hence the name growth stocks. This category of stock funds is further broken down into aggressive growth and growth. Other companies tend to distribute their profits in the form of dividends. The stocks offered by these companies are called value stocks.

Besides the size of the company and its business style as it pertains to investments, stocks can be further broken down into specialties:

- Sector funds, which concentrate on certain industries or sections of the economy
- Index funds, which invest in companies listed on the indexes, most notably the S&P 500 index

157

This chapter covers these divisions in greater detail to help you decide which types of funds will best match your investment needs.

All about stock mutual funds—a short synopsis

Mutual funds fall into one of three general categories:

1. Equity funds, which invest in shares of stocks

2. Fixed-income funds, which invest in government or corporate debt instruments like bonds that offer fixed rates of return

3. Balanced funds, a portfolio of both stocks and bonds

Each mutual fund has specific goals and objectives that its managers try to achieve. These are stated in its prospectus, and include the following:

▪ Capital growth

▪ Preservation of principal

▪ Current income, which can be tax-exempt income

Timesaver
To get a quick feel for how mutual fund performances compare, take a look at one of the many quarterly report tables that hit the press listing fund performances over the past year.

Each fund's portfolio varies widely, and so does the balance of its investments, as you will see. Furthermore, just because a fund is labeled as capital growth does not mean it will not contain bonds or derivatives. You must research each fund to see if its portfolio will match your investment goals.

Equity funds are made up shares of stocks in large, mid-size, and small companies. In exchange for investing in the company, investors receive a part of its profits, either in the form of increased share prices or dividends, which are similar to receiving interest on a bank account.

Equity funds are further broken down by investment style, such as aggressive, and type, such as growth. Within each category are large-cap, mid-cap, and small-cap stocks, which are investments in large, medium, and small companies. Usually, the size of the company equates with risk and return (see Table 8.1). Larger companies oftentimes are associated with less risk than small start-ups.

Equities can also be divided into sectors, such as health or technology. Furthermore, they are divided into domestic, international, and world funds. International and world funds will be discussed in Chapter 9.

Buyer beware

Not all funds are what they say they are—a "value" fund might simply include only large caps, warn some experts.

Look at a fund's holdings each quarter, suggests Liz Davidson, CEO of Davidson Andrade, a hedge fund. Look at its charter: What are the turnover restrictions?

Value funds

Value funds are invested in sound, profitable companies that are paying relatively high dividends—that is, they distribute their profits to shareholders. These companies don't reinvest their profits to increase the size of the company. Most of these companies are already big and therefore cannot grow at the rate smaller companies can grow at, but even small companies can offer value stocks if they choose to distribute their profits through dividends to shareholders rather than re-investing for rapid growth.

Managers of value funds look for "undervalued" stocks, such as those with low price-to-earnings ratios (P/Es). (Low is considered 15 and below.)

Watch Out!
When you buy a fund, you're agreeing with all the terms and conditions set forth in the prospectus. Read it carefully.

Note! →
Different types of funds, based on historical performance, produce different returns. They also carry risks associated with their returns. In theory, the higher the risk, the higher the potential return.

TABLE 8.1: RETURN FOR SEVERAL DIFFERENT TYPES OF FUNDS

	6 months 12/31/97 to 6/30/98	1 year 6/30/97 to 6/30/98	5 years 6/30/93 to 6/30/98	10 years 6/30/88 to 6/30/98	15 years 6/30/83 to 6/30/98
Capital Appreciation	12.85	22.12	16.82	15.13	12.59
Growth Funds	15.11	25.38	19.25	16.50	14.33
Mid-Cap Funds	10.66	22.22	16.95	15.85	12.75
Small-Cap Funds	6.48	17.68	16.97	15.74	11.91
S&P 500 Index	17.37	29.39	22.55	17.94	15.94
Growth & Income	12.11	22.86	19.03	15.78	14.68
Equity Income	9.13	20.95	17.64	14.72	13.88
General Equity Funds	11.75	22.52	18.45	15.87	14.02

Source: Lipper Analytical Services, Inc.

Value investing presents a huge opportunity, Davidson says. These funds have lower risk and better long-term performance records than other fund categories. They use a tax-efficient buy-and-hold strategy.

Growth funds

Growth funds are invested in mostly large companies that are growing at a fast rate (or whose industries are thought to have growth potential). Increasing profits will commensurate with their rate of growth. They plow their earnings back into the company to make it grow. These companies don't distribute much in dividends. Prices of their stocks tend to go up faster in good times. And although these funds are subject to volatility, over the long term, historically, they've performed well.

Some managers may include some less stable small-cap stocks in their portfolio to add more growth potential, but that strategy can backfire into volatility and losses. That's why it's important to check the makeup of the portfolio.

Growth funds are divided into growth and aggressive growth. Aggressive growth fund managers take more risk than growth fund managers. The managers of aggressive growth funds may buy small-cap stocks, stocks in small companies that have the potential for big payouts. These smaller companies are hard to research because less is known about them. Oftentimes managers evaluate these companies onsite, which is time-consuming and costly to investors in terms of higher management fees charged to compensate for additional labor.

Aggressive growth funds are considered volatile because of the instability of the companies in which

Moneysaver
Save hundreds of dollars on furniture by buying it directly from the manufacturers in, for example, North Carolina. You can use these savings to add to your investments.

they invest. Further volatility may be possible if they concentrate their investments in sectors, which tend to fluctuate.

Another twist on growth funds are growth and income funds. In this type of fund, managers invest mostly in companies with well-known track records to produce both a gain in share value and a paying out of dividends. These funds are useful to the long-term investor, but are tailored to those who want to add to their current income, as well. Investment strategies vary among funds. They may invest in a combination of stocks, both growth and income, as well as bonds and money markets.

Note that while you may be receiving steady income via dividend checks from an income fund, your investment may be faltering. Be sure to check the fund's total returns, which reflect both dividends and share price changes.

Balanced funds, also referred to as balanced/equity income funds, include both stocks and bonds in their portfolios to balance the growth potential of stocks and relative stability of income from bonds. The funds are geared toward conservative investors who want high current yield and some growth, according to AIM, a fund family.

Value versus growth funds

Citing data from Moody, Aldrich & Sullivan, LLC, Davidson illustrates the growth of $1 in the 22 years between December 31, 1975, and December 31, 1997, on three indices: the Barra Growth, S&P 500, and Barra Value.

The Barra Value index outperformed the other two. Over this 22-year period $1 grew to $41.92. With the S&P 500, $1 grew to $34.15, and the Barra Growth came in third place at $26.45, she says.

What's interesting is that while the Barra Value outperformed the small-cap growth index, it did so with lower risk, about 4 percent. For large caps, value also outperformed growth, and also at a lesser risk rate, about 5 percent, Davidson says.

Davidson cites another article, this one in the April 1996 *Journal of Accountancy*, which also concludes that value funds outperform growth funds.

The authors explain that a growth investor must be able to predict both earnings and earnings growth. But even professional analysts are poor predictors of earnings.

The article states that studies show the value approach to investing has outperformed both the Standard & Poor's 500 and growth stocks over the past 25 years. In addition, it has done so incurring lower risk.

According to the article, there are eight criteria you should consider for value investing:

- Price-to-earnings ratio
- Price-to-cash flow ratio
- Price-to-book value ratio
- Dividend yield
- Private market value
- Adjusted net working capital
- Insider buying
- Stock repurchases

According to Craig Israelsen, associate professor of consumer and family economics at the University of Missouri-Columbia who studied the 10-year period ending December 31, 1997, value portfolios in the Wilshire Equity Style Index outperformed growth portfolios in every instance except for large-company stocks. Over a 20-year period ending

Moneysaver
It costs $28 for a family of four to go to the movies. You can save $25 (and invest it) if you wait a few months and rent the video instead. Plus, you can watch it over and over for 48 hours.

December 31, 1997, Wilshire value portfolios out-performed the growth portfolios in terms of risk and return. The study, "Higher Returns on Far Horizons," was published in *Financial Planning* (June 1998).

According to this study, during the 10-year period ending December 1997, "the Wilshire large-company growth portfolio produced the highest annualized rate of return and had the lowest deviation of the three growth (large-cap, mid-cap, and small-cap) portfolios."

Bright Idea
Want to know what sector might be next in line for high performance? Think ahead to what today's business will need tomorrow.

Over the 5-year period ending December 1997, the small-company portfolios for both growth and value had the lowest returns. The large-company growth and large-company value portfolios produced comparable returns and equivalent levels of risk, but he added that "in both cases it exceeded the return and risk of mid-cap and small-cap portfolios." So, during this period "there was a risk/return trade-off that rewarded large-company portfolios and penalized small-company portfolios." According to Israelsen, this pattern is contrary to the classic theory and to the typical risk/return behavior of value portfolios over a 20-year period.

Using the Morningstar equity style box, Israelsen found that the five largest large-company growth funds outperformed the equivalent value funds over the 10-year period ending December 31, 1997. The five largest mid-size and small-company value funds outperformed their growth fund counterparts.

"Among value portfolios, mid-cap portfolios produced higher returns with additional risk compared to large-company portfolios," Israelsen says. "In both cases, small-company value portfolios produced lower returns than mid-cap company portfolios, and with slightly less risk. In the case of growth portfolios, mid-cap portfolios produced lower returns than large-company portfolios and with more risk. Small-company portfolios offered more risk and even less return than mid-cap portfolios."

Israelsen found that when style (value versus growth) was taken into account, small-company value portfolios were more likely to outperform the small-company growth portfolios over a 20-year period. He stated that those who want to emphasize growth over value should consider investing in large- or mid-cap equities.

Brandon Thomas, director of equity funds at John Nuveen & Co., an investment firm, echoes these findings. He says that annualized returns over 20 years of value funds have slightly higher total returns with slightly less risk. Looking at shorter period subsets, he says that for 1- and 10-year periods, growth stocks outperformed value stocks. But for 5- and 15-year periods, value outperformed growth.

Thomas attributes these performance reversals to the cyclical nature of the economy. Value funds are more cyclical in their makeup (they often hold stocks from well-established large companies that manufacture things such as automobiles), so they perform better when the economy is coming out of a downturn, he says. When the economy picks up steam, growth stocks outperform value stocks.

You can make use of this data by fine-tuning your portfolio and by adding value funds to reduce risks and increase long-term performance, according to Thomas. But often what you see is that people invest in value funds, which have low price-to-earnings ratios and are therefore considered good buys,

Watch Out!
Just because a
fund has had a
stellar perfor-
mance one year
doesn't mean it
will get a stand-
ing ovation the
next year. Check
out the fund's
history and man-
ager's track
record.

during market downturns. When the correction is over, investors head to large-cap growth funds.

If you look at the S&P 500, you'll see that it's heavily weighted toward growth stocks, notes both Thomas and Kacy Gott of Kochis Fitz investment planners. Gott says that one investment strategy is to buy a passively managed large-cap value fund to counter the S&P 500 growth orientation (if you're invested in an index fund). For instance, if 60 percent of your allocation is in the S&P 500 index, he suggests putting 30 percent in a passively managed large-cap value fund.

Large-cap, mid-cap, and small-cap funds

The labels "large-cap," "mid-cap," and "small-cap" refer to the size of the companies in which these funds invest. Large-caps are stocks in large companies, and so on. Large-cap funds are generally less risky than the funds invested in smaller companies for at least two reasons:

1. Large companies are better established and have known track records.

2. Because large companies are better established, there is more information available for fund managers to study, giving them solid ground on which to base their investment decisions.

According to Gott, it is better to buy large-cap funds than single stocks from large companies. It's just too hard for the individual investor to get a leg up on the competition, he says. What are the chances that an individual investor is going to find a hot large-cap stock that a fund manager has overlooked?

For the same reason, it doesn't make sense to hunt for a manager who can outperform, on a consistent basis, large-cap stocks, Gott says. With a large portfolio, they'll be holding most of the index, anyhow, he points out. Why pay the higher management fees large-cap funds have over index funds? It just makes sense to hold index funds in the large-cap area, he says.

But if you want an actively managed fund in large caps, Gott suggests getting a sector fund or a concentrated fund, because it would be hard for one person to outperform the market with his or her own diversified portfolio. Such a manager can't hold the index and outperform it at the same time, he says. Go for 20 to 30 best bets, he says, adding that the sector funds should make up only a small percentage, say 10–15 percent, of your large-cap allocation. For the majority of your large-cap allocation, he stresses buying into an index fund.

Small caps, on the other hand, do better than larger companies' stocks over the long run because they must pay out better in order to attract investors. They also pay better because small stocks are generally priced cheaper than large company stocks. However, they are harder for managers to research because less is known about each company. Oftentimes, these funds have higher fees, as a result, and, over the short run, are more typically volatile and carry more risk.

Income funds

Income funds invest in companies with track records of distributing dividends and/or corporate or government bonds, which, by definition, have a fixed rate of return. Income funds are an investment tool you can use to increase your current income while preserving your capital.

Although this type of fund usually carries a lower risk than stock funds, it does contain some risk because bond prices fluctuate with changing interest rates. Risk also relates to the type of investments in the portfolio. High-yield funds use lower-rated bonds with longer maturity dates to produce higher incomes. However, those are subject to much more volatility.

Gott says that income funds don't make much sense as an investment tool given the availability of today's investment alternatives. Originally, they were created to entice investors on fixed-incomes to buy stock. Now we look for capital appreciation, which the tax law favors, he says. On dividends, you pay income taxes at your normal tax bracket. But if you hold onto a stock (or bond) fund that has capital appreciation for at least 12 months, you pay only a 20 percent capital gains tax when you sell shares from the fund (or when the fund realizes capital gains).

Gott suggests that if you have a portfolio that generates income, you should have it in a tax-deferred account, like an IRA. For non-tax-deferred accounts, he suggests getting into index funds, which don't realize much in the way of capital appreciation, rather than large-cap dividend funds.

Specialty funds

Sector funds invest in stocks that concentrate on sectors of the economy like technology or in industries such as airlines. Some of the sectors are:

- Consumer products
- Environmental

- Financial services
- Health care and biotechnology
- Natural resources
- Precious metals
- Real estate
- Technology
- Transportation
- Utilities

While these funds diversify by investing in a number of companies within the industry, they have an inherent risk because they are not balanced with stocks from other sectors. Therefore, they may do very well in one economy or at a given time in that industry's history, but at other times, they may perform poorly for substantial periods of time, regardless of overall market performance. (See Table 8.2.)

Fidelity Investments says investing in sector funds should be approached with caution. "Even though Morningstar recognizes seventeen financial-sector categories, the nearly 200 sector funds within these categories differ widely in terms of investment style and performance history," according to a Fidelity document.

"Investors choose the industry, and a professional manager picks the securities. Sector funds tend to perform like individual stocks, offering the potential for substantial returns, but with a high degree of risk," according to Fidelity.

Sector funds are highly volatile because of their narrow focus. Furthermore, sector funds hold a relatively small number of stocks. Therefore, the performance of just two holdings can have a significant impact on the performance of the entire fund.

Fidelity gives these guidelines for investing in sector funds:

Note! →
Sectors are good
bets if you're
invested in them
during their
"economic hot
cycle."

TABLE 8.2: DIFFERENCES IN PERFORMANCE OVER THE YEARS FOR DIFFERENT SECTORS

	6 months 12/31/97 to 6/30/98	1 year 6/30/97 to 6/30/98	5 years 6/30/93 to 6/30/98	10 years 6/30/88 to 6/30/98	15 years 6/30/83 to 6/30/98
Health/Biotech	9.72	17.97	21.64	21.78	18.22
Natural Resources	-7.29	-10.98	8.25	9.11	10.07
Science & Tech	20.96	22.70	22.97	19.98	14.32
Telecommunication	24.71	38.23	18.24	16.64	——
Financial Svcs	12.19	35.16	25.91	22.93	18.45
Utility	8.44	25.93	12.30	13.44	14.54
Real Estate	-4.39	9.07	9.76	10.20	10.77
Sector Equity Funds	5.67	17.21	16.60	17.17	14.65

Source: Lipper Analytical Services, Inc.

- Research the industry
- Research the funds themselves
- Follow the market, economic trends, international events, and industry breakthroughs, as well as government actions. Understand the industry's market dynamics

Index funds

Index funds are made up of many of the stocks listed on one of the indices and are designed to reflect the index's movement. When the market does well, so do these funds. Likewise, when the market tumbles, these funds follow suit. Investing in index funds is, essentially, investing in the market. By definition, index funds are passively managed and therefore usually have low fees.

According to Maria Crawford Scott of the American Association of Individual Investors, "To outperform an index fund without added risk, an active manager must better the index by an amount greater than his added expenses and transaction costs."

She also notes in "Simple Index Concept Takes Numerous Forms" (*AAII Journal,* July 1992) that "active management can skew a portfolio toward a particular market segment. An index fund that tracks a broad-based index is, by definition, truly diversified. And it is always fully invested in the market."

When considering which index fund to invest in, Crawford says, "probably the most important consideration is the index that you want to track." The most popular index among funds is the Standard & Poor's 500. This index, which emphasizes large-cap companies, represents about 70 percent of the U.S. stock market, she says.

Bright Idea
Funds have a wide array of returns. If you diversify your portfolio, when one fund's performance lags behind, another may take up the slack.

There are several advantages, Crawford points out, to using the S&P 500 index, including the wide availability of information on the stocks composing the index and its performance record.

An index fund doesn't necessarily own every stock on the index it tracks. "Instead, many use a 'statistically select' group of stocks that are representative of the index as a whole," Crawford says. "The funds most likely to use statistical sampling rather than complete representation are those that track a large number of stocks and those that have a smaller amount of assets under management, in particular the newer funds," she says.

"Obviously, the more successful the fund is at statistical sampling, the better," Crawford says. "And the only way to check this is to see how closely the fund's performance parallels the index it is tracking." She says a fund should underperform the index by an amount close to its expense ratio.

In general, larger funds will have lower expense ratios because of economies of scale. Crawford says the expense ratio should be below 0.50 percent. Management fees vary, too.

Israelsen found that in 1990 the S&P index lost 3.2 percent. From 1992 to 1994, annual returns were 7.7 percent, 10.0 percent, and 1.3 percent, respectively. During the 5-year period from 1990 to 1994, the annualized return for the S&P 500 was 8.7 percent, which is considerably below the long-term annualized return of 12.5 percent. However, between 1995 and 1997 the average annualized return was a soaring 31.2 percent.

Israelsen published his findings in an article titled, "Index Funds: Fair-Weather Friends?" published in *Financial Planning* in April 1998.

Moneysaver
Index funds are usually very tax efficient. This is because by their nature they use a buy-and-hold strategy. The only time they sell is if a company in the index changes.

The large-cap blend equity style is the most dominant among index funds, according to Israelsen. This is because the S&P 500 index is a large-cap blend index, and most index funds mirror the S&P 500 index, he writes. Compared with non-index funds in the same equity style between December 31, 1992 and 1997, on average large-cap blend index funds have significantly:

- Smaller front-end loads
- Lower 12b-1 fees
- Higher load-adjusted 5-year annualized returns
- Higher average Morningstar ratings
- Lower turnover ratios
- Shorter manager tenure
- Lower expense ratios

While index funds seem to fluctuate more than actively managed funds, they often outperform them.

Index funds have several advantages:

1. Because they reflect the stocks listed on the indices, they are diversified not just among many companies but also among many industries.

2. Index funds are passively managed and therefore often have lower overhead, resulting in lower fees.

3. Passively managed funds use quantitative analysis, which takes out the emotion. These managers are not trying to outguess the market in the way that actively managed fund managers must.

4. Index funds are tax efficient, especially during market inclines when there's a steady inflow of

Watch Out!
When you are
researching a
fund, be sure
that you are
measuring it
against an
applicable index
comparing its
returns.

cash, a rise in stock prices, and few redemptions by shareholders. In contrast, actively managed funds are always buying and selling their holdings to beat the index they are measuring themselves against. Selling stocks that have capital appreciation forces investors to pay capital gains taxes. Although index fund share prices increase in value as well during bull markets, the gains go unrealized until you sell your shares.

Of course, index funds have disadvantages, too. When the market swings downward, investors often redeem shares, forcing the fund to realize gains.

An index fund that's growing doesn't have as much embedded capital gains as one that's older and lacking in new money. Gott says that if an index fund gets a lot of cash coming into the fund, there won't be a lot of embedded gains because they're buying stocks at today's prices, too. But in a down market, you want index funds in your tax-deferred retirement portfolio, he says.

Asset allocation funds are another specialty fund. Managers buy and sell stocks depending on what's "hot" with a goal of beating the indices.

Social responsibility funds make it their primary goal to invest in what they have determined to be ethical or of value. This may mean buying stock from companies that don't have anything to do with the tobacco industry or buying only stocks from companies run by African-Americans. Capital growth is a secondary goal for these fund managers.

If you decide to invest in a socially responsible fund, be sure to review its makeup because what you might consider socially responsible might not be what the fund manager thinks is socially responsible.

Money market funds

Most money market instruments "are just short-term versions of bonds," according to AIM, a fund family. "They're considered short-term investments because the debt they represent must be paid back within a relatively brief period of time, no more than one year. With such short maturity periods, the prices of money market instruments are generally more stable than prices of longer-term debt securities. However, money market securities usually pay less interest than longer-term bonds."

"Most money market funds are at inflation," Gott says. If you're getting a higher-than-average rate, check to see if the fund is temporarily waiving its fees. If that's the case for the time you'll be invested in it, go ahead, Gott says. But if you stay and the fees are reinstated, your performance is going to drop. In that case, you may want to find an alternative investment.

Money market funds invest in short-term papers like government Treasury bills, Treasury notes, Fannie Maes, and Ginnie Maes. Or they can be in short corporate obligations. Shareholders receive current money market interest rates and retain asset liquidity. Some funds offer tax-exempt money market securities.

Tax-exempt money market funds are useful if you would have otherwise placed your money in a money market fund, but your income is high enough that your income tax bracket would more than compensate for the lower yields put out by these funds. Essentially, the tax savings more than compensate for the lower yield. By not paying tax, you can accept a lower yield and still come out ahead.

Money market funds are practically risk-free and provide a constant interest rate (although yields fluctuate because they include fees), but they also provide no potential for increasing your capital and are best used for short-term holdings—that is, when you need access to your money.

Just the facts

- Mutual funds are divided into many asset classes and style types.

- Contrary to popular belief, value funds outperform growth funds.

- Small-cap funds are great performers if you can stomach the ride.

- Index funds have lower fees, and their performance is hard to beat.

- Money market funds are safe, but they barely keep up with inflation.

GET THE SCOOP ON...
How stocks and bonds differ ▪ How you should
mentally approach buying bonds ▪ How bond
and bond funds differ as investing instruments
▪ The differences between international and
global funds ▪ How you can buy into corporate
real estate

Balancing Your Portfolio with Other Types of Funds

The more you diversify your portfolio—within limits, of course—the more you reduce your exposure to risk. Many investors turn to bonds and bond funds, which can provide a safer haven from the volatility of the stock market, to balance their investments. You can also balance your domestic portfolio with international mutual funds, because when the U.S. economy suffers, foreign ones may be healthy, and vice versa.

You might also find money market funds a safe place to stash your cash. Some are invested in federal government securities. Or, if you want to take a swing at corporate real estate, you can invest in office space or mortgages through Real Estate Investment Trusts (REITs) or REIT funds. This chapter gives an overview of these types of mutual funds.

Bond funds

A bond is a debt instrument; that is, you are loaning out your money to a corporation or government. Essentially, you are acting like a bank. In return, you get interest on your loan, at a set percent for a set amount of time until the bond matures, at which time the borrower must pay back the principal.

With stocks (and hence stock mutual funds), you're buying part ownership into companies through shares; with bonds (or fixed-income securities), you're lending out money but won't reap any of the borrower's profits. It is the same as when your home appreciates; your mortgage lender doesn't get to share in your profit.

And just like a mortgage lender, you must look into the credit of the bond issuers to decide how much risk they will present to your portfolio. You will get a higher yield from those bond issuers that pose a higher credit risk.

There are many types of bonds, including U.S. government bonds, corporate bonds, high yield (junk) bonds, and bonds from emerging markets. There are also bonds issued by international governments or corporations, tax-free bonds, and more.

Not all bonds are equal, though. Some carry significantly more risk than others (See Chapter 6). For instance, bonds issued by small, upstart businesses carry much more risk than bonds issued from the federal government. After all, a high percentage of new businesses file for bankruptcy.

Because some bonds, like those issued by small businesses, carry more risk, they usually offer higher yields. However, if they go under, you've lost your investment.

Watch Out!
Foreign government bonds are more risky investments because many foreign governments lack stability.

Time is a factor, too. The shorter the time horizon, the lower the risk. Therefore, you'll get lower
interest rates for shorter time horizons.

How do you tell the difference between a high-
risk bond and low-risk bond? Bonds are rated from
AAA on down. The higher the rating, the lower the
risk and the lower the income they will produce for
you.

A bond fund is a collection of bonds. They come
in many different product lines, such as municipal
bond funds. They also come in different time horizons—short-term, intermediate-term, and long-
term. However, unlike a single bond, these bond
funds have no single maturity date because the manager is always buying and selling. So if you invest in
a single bond, you know at least two things:

1. When the bond matures, you will get back the
   face value.

2. You will receive interest payments at specified
   intervals at a specific interest rate.

However, that does not mean bonds are a sure
bet. No investment is guaranteed. Moreover, single
bonds don't hold their value if interest rates rise in
the marketplace. If you're holding a $1,000 bond
that pays 5 percent interest, and interest rates jump
to 10 percent, you've lost 50 percent of your investment if you turn around and sell that bond in order
to invest at 10 percent. This is why they're often
used when you have only a short term to invest.
(Note: Historically, when interest rates rise in the
U.S., it is over a long period of time. This example
is used for illustrative purposes only.)

There is another factor that differentiates bonds
from bond funds. With individual bonds, the interest rate is set. You know what your interest checks

Watch Out!
This month's best fund pick may be next year's dud! Why? The manager could have been heavily invested in a well-performing sector. That sector may not have an encore performance the next year.

will be and how much your investment will be worth when the bond matures.

Bond funds don't mature on a specific day. They have the dollar-weighted average maturity. The average maturity indicates how sensitive the fund is to changes in interest rates. Long-term funds are more sensitive to interest rate fluctuations than short-term funds.

"Another measure of the bond's volatility is duration, which measures the weighted average time until the interest in principal from a security are received," according to Fidelity documents. Duration is considered a better indication of bond interest-rate sensitivity than average maturity because it accounts for both the bond's maturity and frequency and amount of interest payments. The duration typically is shorter than a securities maturity. Fidelity gives this example: "A 30-year bond paying 8 percent interest has a duration of roughly 12.5 years. Thus, it will take 12.5 years for you to earn back the present value of your investment."

Bond funds also do not give regular payments. Investors get a prorated share of the earnings or dividend payments and any capital gains. The share prices fluctuate daily, so when you sell your shares they may be worth more or less than what you paid for them.

The advantages that bond funds have over individual bonds are the same as those mutual funds have over stock portfolios picked by individual investors. In both cases the funds are professionally managed and diversified, at least to some degree. Bond funds, like money market funds, have the benefit of liquidity, in case you need quick access to your money. Bond funds also provide a regular income

with less volatility than stocks. Bond funds, at least
those invested in federal government bonds, are also
considered relatively safe investment instruments.

There are a few additional reasons investors turn
to bonds:

- They are safe relative to stocks.

- They provide a steady income in the form of
  dividends.

- Analysts are anticipating sharply lower interest
  rates in the general economy.

- In a shaky market, they are used to reduce
  volatility.

Bonds and stocks can react differently to
changes in the economy. Plus some bonds provide
tax-free income. Bonds and bond funds also provide
alternatives to money market funds whose yields are
usually lower.

But there are disadvantages. During market fluctuations, you may not receive the amount of income
from the bond fund that you expected. And since
bond fund share prices fluctuate, you may realize a
loss when you sell your shares.

What attracts investors to bond funds is the
yield. (The Securities Exchange Commission makes
funds calculate quoted yields by a uniform formula,
making it easier for investors to compare funds.)
Bond yields move in the opposite direction of their
price. When prices go up, yields go down and vice
versa. So, if the economy turns upward and interest
rates rise, a bond fund portfolio filled with low-yield-
ing bonds won't attract new investors.

Competition leads bond managers to sell the
lower yielding bonds, taking a loss, to get higher
yielding bonds in their portfolio. These funds pay

you more but the bond fund gets smaller (in terms of principal) so they can pay more dividends, and the value of your holdings diminishes.

Bond funds are either yield-oriented or total return/value-oriented. When choosing a bond fund, look at both the yield and total return.

Fidelity defines yield as "the interest income a fund produces ... measured as a percentage of its share price and expressed as an annualized percentage rate. The quoted yield may change on a daily basis. Yield calculation methods are standardized for all stock and bond funds." Fidelity defines total return as "the sum of the bond's yield and its capital return." It measures the total gain or loss over time and includes share-price fluctuations and any dividend or capital gains distributions that have been reinvested.

Note that the highest yield investment tools may not be the way to achieve your investment goals. The manager may be taking added risks to get those high yields.

Of course, it's not just increased market yields that force bond managers to buy new bonds. Bond managers must continually sell bonds as they become due. They have little choice but to replace them with bonds with yields at the going rate, which may be yielding less than those they are selling.

Many investors use bonds and bond funds to balance out their portfolios. Bonds balance the risk associated with stocks and stock mutual funds, as well as create a steady income while another portion of the portfolio is invested for capital growth. Bonds and bond funds also add balance because they gain value when the economy is slow, while stocks gain value when the economy is growing. But the type of

Bright Idea
If you want to save a story from one of your favorite financial magazines or newspapers but don't want to add more paper to your desk, see if the story is posted on its Web site, copy it and store it on your computer.

fund you choose can be a critical factor in matching your goals. Remember, at times, some bond funds may be paying out dividends while at the same time your principal investment is dwindling relative to a rise in interest rates.

Interest rates affect bond fund prices; usually the price for bond funds moves in the opposite direction of interest rates. Fidelity gives this example: you have a 20-year or $1,000 bond paying 6 percent interest. After 5 years, you decide to sell the bond but interest rates have risen and the new bonds are now paying 8 percent interest to buyers. New buyers would not want a 6 percent interest bond when they can get an 8 percent one for the same price. So, you would have to sell your bond for $750 for the buyer to get an effective yield of 8 percent (6 percent of $1,000 = 8 percent of $750). The same relationship works for bond funds as well.

Some stock fund managers also use bonds to balance their portfolios. So while you may think you're investing in a stock mutual fund, you may actually have as much as 35 percent of your investment in that fund in bonds rather than stocks.

Bond fund managers usually have bonds of similar qualities, such as maturity, credit ratings, and issuer (government, corporate, etc.), in their portfolios. There are four types of issuers, and hence, four types of bonds: government bonds, mortgage-backed bonds, corporate bonds, and municipal bonds.

Besides interest rate risk, bond funds have another risk. Prepayment risk is "the risk that a bond issuer may decide to pay off the principal of (an) existing bond before it matures," defines Fidelity. If that happens, the fund manager must

reinvest the assets at the current rate (which is usually lower during periods of widespread prepayments
or borrowers would have little reason to prepay).

There's also an inflation risk, which is tied to
interest rate risk. As interest rates rise, bonds, especially long-term bonds, become devalued.

Municipal bond funds

Municipal bond funds, called munis for short, are
one of the safer types of bond funds. They invest in
local government-issued bonds. Munis pay off in
high tax brackets because income from these bonds
is tax exempt. However, gains from price appreciation are taxable.

The quality of bonds in these portfolios varies. In
short, the lower the quality (the lower the credit rating of the issuer) of the bonds, the higher the
potential yield and, along with that, the higher the
potential risk to lose part or all of your investment.

For investors in the middle to high income tax
bracket, these bonds will often have higher after-tax
yields than income funds of similar credit ratings
and maturity dates because of the tax break they
give.

Other tax-exempt bonds

Double tax-exempt bond funds give an even greater
tax advantage if you live in a state or city that has
high income taxes. These funds invest in municipal
bonds of just one state. However, by investing in
bonds of just one state, you're investing in a concentrated portfolio, and by definition, that makes it
riskier.

If both the city and state where you live have
high income taxes, you may consider investing in
triple tax-exempt funds. These funds are exempt
from income tax in a specific city as well as federal

and state income taxes, if you live in the state and city where the money is invested. Note again, however, that by concentrating any investment—in this instance in a single geographic area—you are increasing risk by decreasing diversification.

Buying bonds and bond funds

When you look into a fund, look at performance, expenses, and fees. These will be higher for funds that take on more credit risk because they will take more time to monitor the holdings in the portfolio. Some bonds have sales charges—that is, loads—and some charge a redemption fee, or back load. Also, check out the manager's style and track record.

Kacy Gott of Kochis Fitz investment planners suggests buying individual bonds to meet your income needs by matching bond maturity dates to the dates you will need the cash. For instance, if you are going to depend on bond income every year, get bonds that mature in 1, 2, 3, 4, and 5 years. Each time a bond matures, you can buy another bond to replace it; that is, you buy a bond with a 5-year maturity date. This technique is called laddering and is the safest way to use bonds as an investment tool because you are using them for short-term investments.

Investors buy bonds to be more conservative or defensive in their investment style because individual bonds have a specified interest rate and a maturity date. If you buy a bond mutual fund, you're buying shares of stock in the bond fund and you lose both those "guarantees," says Jeff Cummer, president of Cummer Moyers Securities. You end up buying stocks either way, he says. Studies show stock funds outperform bond funds in the long run, he says.

Bright Idea
Did you see a "teaser" headline of a story you'd like to read in one of the popular financial magazines but you don't want to buy it? Check out their Web site. Some publications post their features.

Other financial advisers echo his concern about bond mutual funds, especially those investing in long-term bonds to counter inflation risks. Cummer, who specializes in fixed-income investments, says people buy bond funds because it's convenient, and they don't know how to buy bonds directly.

But if you do decide to invest in bond funds, experts suggest finding out what's in the bond portfolio before investing. If the funds have performed exceptionally well historically, you can presume they've probably taken additional risks. In the long run, investors in these types of funds will find their dividends growing as a result of management selling off bonds to buy new ones with higher yields, which causes their principal to shrink, Cummer says. That's not much security, he points out. These types of managers are referred to as "bond chasers." This quick buy-and-sell strategy also leads to increased taxes.

Next, check the credit ratings. Top bond ratings are those with an AAA rating. As the ratings drop, both risk and yields increase. Then note the maturation horizon; the longer the horizon, the lower the value of the fund when rates go up.

Municipal bond and bond fund yields are usually lower than their taxable counterparts. In order to figure out how they compare after taxes, you need to do some calculating. Money magazine's Internet site has a municipal bond calculator that can help you figure out the taxable equivalent yields.

Unless you have a lot of money to invest, mutual funds may be the best way to buy munis. In an article in the September 28, 1998, issue of Money, Susan Scherreik explains that you'll need "at least $75,000 to build a diversified portfolio of individual bond issues, but for an initial ante of $3,000 or less, you can find a solid bond fund."

(Note: If you're investing to balance your portfolio with 20 percent bonds/80 percent equities, you'll need a total portfolio of $375,000 to diversify your entire portfolio if $75,000 is invested in bonds versus a $15,000 portfolio balanced with $3,000 in bond funds.)

Another benefit of bond funds is that international and high-yield bonds are not easily obtainable by individuals.

Some experts say that bonds and bond funds are best suited for an IRA, because you won't have to pay taxes right away on the dividends.

International funds

International investing is becoming more popular because the percent of U.S. securities in the world marketplace has dropped. According to Fidelity, in 1983 U.S. securities constituted 57 percent of the world total, but 10 years later that number had dropped to 38 percent. The shift, Fidelity says, is due to burgeoning overseas economies, and not poor economic performance stateside.

In addition, some foreign stock markets have outperformed the U.S. markets even during its stellar bull performance over the past decade. But their performance overall varies widely. (See Table 9.1.)

Sometimes, when the U.S. market falls, markets outside this country do well. Some international stock markets have outperformed the U.S. market over time. Therefore, some investors like to balance their portfolios with foreign securities.

There are two main types of funds in this asset class:

Note! →
Examine the
funds and where
they're invested
before purchas-
ing shares.
Performance in
international
and global
funds varies
significantly.

TABLE 9.1: THE RANGE OF PERFORMANCE AMONG INTERNATIONAL AND GLOBAL FUNDS

	6 months	1 year	5 years	10 years	15 years
	12/31/97 to 6/30/98	6/30/97 to 6/30/98	6/30/93 to 6/30/98	6/30/88 to 6/30/98	6/30/83 to 6/30/98
Global	14.06	14.05	15.31	12.40	14.36
Global Small-cap	10.57	6.18	14.37	10.85	10.32
International	15.50	8.19	12.41	10.57	13.73
International Small-cap	22.16	11.21	10.91	—	—
European Region	27.64	33.00	21.19	12.40	—
Pacific Region	–13.70	–40.37	–3.14	2.38	14.64
Japanese	1.26	–24.98	–5.90	–2.04	8.79
Emerging Markets	–15.60	–31.86	–0.53	—	—
Latin America	–18.11	–24.20	4.60	—	—
Canadian	–8.83	–16.35	1.32	4.64	—
World Equity Funds	6.14	–3.96	10.08	8.52	11.4

Source: Lipper Analytical Services, Inc.

1. International funds, which hold securities outside the United States

2. Global funds, which include both domestic and
   international securities

There are several reasons why it's best to invest
in international mutual funds as opposed to individual foreign stocks:

- Automatic diversification. As with domestic
  mutual funds, international mutual funds are
  diversified by their very nature.

- U.S. management expertise. International
  investing is one area in which the research management expertise of mutual funds is especially
  valuable, not only because of the additional
  risks, but because there is little published
  research on many foreign markets, and business
  customs, culture, currencies, and languages differ among countries. You also may not understand how economic and political events can
  affect your foreign investments.

- Reduced paperwork and other annoyances. If
  you're invested in foreign securities through a
  mutual fund, you won't have to worry about
  time zone differences, nor do you have to be
  concerned about trading laws in other countries. You can also avoid tiresome record
  keeping.

Mutual fund managers have experience with foreign markets and have greater access to investment
opportunities not readily available to individual
investors.

The results of a Morgan Stanley survey conducted for Fidelity showed that the industry had
more impact on stock prices than the country, says

Rick Spillane, senior vice president and associate director of Fidelity's International funds in Fidelity's online presentation about trends in international investing. Two periods were reviewed—from 1989 to 1991 and then from 1995 to 1997. The survey found a significant shift by the second period. "The impact that industry had upon a stock's price grew from less than 28 percent to nearly 40 percent," Spillane writes. The study found that the impact of industry was even higher in more diversified areas.

Spillane cited Honda and Ford as an example. Honda's stock price over a 10-year period generally rose while the Nikkei Stock average was flat or down over that same time period. Ford, a U.S.-based company, showed similar fluctuations in stock prices during the 10-year period studied.

Timesaver
Listen to the news often to learn about international current events. This will tip you off on shifts in the economy.

"This relation between industry and price suggests researching stocks on a fundamental level, with a focus more on the company's financial situation and less on local market conditions," Spillane says.

International and global funds invest in both stocks and bonds worldwide. Most of these funds are considered aggressive growth or growth investments and carry risks associated with growth funds as well as added risks associated with investing in less stable markets. Some funds concentrate their portfolio in a specific country or region, which may increase or decrease risk and returns, depending on the specific area, economy, and political situation.

International stocks can be divided into three distinct assets classes:

1. Core holdings. These are large companies in mature economies, like Sony in Japan.

2. International small caps. There's not as much historical information for this category and

therefore expectations for return in this class are more theoretical. Analysts transfer trends in historical data from domestic small caps to the international market.

3. Emerging markets/equity investments. This category is made up of large companies in very immature economies.

The first two categories are in mature economies.

There's more evidence on expected rates of return domestically. International securities haven't been tracked as extensively, so returns expectations are less confident.

Investments overseas, especially those in emerging markets, carry greater risk than domestic investments. These risks include:

- Political uncertainty. Foreign governments don't offer the stability the U.S. Government does. This can lead to economic uncertainty.

- Currency fluctuation. Foreign currencies may fall, lessening your spending power.

- Market vulnerability. Many overseas markets are smaller and more volatile than the U.S. markets, and as a result a relatively small crisis (a drought, e.g.) could have a significant impact on market performance.

- Liquidity(pertaining to stocks only). Since the trading volume is lower in foreign markets than in the U.S., it may be more difficult to sell your securities, especially if you've invested in small caps. This is a good reason to invest in mutual funds.

(See Chapter 6 for more detailed information on risk and how to deal with it.)

Bright Idea
Want to teach your kids about other cultures? Buy an international fund and study the cultures in the countries where the fund has its investments.

World funds, which can be include both domestic and foreign investments, are good for people who don't have time to do their own domestic and foreign asset allocations, Gott says. The funds do this for you. (See below for specific guidelines on which investment might be right for you.) But, he warns, unless you're getting an extremely good manager, you should limit your exposure to world funds because someone else is deciding on the asset allocation. It may not be appropriate to you as an investor, he says. You don't know if the portfolio has large or small caps, etc., or if the manager is moving in and out of these classes. "It's contrary to the process of trying to match funds to your own personal asset allocation," Gott says. Also, if you have few assets or are on a fixed income, international investments are not a recommended investment tool.

Which international investment may be right for you? Use the guidelines below to determine which international equity fund category best suits your investment profile and goals, and your tolerance for risk. As with any equity fund investment, domestic or international, you should have a long-term time horizon.

Hybrids and funds of funds

A hybrid fund invests in a combination of both stocks and bonds. They're usually split 60–40 between stocks and bonds (mostly taxable), so this type of fund allows you to diversify and reduce risk with one investment. These funds allow you to expose yourself to growth through the equities but gives some protection against market volatility through the bonds.

WHICH INTERNATIONAL INVESTMENT MAY BE RIGHT FOR YOU?

← Note!
Make sure you pick international funds that match your investment goals.

A broadly diversified global or international equity fund

Investment Profile	Investment Goal	Risk Profile
You already have a well-diversified domestic portfolio. You want to make your first international investment.	To diversify internationally to achieve broad exposure to foreign markets with an emphasis on established markets.	Risk tolerance is above-average.

A targeted country/region equity fund

Investment Profile	Investment Goal	Risk Profile
You are a more aggressive investor who has specific geographic interests. You already have a well-diversified domestic portfolio and you own a broadly diversified international equity fund.	To further diversify internationally. To have the ability to focus on a country or region.	Risk tolerance is above-average and you can accept the volatility associated with regionally focused funds.

A targeted emerging markets equity fund

Investment Profile	Investment Goal	Risk Profile
You are a very aggressive investor. You are looking to target a small portion of your already well-diversified international portfolio to pursue very aggressive growth.	To seek the exceptional growth opportunities of newly industrializing economies.	Risk tolerance is considerably above-average and you are prepared for extreme swings in performance.

If you know how much exposure you want to specific asset classes, then this type of investment is not for you, Gott says. The management decides what's in these funds and it matches their goals, not yours. There is one exception. Hybrid funds are good for mid-term money, like college accounts, with an investment horizon of 5–7 years.

Buttonwood Financial Resources's Web site tracks performance records of hybrids and globals for up to 10 years.

A fund of funds is a mutual fund that invests in other mutual funds. It's used to cut risks and increase diversification but has additional fees because of the management layers.

However, some fund families offer funds of their own funds and don't charge these double fees.

There are two possible added benefits that funds of funds have:

1. Some managers can buy load funds without paying a load.
2. Some managers can invest in institutional funds.

The Funds of Funds Association list many funds of funds on their Web site. The association has subdivided them into three categories based on volatility:

1. Conservative, which have relatively low volatility and emphasize capital retention.
2. Moderate, which balance low volatility and total return.
3. Growth, which target total return, while disregarding short-term volatility.

There are single asset funds of funds. "At least 65% of the underlying mutual funds owned by these

funds of funds are in the same asset class," according to the association.

Funds of funds should be used for lower-level
goals, Gott says. Investors tend to use them for easy
asset allocation, ease of investing, or exposure. But,
he says, they add a layer of expense because you're
buying funds X, Y, and Z, all of which have managers and management fees. These funds are pack-
aged into a fund of funds, which also has manager
and management fees.

Watch Out!
Although some
international
funds have out-
performed
domestic funds,
they carry more
risk.

REITs and REIT mutual funds

Real estate investment trusts (REITs) own a portfolio
of professionally managed commercial properties
or mortgages. REITs, like mutual funds, generally
don't pay corporate income tax. REIT mutual
funds, of course, have a collection of REITs in their
portfolios, and so offer instant diversification of
these trust-like stocks.

There are three broad REIT categories:

- Equity REITs. These REITs own real estate.
  Their revenues come primarily from rent.

- Mortgage REITs. Most of these REITs make
  loans to property buyers. Their revenues come
  primarily from interest on the mortgage loans;
  others invest in residuals of mortgage-based
  securities.

- Hybrid REITs. These REITs invest in a combination of equity and mortgage REITs.

REITs are further subdivided by property types,
including:

- Office/Industrial
- Residential
- Retail

- Healthcare
- Self storage
- Hotels

Some REIT portfolios include several types of property, like office buildings, shopping centers, and apartments. Others are more concentrated, focusing on just one property type, like healthcare facilities. Still others have a geographic focus.

There are more than 300 domestic REITs with more than $130 billion in assets, according to Cohen & Steers. There are 105 REITs included in the S&P REIT Composite Index, according to Wells Real Estate Funds, which was the first investment company in America licensed by Standard & Poor's to market this index in a mutual fund.

According to Cohen & Steers, who sell REITs, by federal law a REIT must satisfy the following requirements:

- Invest a minimum of 75 percent of their total assets in real estate.
- Get a minimum of at least 75 percent of their gross income from rents from real property, or interest on mortgages on real property.
- Pay at least 95 percent of REIT taxable income in dividends.

"[REIT mutual funds are] a painless way to own real estate," Gott says. You don't have to hire managers to deal with tenants. But, he says, expected returns from this type of a real estate investment are not as good as those from equity investments, and REITs carry a higher level of risk than large-cap domestics. REITS also have lower expected rates of return than large caps or small caps, Gott says. Further, there are many layers of management, so there are additional layers of expense. But, he says, REITS get around the liquidity issue.

REITs also come in index funds. This is a relatively new type of fund, just hitting the market in 1997. The S&P REIT Index tracks the total return of domestic REIT stock performances. REITs often yield high dividends, but are highly dependent of economic cycles.

It is this latter reason that makes REITs a poor investment during slow economies when demands for office space falls. Also, it's difficult to raise apartment rents during down economies. On the other hand, while bonds deliver the same dividend every year, REITs tend to rise, at least during good economies.

REITs are required to distribute nearly all of their earnings in capital gains if they sell property at a profit. If you decide to invest in a REIT or a REIT mutual fund, in order to profit, you must consider it a long-term investment because real estate investments are heavily dependent on economic cycles. REITs vary in payout according to real estate cycles.

The advantages of REITs include:

- Dividend checks to increase your current income

- Liquidity

- Professional management and asset diversification (as with all mutual funds)

REITs attract investors who want to increase their income through dividend distributions while at the same time investing for long-term potential principal appreciation.

If you decide to invest in REITs, check the funds from operations (FFO), which is the net income

Moneysaver
Surf the Net at the library, and save on costly monthly access fees.

minus capital gains or losses plus depreciation. The FFO ratio is like the price-to-earnings ratio for conventional stocks. Since it's difficult to check individual REIT portfolios, it's best to invest in real estate through mutual funds.

Just the facts

- Bond funds lack the control individual bonds provide.
- Government bonds, bond funds, and money market funds are considered the safest investments around.
- Bond funds may be paying out lofty dividends and reducing your principal at the same time.
- International funds are high in risk but are good for balancing a domestic portfolio.
- REITs and REIT mutual funds can be good investment tools in certain economical cycles.

Getting into the Market

PART V

GET THE SCOOP ON...
Ways to purchase shares ▪ What to ask a financial planner before signing on ▪ The kinds of
personal questions a financial planner must ask
▪ Three methods you can use to track your portfolio ▪ Why you should consider joining an
investment club

Buying Mutual Funds

Chapter 10

Once you've decided on the mutual funds you would like to invest in, there are three ways to buy shares. If you decide to buy them directly, you can save money on commissions. If you hire a financial planner, you will get the added benefit of having someone who will help you develop an entire financial plan, not just your investment portfolio.

This chapter will give you tips on how to hire a financial planner, what standards you should look for, and what questions you should ask. If you want to handle your own portfolio, this chapter gives various methods for tracking your funds. Finally, the advantages and disadvantages of joining an investment club are also discussed.

Ways to purchase funds

There are a few ways you can buy shares of mutual funds. You can call the fund directly and they will send out paperwork for you to fill out and return along with a check for the purchase. Once you invest with a fund company, some allow you to purchase more shares over the Internet.

Another way to purchase shares is to go through a brokerage supermarket, where funds from many fund families are sold without transaction fees.

Finally, you can use a financial planner/adviser to help you develop your financial goals, design a portfolio, and purchase shares.

How to pick a financial adviser

Perhaps the idea of creating your own investment plan or riding out market storms is too overwhelming, and you've decided it's worth the cost to hire a financial planner. What can this professional do for you and how do you select one?

Investors often look at their portfolio as a collection of units: a pot for buying a home, a pot for their next car, a pot for their children's education, a pot for retirement, etc. But it's wiser to look at the portfolio as a whole and consider risk and return for the overall portfolio. A good financial planner can help you do this.

Financial planners, when they make these pots, are trying to think in terms that are comfortable to the people they are representing. But, says Meir Statman, a researcher at the Leavey School of Finance at Santa Clara University, it is the planner's role to make sense of the whole meal while the investor sees it as dinner and dessert. The planner should make sure the whole diet plan is nutritious, he says.

Before choosing a financial planner, ask friends and family members for referrals, contact professional associations, or use a trust officer or investment adviser at a bank. Whichever method you use, be sure to ask for references, and call them. That will narrow down the pool. Out of that pool, to find an adviser who will fit your needs, there are a number of things you must consider:

Personality

This is a person you're going to share very personal information with, so you need to feel comfortable with him or her and have reason to believe that he or she is trustworthy. The planner will need to know the following information:

- Your salary
- Your spouse's salary
- Other forms of income and how long they will last
- Assets, including your home if you own it
- Debts and your repayment plans
- Your monthly, quarterly, and annual expenses
- Expected inheritances
- Insurance policies and coverages
- Whether you have a will and/or a trust
- If and how you plan to take care of your parents
- Medical problems that you or your dependents may have
- Upcoming short- and long-term financial goals, like braces or college tuition
- Risk tolerance

Listening skills

In order to gather that information, your financial planner must be a good listener. You can assess listening and evaluation skills during your first appointment, which is usually free. After listening carefully for several sessions, the adviser should be

Bright Idea
If you think you might panic and cash in on your investments during market downturns, hire a financial adviser to help you stick to your long-term plan.

able to create a plan that meets your goals and your risk tolerance level. If the adviser asks you only a few questions before telling you what you need, it is likely that he or she is more of a salesperson than a professional investment adviser or planner.

Method of payment

Before choosing a financial planner, find out how he or she is paid. Ask for a copy of the firm's commission schedule or a disclosure of its fee structure.

Some firms have their own investment products and the planner may get added compensation for selling one of them to you. But those investments may not best meet your needs.

A diversified portfolio should be tailored to your needs and not a sales professional's goals, says Peter F. Mackie, president of the Investment Management Group, which has investment responsibility for the Commerce Funds Family. It may be that such products might help you to achieve your goals, but your goals must be primary, he says.

Mackie suggests looking at the adviser's fee schedules. Are they transaction-oriented or asset-based? Someone who is compensated on the basis of the number of transactions performed has an added incentive to move you in and out of funds, which puts you into the position of having to realize capitals gains, if there are any, and pay taxes on them.

This type of trading has additional consequences. Frequent trading forces you to pay high back loads, if that's how the fund is structured, because many back loads phase out only after you've held your investment for 5 years. Moving in and out of front-loaded funds also costs you in up-front commissions. Some funds also have transaction costs, redemption charges, and frequent-activity fees. By paying any of these commissions, fees, and taxes, your principal investment is reduced and, as a result, your earning power is reduced as well.

In contrast, asset-based commissions give no incentive for the planner to move you in and out of funds. In fact, it gives him or her an incentive to put you in the funds that would give you the most gains because the more you have invested, the more he or she profits from your investment. However, you must be careful not to allow your adviser to heavily weight your portfolio with aggressive funds in order to get quick gains (taking high risks) if your risk tolerance is not on that level or if such aggressive investments don't meet your investment goals.

The problem with asset-based commissions, though, is that you don't necessarily get additional benefits with additional assets, but the commission is higher. It takes no more effort for the financial planner to make a transaction on a $100,000 account versus a $500,000 account. Therefore, some people with hefty assets request that the commission be based on a lower percentage (say 1 percent versus 2 percent) of total assets.

There are financial investors who work on a fee basis, as well. If you have significant assets, this form of payment might be more economical, especially if you don't need much hand-holding when the market dips.

But the flat-fee structure of payment may lessen the financial planner's incentive to place you in funds with the very best performance records, since researching funds takes time.

If the fee is charged on an hourly basis, you must consider whether the amount of time charged is appropriate. If you're worried about spending

Watch Out!
Too many transactions can be considered churning, an unethical and sometimes illegal practice used by some unscrupulous salespeople to increase their commissions by turning over securities more frequently than needed to meet the investor's goals.

money on this service, this might not be the best payment method for you because each time you call your adviser, the clock starts ticking.

Rather than a fee-only basis, the firm might be compensated on a commission only, fee and commission, or fee offset-basis. Michael Leonetti, a certified financial planner and president of Leonetti & Associates, a fee-for-service financial planning firm, suggests asking if the fees are capped. If the firm charges on a fee-offset basis make sure that if commissions exceed the fee that that part of the fee is returned to you. Also check to see if anyone employed by the firm acts as a general partner, participates in, or receives compensation from investments he or she may recommend, he says.

Besides the planner's fees or commissions, ask if there are any charges for opening, maintaining, and closing an account. (See Chapter 13 for more fees associated with investing.)

Typical client profile

Check to see what population the planner serves most. People with similar income levels tend to have similar problems. By specializing in a specific sector, the planner may be better able to help you.

Educational background

Ask if he or she is a CFP (certified financial planner) or has a business or law degree. Check to see if he or she enrolls in courses and earns continuing education credits. By asking about financial planning education and designations, you may be able to distinguish between the insurance salesperson and the financial planner, Leonetti says.

Leonetti suggests finding out how many years of financial planning experience the adviser has and if he or she belongs to any professional financial

"
Money is the most egalitarian force in society. It confers power on whoever holds it.
—Roger Starr
"

planning associations. He suggests inquiring as to whether the planner has been disciplined by a professional or regulatory governing body. (This may be a tough question to ask, but remember, you are entrusting your savings to this person.) You should also ask if his or her firm is registered as an investment adviser with the U.S. Securities and Exchange Commission (SEC) and with the state securities office.

Legal paperwork

Many brokerage firms will require you to sign a new account agreement. Read this document carefully. It could affect your legal rights.

Don't rely on verbal agreements. Insist that everything be placed in writing before signing the agreement.

According to the SEC, completing the new account agreement requires making three critical decisions:

1. Determining who will control decision-making for your account. You will maintain control unless you decide to give discretionary authority to your financial adviser. With discretionary authority, the financial planner can make investment decisions "without consulting you about the price, the type of security, the amount and when to buy or sell," according to the SEC.

2. Payment method for your investment.

3. Amount of risk you'll assume. In a new account agreement, you'll specify your investment objectives, such as income, growth, or aggressive growth, which determine level of risk.

According to the SEC, when you open a new account, "the brokerage firm may ask you to sign a legally binding contract to arbitrate any future dispute between you and the firm or your sales representative." This contract may be part of another document. "The federal securities laws do not require that you sign such an agreement," according to the SEC. By signing, you give up the right to sue your adviser and the brokerage firm in court. Furthermore, if you don't sign that contract, you can still choose to arbitrate a dispute for damages without going to court.

Advantages and pitfalls of one-stop shopping

Somehow, full-time, 40-hour-a-week jobs become 50- and 60- and sometimes even 80-hour-a-week jobs, not counting commutes of 10 to 20 hours a week. No wonder people have little time for their families and outside interests, much less investing.

Moneysaver
If you're retired, have your pension and Social Security checks deposited electronically into your mutual fund. That way the money can start earning interest right away.

Many businesses created conveniences for people who have a lot of money but not much time. There are convenience stores, which charge more, but are small enough that you can run in and get what you need fast without having to wait in long lines. There are apartments and condos with concierge services that water your plants, take your clothes to the dry cleaners, do your grocery shopping, and more. So it should come as no surprise that Wall Street, known for its stressful, long days, created a convenient way to invest: one-stop shopping.

"Prior to 1984, the only way that you could buy no-load mutual funds was by going directly to the mutual fund company," says Jeff Lyons, senior vice president of mutual funds marketing at Charles Schwab, a brokerage firm. Back then, if you wanted to invest in a number of funds in different fund families you had to establish a relationship in each company. So, if you wanted to sell from a Vanguard fund, for instance, and use that money to buy into a Janus fund, you'd have had to go through all the paperwork, and the transaction itself took days, Lyons says. Plus, you'd have had to pay transaction fees, which added up.

In today's marketplace, you have a choice. Mutual fund supermarkets, where you can buy into no-load funds from a list of fund families without incurring any transaction fees, popped up in 1984 when both Charles Schwab and Jack White came out with their programs. Now all it takes is one phone call to make transactions and, rather than poring over numerous monthly statements written in a variety of forms, one-stop-shopping investors can monitor their entire portfolio with greater ease. They get one monthly statement with all of their mutual funds and other securities listed that are sold through that brokerage. There are dozens of brokerages offering supermarkets today.

By using a supermarket like Schwab's One Source, you not only save on transaction fees and get a single statement for your entire portfolio, but if all the funds and other securities are bought through that brokerage, you get added services that a smaller brokerage can't offer. Many of the larger fund families also have added valuable services such as the following:

- Check writing
- Automated investment programs
- Bill-paying conveniences
- Ability to get quotes off an automated service
- Local branch offices

- Electronic transfers over the Web or through desktop software via a modem
- Selection decision tools (Schwab offers a performance guide on more than 1,000 funds and other planning tools to evaluate different funds among fund families.)
- Automatic Transaction Machines
- Touch-Tone telephone transfers
- Computer access to buy and redeem shares, check your account balance(s), review the fund's portfolio, and tap into research

If you already have an established portfolio, can you move it into a supermarket? Funds can be moved directly from a fund company to a brokerage firm or from one brokerage to another, assuming the broker can handle the operational detail of the funds, Lyons says. For those funds listed in the supermarket of funds there would be no problem and no fees involved, he says. For example, if you have a selection of Fidelity funds and Janus funds, and those funds are part of the 1,000 funds in One Source or a similar supermarket, you can move them to the supermarket, making it easier to track your portfolio. Once you're in a supermarket, you can move in and out of those funds without incurring transaction fees.

Looking back, Lyons says many analysts predicted there would be a lot of consolidation among mutual funds companies. He believes that supermarkets prevented this consolidation because it gave many medium and small companies a way to put their products on the shelves, making them better able to compete.

There are drawbacks, however. You may not get the in-depth expertise on a specific mutual fund by calling a supermarket representative. In contrast, by calling directly to the fund family you might get a more informed answer on a complicated question.

Lyons summed it up this way: Fund families do a great job managing money and supermarkets do a great job servicing investors. It's a synergistic relationship.

Keeping track of your portfolio

Keeping track of your portfolio is important, regardless of whether you're a long-term investor or short-term trader. Both types of investors must keep abreast of capital gains and losses because of the tax implications (see Chapter 12). Both types of investors need to be aware of how well your portfolio is performing. If you're a long-term investor, you might want to sell a fund that doesn't perform well over a long period of time, especially if you believe it has to do more with poor management rather than the economic cycle.

Furthermore, over time some of your investments will better others, changing the balance of your portfolio. So, if your financial plan calls for 50 percent small caps and 50 percent large caps, and the small caps did exceptionally well, the balance of your portfolio may have shifted. Due to the increase price of the shares, your portfolio now may be 70 percent small caps and 30 percent large caps. To rebalance your portfolio, you will either have to buy some large caps or sell some small caps.

If you're a short-term trader, you must stay abreast of your portfolio in order to know what you should buy and sell. Your approach to tracking your funds may differ from that of a long-term investor because you'll need more up-to-the-minute standings.

Bright Idea
If you see your investments making money and that tempts you into cashing in some shares and buying things you hadn't planned on, hire an investment adviser to remind you of your long-term goals and how compounded growth works.

If you're a long-term investor, the cheapest way to keep track of your portfolio is on paper at the end of the year. This, however, can be a tedious process.

Monthly and/or quarterly statements will include details of transactions for that month or quarter. Yearly statements will have all transactions for that year. Current share prices, or net asset values, are listed in the business sections of daily newspapers. You also can let your fingers do the walking and phone each fund to keep up to date.

At the end of the year, you'll receive a 1099-Div form for tax purposes. You can estimate how much you'll owe in taxes using the year-end statements, which tell you how much you've received in dividends and capitals gains. The tax rates are not broken down in that form, however. Some of those gains may be long term, while others may be short term.

One way to check the balance of your portfolio is to list all your funds by category—large caps, small caps, etc.—and then use the year-end statements to determine the value of each fund and add up the categories. Check what percentage each category totals and rebalance at the beginning of the year, if necessary.

You can automate this process by using software to easily update your records five days a week, if you have the desire, by entering the share prices listed in the business section of daily newspapers. At the end of every quarter the newspapers report if the funds gave out dividends, although you'll have to wait for your statements to find out how much in dividends your investment earned.

Computer software, like Quicken and Microsoft Money, also gives you the benefit of seeing your portfolio changes in the form of graphs, not to mention lively colors.

Many of the fund families and brokerages have Internet sites where you can download your fund's market performance into your software. Each site's timing differs. Some sites have a 20-minute delay, while others are shorter. All you have to do at these sites is enter the fund symbol. If you don't know the symbol, you can look it up right on the Web site.

If you sell a mutual fund, it's easier to figure out your cost basis and what you invested (plus dividends) versus your earnings using computer software. If you're using paper and your investment over 30 years is $5,000, for instance, and you sold $1,000 worth of shares, you would have to go back over your paperwork to determine how much the shares were worth when you bought them. If you don't specify which shares you're selling, the IRS will assume you're selling the oldest ones first.

Of course, this is not always to your advantage. The oldest shares might have the highest gains and that means you'll have to pay more taxes.

By using software, you can quickly determine which shares were bought at which price and figure out which ones you can sell at the greatest tax advantage. (See Chapter 12.)

The calculation is further complicated because to withdraw $1,000, you will likely be withdrawing a fraction of a share, such as 256.66 shares. Software relieves you of this difficult computation.

Computer calculations also will tell you what percentage rate increase or decrease your investment has earned or lost. Some software, like Quicken, has a compatible tax program, eliminating the need to re-enter data and thereby reducing chances for error and saving time.

Timesaver
By using a mutual fund supermarket, you can get one statement for your entire portfolio. That way you'll only have to decipher one company's method of displaying the information.

In addition, some fund family and financial magazine Internet sites allow you to track your portfolio online. However, by using this method, some of your privacy is lost (because the site knows your e-mail address and can use it to watch your portfolio).

Investment clubs

You learn by doing; this is the basic premise of investment clubs. Investment clubs are used to help individual investors who don't want to make a go of it alone, or at least not completely. When investing in stocks, such clubs can combine money from its members and therefore can afford a better variety of stocks than each member could alone, much like a mutual fund. Although typically these clubs aren't oriented toward mutual funds, they can be used the same way for those mutual funds whose initial minimum investment far exceeds what some individuals can afford.

Investment clubs and mutual funds also share certain other similarities. Both provide you with a diversified stock portfolio, although often to differing degrees, and both allow you to withdraw money at any time. (Most clubs use the evaluation unit system of accounting, which makes it similar to cashing in shares of a mutual fund. And just like mutual fund shares, the value of club "shares" changes over time.)

But there are several differences between investment clubs and mutual funds. An investment club's portfolio is diversified over time, as the members purchase stocks. Investing in a mutual fund provides instant diversification.

Each member of the investment club shares in the role of the mutual fund manager, researching industries, individual companies, and the potential they hold for investors. But unlike mutual fund managers, who have extensive knowledge of economics and industry sectors as well as easy access to company historical performances and analyst predictions, members of an investment club rarely have any background in investing. Oddly, this is one of the greatest benefits investment clubs have to offer. Investment clubs serve as an introduction to the stock market.

Investment clubs also serve another useful purpose. Misery likes company, but only company that's miserable. During market downturns and bear markets, who better to comfort you in your losses but others who have taken the exact same hits? And what better way to remember your investment goals but from a group who shares similar goals? A club can become a support group when the Dow dips, as it eventually will during any long-term investment horizon.

Investment clubs are a great place to learn, says Maurice Elvekrog, a licensed psychologist and chartered financial analyst. Members learn about investing and acquire leadership skills.

But there is a control issue: You must go along with others because the group invests as a whole. And you may have to deal with those who lack initiative. Some members are careful and do their homework, and others want a free ride, Elvekrog cautions. Before joining a group, ask how these different personalities are handled.

There are 37,500 investment clubs that are members of the National Association of Investment Corporations (NAIC). Each of these clubs have about 16 members. Of those 16 members, on average, only one person had investment experience

Timesaver
Everyone in an investment group is assigned a fund or stock to research. But if your time is restricted you may want to stick with investing in mutual funds. You won't have to research each stock.

when the club started out. But after 5 years, 15 of the 16 club members are investing on their own in addition to investing with the club, and they invest about three times as much personally as in their investment club, according to Kenneth S. Janke, Sr., NAIC's president and CEO.

Janke says you can take courses and read publications and news articles about investing, but "until you risk some money on your own, you're really not going to learn."

Besides hands-on experience, members who might be embarrassed to ask a broker some basic questions can comfortably bring these questions to their peers. "Everyone is really learning at the same pace," he says.

There are two main reasons people join investment clubs:

1. People want to invest to get gains but have no knowledge of the stock market.

2. Being a club member forces you to think about investing once a month and forces you to keep up with your own portfolio at least as often. And you can't just take a superficial glance at the market or at your portfolio. You must do your homework to prepare for meetings. As stocks are purchased, they are assigned to members who are responsible to keep abreast of their performance and growth prospects. When a stock price changes, the member responsible for tracking it must explain it to the group, Janke says.

Note that because it is extremely difficult for individual investors to research foreign stocks (as discussed in Chapter 9), investment groups use

Watch Out!
If you own stock, you could have a sticky situation on your hands if you lose the stock certificate. With mutual funds, you don't have to worry about them. The fund takes care of all paperwork.

global funds to satisfy the international aspect of a fully diversified portfolio, Janke says.

So if you want to learn firsthand how to invest while surrounded by the security of your peers, have the motivation to do some of the legwork, and are willing to trust others to do likewise, the question is, how do you join one of these clubs?

The answer is: more legwork. It's hard to get into a club if you don't know of one, Janke says. You must be invited to join.

NAIC suggests organizing your own club of 15 to 16 people. Since it's a challenge to find this many future investors, Janke suggests talking to two or three people and letting them talk to two or three people. This not only lessens the burden on you to find so many people, but it serves to decentralize the power so no one person dominates the club.

NAIC suggests recruiting club members from a variety of professions. You want to have a diversified membership so each member can give the inside scoop, so to speak, about his or her industry. If the group is homogeneous—say, all doctors—the members' collective expertise lies in health care, and it will be tempting for the group to concentrate their investments in this industry.

Initially, when a club is formed, members are not focused on building a portfolio, Janke says. The first reason people invest is because they know of a "hot" stock, one which they think will make money. They're not thinking of diversifying, he says.

But as time goes on, things change. Here's why:

- NAIC instructs its members to research a different industry each month.

- After researching the industry, members are instructed to look at the companies within it.

- The third step is to look at the stock prices for these companies and determine if they're reasonable.

- Once the industry is understood and a company within it is well-researched and priced with a low enough P/E that it shows growth possibilities, the group purchases shares.

As months pass, more and more industries are examined and more and more stocks are bought from companies in a variety of sectors. That's how the diversification begins. Eventually you build a portfolio that makes sense to you, Janke says.

NAIC teaches three basic principals:

1. Invest regularly. Don't try to predict the market. (If you look at any popular index average, you'll see there are many ups and downs. The general trend is up.)

2. Have faith in the power of compounding, or reinvesting earnings. (See Chapter 1 for more on the power of compounded growth.)

3. Study companies on a fundamental basis, not on price. NAIC suggests clubs buy stocks in companies that are growing more rapidly than the economy. This is accomplished by:

   - Looking at management

   - Looking at price, and making sure the stock is not overpriced at that moment

Investment clubs have their drawbacks. "Whenever you get more than two personalities together, you're going to have a problem," Janke says, especially if you have all leaders and no followers. You need followers.

Other problems can occur if club members don't have a long-term view of investing, or if they become discouraged by a loss. Many clubs initially lose money. But if members have a long-term view, their risk tolerance will be similar, and most likely, their stock selections will pick up speed since the market historically rises over time. "You must check your performance from one peak market to the next," Janke says.

Having members who want to move in and out of stocks is another possible problem which could cause the downfall of a club, Janke says. The investment philosophy must be the same among all members for the club to do well. Traders should probably not be in a club because the club only meets once a month, Janke says.

If you're interested in forming an investment club, call (248) 583-NAIC. NAIC provides member clubs with an official guide to operating a club, including agreements, agendas, and procedures. The guide teaches investors how to analyze securities from the point of view of what the company is doing—not what prices are doing.

Since accounting can be a burden for the club treasurer, NAIC provides accounting software to its members. "If there's one reason for an investment club to go out of business, it's because no one wants to become the treasurer," Janke says. The software even includes tax returns.

NAIC first-year dues are $35 for the club plus $14 per member.

Carol Nemec, a professor of accounting and finance at Southern Oregon University who has served as a director of an area council of NAIC, cautions club members to learn about the market and consider its risks.

Moneysaver
By joining an investment club, you save money because management fees are indirectly split among members.

Bright Idea
Since you must invest a specific amount each month in an investment group, you automatically dollar cost average, thereby buying at market lows as well as highs.

Clubs should be used to learn as much about your investments as possible and about risks, the economy, and the market.

Just the facts

- In order to get solid financial advice from an investment planner, you must reveal personal information such as salary and any health problems.

- Brokerage fund supermarkets allow you to invest in a variety of fund families without incurring transaction costs.

- Fund supermarkets simplify bookkeeping by providing just one statement for all your funds and other securities held through that brokerage.

- You can keep track of your portfolio with computer software, making tax time less taxing.

- An investment club is a good place to learn about investing, but conflicts in members' personalities can pose problems.

GET THE SCOOP ON...
Why you benefit from dollar cost averaging ▪
Why you should stick with a buy-and-hold
strategy ▪ Why timing the market is so difficult
to do ▪ Which economic indicators say "buy"

Understanding Investment Strategies

Chapter 11

Not many people have large lump sums of money that they can invest when they are young, freeing them to use their salaries purely for pleasure. Therefore, the best strategy for the vast majority of individual investors is to dollar cost average—that is, make regular investments over time. An adjunct strategy you can use is to buy and hold investments. This strategy has several benefits, a tax advantage notwithstanding.

For those of you who are daring and have nerves of steel, you can try to time the market, but most investment experts don't recommend this strategy. In fact, even the experts are not good at playing this game. But if you do decide to try your luck, it's best to go in with a little knowledge of the relationship of the economy to stock market fluctuations. These topics and more are discussed in this chapter.

Dollar cost averaging

By dollar cost averaging, you're making regular investments over time, usually monthly or quarterly. This method of investing has several advantages. First, it's practical. You can arrange for automatic withdrawals to be made by your mutual fund account from your bank account. Some employers will make direct deposits for retirement plans.

Second, many mutual fund companies will waive or reduce the minimum initial investment amount if you make arrangements for automatic investments because it assures them that over time you will reach that dollar amount.

Automatic investing also makes it possible for you to be a disciplined investor. It is especially helpful if you have trouble parting with your hard-earned dollars (that is, taking them from the safe haven of an insured bank account), or if you don't have any trouble parting with them to buy unnecessary things.

The dollar-cost-averaging investment strategy takes much of the guesswork and anxiety out of investing. Using this strategy, you don't have to wonder if you're buying shares at peak prices or if the market might fall a little more. You'll likely buy shares at their peak, at their lows and everywhere in between. When you buy at market highs, you will get fewer shares, and when you buy at market lows, you will get more shares. The amount you invest remains the same, unless you decide otherwise.

The idea behind this method is twofold: first, that the price you paid for all your shares will average out over time so you won't kick yourself for buying at peak prices, and second, you can take advantage of buying at market lows.

It also has psychological advantages. If you invest a big lump sum into the market and it falls, temporarily you're down, says Craig Israelsen, associate professor of consumer and family economics at the University of Missouri-Columbia. But if you continuously invest smaller sums, you're apt to buy more shares at a cheaper rate.

Note, however, if you end up buying at a market low, you're better off lump-summing. But it's more likely you'll dollar-cost average because most Americans don't have a large sum to invest, Israelsen says. With lump-summing you need to be able to stomach a possible big loss.

Israelsen says that how you invest—lump sum versus dollar cost averaging—affects the average annualized return. Dollar cost averaging can sometimes produce a higher average annual return, but lump sum investments have more earning power and as a result make more money total.

As noted in Chapter 7, mutual fund returns reported in the popular press assume the investor made a lump sum deposit, rather than dollar cost averaged it, that all dividends were reinvested into the fund, and that the investor made no withdrawals from the fund.

Israelsen gives this example: If you invested a lump sum of $3,000 into T. Rowe Price Equity Index on May 1, 1992, it would have been worth $6,488.06 five years later. The average annual return would be 16.68 percent. If the person invested $50 each month over that same 5-year period, the ending value would total $5,010.92 and the average annual return would then be calculated as 19.45 percent. (Note that $50 per month for 5 years equals $3,000.)

Timesaver
Mutual funds help you save time by providing necessary tax forms and transaction confirmation for easier tax reporting.

Israelsen says when you consider reported return figures for mutual funds, they will only be accurate if:

- You were invested during the entire 5-year period.

- You had invested a lump sum and did not invest additional amounts.

- You reinvested all dividends back into the fund.

- You didn't make any withdrawals during that time frame.

Buy and hold

The reasons for using the buy-and-hold strategy are plentiful, make a lot of sense, and are backed by historical data showing that those investors that buy and hold fare much better over time than those investors who try to outwit the market.

> 66
> I never attempt to make money on the stock market. I buy on the assumption that they could close the market the next day and not reopen it for five years.
> —Warren Buffett
> 99

Remember Anne Scheiber (Chapter 1), the woman who started with nothing, but by making relatively small investments over time and using a buy-and-hold strategy, ended up with a reported $20 million? She picked investments and stuck with them no matter how badly they did at times, and she lived through some deep dips and rough bear markets. She even had the living memory of the crash of 1929 to dissuade her from keeping her money invested at all, let alone through rocky rides. Plus, she didn't have the benefit of hindsight in her earlier investment days—that is, she didn't know that the market, over time, would return 10–12 percent on average.

But the buy-and-hold strategy paid off for her, and it can pay off for you, too, provided you do your research and pick solid investments. Scheiber spent a great deal of time researching the companies in which she invested.

(If this example doesn't convince you of the strength of the buy-and-hold strategy, consider that this is the method Warren Buffet used to make his fortune.)

So, what are the various reasons investors use the buy-and-hold strategy? It goes without saying that some have looked over the historical performance of the market and know that if they sit tight, grit their teeth when there are market corrections and when the market dives or hibernates (the dreaded bear markets), they will be paid handsomely.

Then there are those who don't have the time or don't have the desire to play with the market, and the buy-and-hold strategy is simply a default method of investing.

Others know that just one mistake in market timing could cost them all their winnings from previous lucky guesses (for that is what market timing is for the vast majority who play with fire). Then there are those who have been burnt and turn to the buy-and-hold strategy as a painful lesson learned.

Making just one mistake, or thinking that you might make one mistake with dire consequences to your life savings, will probably cause you a lot of sleepless nights and result in a kind of obsession with the market, the economy, politics, world events, global weather, Federal Reserve Board Chairman Alan Greenspan's facial expressions, and more.

Considering that even those who make a profession out of timing the market and are supported by a staff of economists and other experts are more often wrong than right, this is a tough row to hoe single-handedly.

But even a few lucky wins timing the market can be offset by expenses. Each time you redeem shares in a taxable account—that is, one that is not sheltered by your retirement plan—you must pay any capital gains taxes owed. There are transaction costs to consider, as well, which may include commissions, front- or back-end loads, frequent activity fees, share redemption fees, and more. As we explain in Chapter 13, these charges eat up your principal investment, which diminishes your earning power.

Buy and hold isn't just a strategy to consider for yourself but for the mutual funds you invest in, as well.

With an assumed 20 percent gross return on all stocks in the portfolio, a 39.6 percent federal tax rate, and local taxes totaling 5.4 percent, a 15 percent turnover rate would produce an after-tax return of 18.7 percent, says Liz Davidson, CEO of Davidson Andrade, a hedge fund. A 200 percent turnover rate would reduce the after-tax return to 2.0 percent. She noted that this is a worse-case scenario because funds will often sell their losers and offset losses with sales of high gainers. However, it's still a factor.

Table 11.1 demonstrates the effect turnover has on an investor's portfolio.

Note! ➡
Table 11.1 assumes a 20 percent gross return on all stocks in the portfolio, a 39.6 percent federal tax rate, and state and local taxes totaling 5.4 percent. Source: Davidson Andrade

TABLE 11.1: THE EFFECT OF TURNOVERS

Turnover	After-tax Return
15%	18.7%
25%	17.8%
50%	15.5%
75%	13.3%
100%	11.0%
150%	6.5%
200%	2.0%

With a turnover rate of over a 100 percent, you're much more dependent on the skills of the portfolio selection staff, according to Peter F. Mackie, president of the Investment Management Group.

With a lower turnover rate portfolio, you're invested as a shareholder in the company, but in a higher turnover fund you're invested in a pool of assets being quickly turned over, he says. It's not the individual company driving the portfolio results but the manager's skill. Furthermore, mutual funds with high turnover rates will have more short-term capital gains, which are taxed at your income tax bracket rate, as opposed to long-term gains, which are taxed at 20 percent for investments held 12 months or longer.

Timing the market

One of the best ways to come out ahead in Las Vegas or Atlantic City is to sit at the roulette table, write down your picks and the amounts you'd bet, and see how much you'd walk away with at the end of the evening if you had placed money on the table. Although it's not nearly as exciting as actually playing, you'll more likely than not be ahead of the game if you keep your hands in your pockets.

Timing the market is like gambling. Few investors come out better than if they would have taken a buy-and-hold position, although some feel more in control of their investment this way.

If you think you can time the market, use the same methodology as described above. Try keeping a running log of your market predictions. Most likely, you'll see that your predictions don't pan out over time. At least in a casino you have some control over the situation. You can decide your moves in

Moneysaver
If you're willing
to spend time
developing your
own investment
plan and
researching
mutual funds,
and if you can
stick to your
plan during mar-
ket dives, you
can invest on
your own, saving
on commis-
sions charged
by financial
advisers.

blackjack based on the dealer's hand, for instance. In timing the market, there are many factors to consider, and even those professionals who spend 5 days a week researching and contemplating don't line their pockets with gold very often.

There is a long list of economic factors that affect the market. You can gain access to current Federal economic indicators at the Economic Statistics Briefing Room (ESBR) (www.whitehouse. gov/fsbr/output.html).

The list of economic indicators includes the following and more:

1. Production, Sales, Orders and Inventories
   - New housing starts
   - New orders for manufactured durable goods
   - Monthly retail sales
   - Advanced retail sales
   - Total business sales

2. Manufacturing and Trade Inventories and Sales
   - Industrial production
   - Capacity utilization
   - Output
   - Gross domestic product
   - Nonresidential fixed investment
   - Residential investment

3. Personal Savings Rate

4. Corporate Profits

5. Personal Consumption Expenditures

6. Total U.S. Expenditures for Research and Development

7. Income, Expenditures, and Wealth

- Disposable personal income
- Per capita income
- Farm sector income
- Household income
- Poverty rates
- Household wealth

8. Employment, Unemployment, and Earnings

- Civilian labor force
- Unemployment
- Unemployment rate

9. Prices

- Gross domestic purchases prices
- Consumer Price Index
- Retail gasoline prices
- Crude oil prices

10. Money, Credit, and Interest Rates

- Bank credit at all commercial banks
- Interest rates and bond yields

11. Transportation

- Revenue passenger miles
- Airline domestic revenue passenger miles
- U.S. truck/rail imports
- U.S. transborder commodity imports by truck and rail

12. International Statistics

- Balance on current account
- Monthly trade balance
- U.S. international trade in goods and services

To time the market—and win—you must keep one step ahead of each market fluctuation. The market is often a wild roller coaster, taking investors on a thrilling ride with sweeping curves that come from seemingly nowhere and deep dips that heave investors' stomachs into their chests. It seems to change direction at whim, with analysts deciding from hindsight what caused its erratic behavior. It's impossible to predict because, in addition to economic factors, its movement is tied to politics, current events, and the emotion of Wall Street investors.

Perhaps this is why, as Liz Davidson puts it, "Market timing is definitely on its way out." She says that today, mutual funds, on average, hold less than 5 percent cash. "Experts say that portfolio managers are remaining fully invested in an attempt to compete with the indices, which have beaten actively managed funds over the last several years," she says, adding that she thinks it goes beyond that reasoning.

"I think most money management firms have come to the conclusion that it is extremely difficult to successfully time the market. This has come from decades of experience," Davidson says.

Furthermore, she notes, "There is a new theory that individuals can hold cash on their own if they choose to do so. When individuals allocate a percentage of their assets to a mutual fund, they are effectively saying that they want that percentage of their assets invested in equities.

"Because individuals have unique risk profiles and liquidity needs, they should be the ones to decide the percentage of their assets that should be invested in equities," she says. "Portfolio managers

Timesaver
By investing in mutual funds versus stocks and bonds, you save time on record keeping. The fund keeps track of transactions, interest, dividends, and short- and long-term gains and losses.

should simply try to find the best opportunities in the market."

Davidson thinks experience has taught investors that you can't consistently make money timing the market. For any one person to think they know more than the aggregate is arrogant, she says.

The market is very reactive to both good and bad news, Davidson says. It's incredibly hard to predict the market because it's defined by so many different factors.

"It's time, not timing, that counts when it comes to your investment return," according to AIM investment literature. "Suppose you made a...$10,000 investment in the unmanaged Standard & Poor's 500 Index for the five-year period ending March 31, 1998. Your $10,000 would have grown to $27,219. Now let's say you tried to time the market and ended up missing its 10 best days (the 10 best single-day performances for the S&P 500 during the period). Your $27,219 would have shrunk to $20,824."

Another problem with timing the market is that you may miss some great buying opportunities while you're waiting for the market to go just a little lower or by waiting until it bottoms out.

When the market falls, it's like buying stock on sale. But how deep will the discounts get? Well, it's like going to a store and the clerk won't tell you if there will be another reduction coming up in a few days, says Kacy Gott of Kochis Fitz investment planners. The only difference is if the prices do go down, you can't return your stock within 30 days and get the better price.

There's no way to figure out which stock classes or sectors will be affected by each market downturn.

Sometimes, small caps will be affected while other times it will be large caps that take a dip. Sometimes certain sectors will get hit hard while others are left none the worse for wear.

66
The entire essence of America is the hope to first make money, then make money with money, then make lots of money with lots of money.
—Paul Erdman
99

If you time the market, you'd better have great reflexes. Bad news travels fast. Take the following *Washington Post* report ("World Stocks Plunge; Dow Off 357"), dated Friday, Aug. 28, 1998, as an example: "Bad economic news ricocheted around the globe today, from Japan to Russia to Europe and then to Latin America, finally exploding in U.S. stock markets and sending the Dow Jones industrial average plunging." In Russia, the central bank suspended trading of rubles for dollars while the country stopped paying foreign loans. Foreign stock markets continued to plummet. Domestic stocks followed suit, continuing a vicious cycle of one market reacting to the next.

"The market will [move] up and down on news, both national and international," says Carol Nemec, a professor of accounting and finance at Southern Oregon University. "The market in the U.S., however, is still learning how to be an international market, in my opinion, and therefore isn't certain how to respond to international news."

Furthermore, she says, "the market is also a different animal from even a few years ago. We [investors] are the market, and we have become a more active investing group, and many have more true information available to use in decision-making." But, she warns, "many think they have more information, and [they] don't! The last two dips of the market were halted and reversed by small investors, many in investment clubs." That's a little scary, she says.

Regardless of who's driving it, the stock market, as we discussed in Chapter 7, is driven by expectations. It's fueled by emotions.

"Prices of stocks are based on fundamentals, but [investors] trade on hunches and emotion along with real...information," Nemec says.

Researchers have studied what is called a "bubble"—that is, prices feeding on other prices—not on true firm values, Nemec says. "The problem, however, is that a bubble cannot be ascertained until after it has burst," she says. "So bubble or not, look to the value of each firm, not what [people] are heralding."

Nemec likens the stock market to an animal, saying that it scares easily and has a herd instinct. Just like cattle, it will stampede without a clue as to why.

There is one thing you can count on: business cycles. No bull market rages forever, nor do bear markets hibernate indefinitely. There's a connection between business cycles and market cycles.

After reading this chapter, if you still want to play the market, consider using just a small portion of your portfolio, an amount you can afford to lose. Consider it gambling money. Also, make sure your funds allow unlimited trades by phone with no transaction fees. You'll probably need the money.

Investing in an uncertain market

Whether you're timing the market or actively managing your portfolio, which is not recommended, you should pay close attention to market cycles.

Older investors know to cling to money market funds, CDs, or Treasuries during market lows and bear markets. They often turn to more risky, more aggressive equities when the bull emerges. That's the simplest way of working with cycles. But you can further refine the strategy.

To best use this strategy, you must understand the interplay between economic and stock market cycles and you must become aware of various market indicators.

Investment cycles

Bright Idea
Check out where corporate executives are flying. At the FAA, flight data is posted on the Internet to see if they're operating efficiently or taking lots of company sponsored vacations.

Some companies are tied to the economy more so than others; If you want to take advantage of economic cycles, you can rotate your investments into what are called cyclical sectors, those that do well in specific economic environments.

In an article titled, "A Sector Rotation: Investing Based on the Economic Cycle," which appeared on the American Association of Independent Investors' (AAII) Web site, author John Bajkowski, explains stock market rotation, the shift of assets from one investment style, industry, or sector to another. He covers top-down analysis, the cyclicals, defensive stocks, and the growth sector.

Top-down analysis gets its name because it starts with a general overview of the economy and ends with the specifics. It is contrasted with bottom-up analysis, which begins analyzing down at the individual company level and builds up to an analysis of industries and finally, the economy, Bajkowski writes.

Using top-down analysis, characteristics of the economy are determined and forecasting changes are examined. Based on the forecast, industries that are expected to perform well are identified. Then strong companies within the desirable industries are selected for the portfolio.

"Top-down analysis is based upon the premise that economic cycles exhibit characteristics that impact industries differently during the stages of expansion and contraction," Bajkowski writes, noting that the economic forecast is often no more than a seat-of-the-pants judgment of the general economic trends.

Bajkowski says you can track and analyze the economy simply by reading publications such as the *Wall Street Journal* and *Business Week*. These publications also are a good for getting a feel of market predictions (or rather, expectations), which, as noted earlier, drive the market up or down.

Bajkowski points out that the U.S. Department of Commerce tracks economic indicators such as the following:

■ Leading indicators showing where the economy is heading

■ Coincidental indicators showing the economy's current standing

■ Lagging indicators showing where the economy has been

There are 11 series that make up the leading indicators of future economic performance. Of those, the stock market has the best track record, he says.

Stocks tend to move in advance of the economy. Specific market sectors "have different relative performance throughout the economic cycle," he writes.

Bajkowski considers three major industry groups: cyclical, defensive, and growth.

1. Cyclical. Cyclical industries are tied closely to consumer demand, and are therefore sensitive to changes in income or interest rates. Consumers tend to defer big-ticket purchases

when incomes go down or interest rates rise. As the economy picks up speed at the end of a recession, capital good producers' performance improves. But as demand out paces supply, additional investments are needed.

2. Defensive industries. These noncyclicals are consistent performers; consumers need their products or services despite economic times. Noncyclicals include such industries as health care, tobacco, and food. But there are some noteworthy fluctuations in purchasing behaviors. Consumers may tighten their belts by buying less expensive food, for example.

3. Growth industries, which change from cycle to cycle, are those expanding rapidly regardless of the economy. Therefore, they are a good bet during recessions. A current example is biotechnology, he says.

Investors move into cyclical stocks when they predict a stronger economy is on the horizon. They assume companies have scaled back, leading to lower break-even points, "so that even a small increase in sales will lead to large profit increases," Bajkowski writes. "The market is also helped by the low interest rates that make alternative investments less attractive."

> **"**
> It's a recession when your neighbor loses his house. It's a depression when you lose yours.
> —Harry Truman
> **"**

If you don't want to research stocks, Bajkowski suggests buying an industry sector mutual fund. You can use this strategy for cyclicals, non-cyclical defensives, and growths. But he cautions that using a sector rotation investment strategy can be challenging because your market predictions could be incorrect.

Market indicators

The classic definition of a recession is when the GDP (gross domestic product) declines for two consecutive quarters. Of course, that's hindsight, and there is no grace period for trading.

But there are a few key indicators you can follow to help you determine where the economy is heading:

- Inflation and deflation pressures. Inflation occurs when the economy grows too rapidly. Lenders raise interest rates, and prices rise. Deflation, which signals an economic contraction, is caused by falling prices as a result of weak demands. Inflation and deflation pressures can be tracked using the Producer Price Index, or PPI, which measures the average change in selling prices received by domestic producers of goods and services (by certain industries and products). The U.S. Department of Labor posts news releases on this topic at http://stats.bls.gov/ppiover.htm. These changes can be used, in part, to forecast future price changes for business and consumers. (The president, Congress, and the Federal Reserve use these data to help formulate fiscal and monetary policies, according to the Bureau of Labor Statistics.)

- Consumer confidence. This indicator is measured by job growth, which is tracked by the U.S. Labor Department (http://stats.bls.gov/eag.table.html). Positive outlooks indicate better economies and vice versa.

- Retail sales. What and how much are consumers actually buying? Consumer spending is reported at the Bureau of Labor Statistics. You can view their press releases at http://stats.bls.gov.

▪ Manufacturing strength. The National Association of Purchasing Managers (http://www.napm.org/) keeps tabs on the specific industry purchasing, such as banking industry purchasing trends. This information can indicate which direction the manufacturing economy is heading. Read the news releases at this site.

▪ Corporate earnings. Corporate earnings are reflected in consumer spending. When consumers lack confidence they scratch off big-ticket items from their shopping lists. This can be the green light for an economic slowdown. Likewise, when consumers start buying big-ticket items—new cars, houses, washers, dryers, etc.—corporate earnings rise, and the economy is strengthened. Wall Street analysts predict corporate earnings at the beginning of each quarter, and companies publish their expected earnings at the end of each quarter. Often, the two don't match, causing movement on the stock market.

AIM literature quotes Harry Dent, an economist, as saying that the most fundamental force driving the market is consumer spending, specifically for housing, furnishings, autos, and appliances. Dent is quoted as having three predictions:

1. Historical evidence shows that the market tends to perform well during generation spending peaks, when the largest population within an age group hits ages 45 to 50.

2. Technology will continue to make business more efficient, making it possible to expand goods and services at the same time boomers

have increased demand for them. This will keep inflation down.

3. Inflation also is dependent on the consumer price index, which tends to rise and fall with the rise and fall of new jobholders, ages 20–25. Dent believes new entrants to the labor force will decline in coming years, due to lower birth rates, keeping inflation low.

Bajkowski suggests reading the Survey of Current Business, which is published monthly by the Department of Commerce, Bureau of Economic Analysis if you want to know more about business cycle activity. This report can be found at http://www.bea.doc.gov and clicking on "Publications."

Newsletter content seems to be another market indicator because newsletters are consistently wrong, says Davidson. When newsletter writers are bearish, the market goes up. This is known as a contrarian indicator. She believes that newsletter content becomes bearish because the market is going down, and the editors think the momentum will continue. All the positive expectations go out of stock prices. Any news that is not bad news is considered good news, and the market reacts, going back up.

Just the facts

- Dollar cost averaging takes the guesswork out of investing, since what you invest went the into market at both highs and lows, creating a balance.

- Timing the market is almost impossible, even for financial professionals.

- The economy and the stock market are cyclical in nature.

- Most market indicators are not useful to investors timing the market because reaction time is too short.

- Newsletter editors are often wrong in their predictions of bear markets.

The Costs of Investing

PART VI

GET THE SCOOP ON...
How many days you work just to pay taxes ▪
Why investing for at least 12 months can
reduce your taxes ▪ Which tax method of selling
shares will benefit you most ▪ The worst time
to buy shares in mutual funds

Taxes

T axes play an important role in your investments. In part, they determine how much
you'll profit from your investment, because
a certain percent of your profit must go to taxes.
And, if you receive dividends, you must pay taxes on
them as income, even if your principal investment is
devalued.

Furthermore, some funds are more tax-efficient
than others. Although taxes alone shouldn't determine your long-term investment strategy, they
should certainly be a consideration.

This chapter discusses how mutual funds are
taxed, how to keep track of the taxes you owe, and
investment strategies you can use to reduce your tax
burden.

How much do you pay in taxes?

Although we don't think of it this way, taxes are
accrued on a daily basis. During a single day at work,
you spend an average of 2 hours and 50 minutes
laboring just to pay taxes, according to the Tax

Foundation. Of that time, 1 hour and 55 minutes is spent working to pay federal taxes and another 55 minutes to pay state and local taxes. The Tax Foundation used the collective national effective tax rate of 35.4 percent in 1998 to arrive at these figures. The Tax Foundation is a nonprofit, nonpartisan policy research organization.

The Tax Foundation notes that the total of 2 hours and 50 minutes is greater than the amount of time you worked to pay for housing and household expenses (1 hour and 20 minutes), food and tobacco (49 minutes), and clothing (20 minutes) combined.

Another way to look at how big a bite taxes take out of your income and savings is to consider how many days you must work before your entire paycheck is yours. The Tax Foundation keeps track of how far into the year you must work just to pay your tax bill. In 1998, Tax Freedom Day was May 10. That means you had to work, on average, 129 days to pay off your total tax bill last year. Add 13 days to that if you include the costs associated with complying with the tax system, like record keeping, etc.

Over the years, Tax Freedom Day has been pushed further into the year, reflecting the increased tax burden Americans carry. The Foundation notes that as your income increases, the number of days you must work to pay off your tax burden also increases due to the progressive nature of the tax system. See Table 12.1 and Figures 12.1 and 12.2.

Where does it all go? If you and your spouse both work, and you're earning $54,910 (the median income for two), 37.6 percent of your income will go to federal, state, and local taxes, according to the Tax Foundation. If you're single, your 1997 tax

TABLE 12.1: TAX FREEDOM DAY

Year	Tax Freedom Day	Taxes as % of NNP (Net National Product	Year	Tax Freedom Day	Taxes as % of NNP (Net National Product
1902	January 31	8.5%	1966	April 16	28.9%
1913	January 30	8.2%	1967	April 18	29.4%
1922	February 17	13.2%	1968*	April 23	31.0%
1925	February 6	10.1%	1969	April 29	32.5%
1929	February 9	10.8%	1970	April 26	31.5%
1930	February 12	11.8%	1971	April 23	30.9%
1935	February 28	16.0%	1972*	April 27	32.1%
1940*	March 8	18.3%	1973	April 27	32.0%
1941	March 18	20.9%	1974	May 1	32.9%
1942	March 19	21.3%	1975	April 26	31.6%
1943	April 7	26.3%	1976*	April 28	32.3%
1944*	April 1	25.0%	1977	April 30	32.6%
1945	April 4	25.7%	1978	April 29	32.4%
1946	April 5	25.8%	1979	April 29	32.6%
1947	April 5	25.9%	1980*	April 30	32.9%
1948*	March 29	24.1%	1981	May 4	33.7%
1949	March 25	22.9%	1982	May 2	33.3%
1950	April 3	25.5%	1983	April 28	32.3%
1951	April 10	27.3%	1984*	April 27	32.1%
1952*	April 10	27.3%	1985	April 29	32.5%
1953	April 9	27.1%	1986	April 29	32.6%
1954	April 4	25.7%	1987	May 3	33.5%
1955	April 7	26.5%	1988*	April 30	33.1%
1956*	April 9	27.3%	1989	May 2	33.2%
1957	April 11	27.5%	1990	May 1	32.9%
1958	April 9	26.9%	1991	May 1	32.9%
1959	April 12	27.9%	1992*	April 29	32.7%
1960*	April 15	28.9%	1993	April 30	32.9%
1961	April 16	29.0%	1994	May 2	33.4%
1962	April 16	29.0%	1995	May 4	33.8%
1963	April 18	29.5%	1996*	May 5	34.4%
1964*	April 13	28.2%	1997	May 9	35.1%
1965	April 13	28.1%	1998	May 10	35.4%

← Note!
Tax Foundation economists researched historical taxes as a percentage of income and determined when Tax Freedom Day fell at various times throughout the 20th century. Source: Tax Foundation

← Note!
*Leap year makes Tax Freedom Day appear a calendar day earlier.

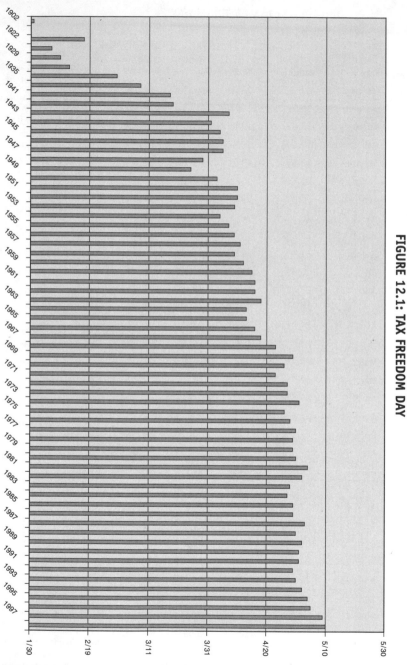

FIGURE 12.1: TAX FREEDOM DAY

Note! ➜   Illustrates progress of Tax Freedom Day.

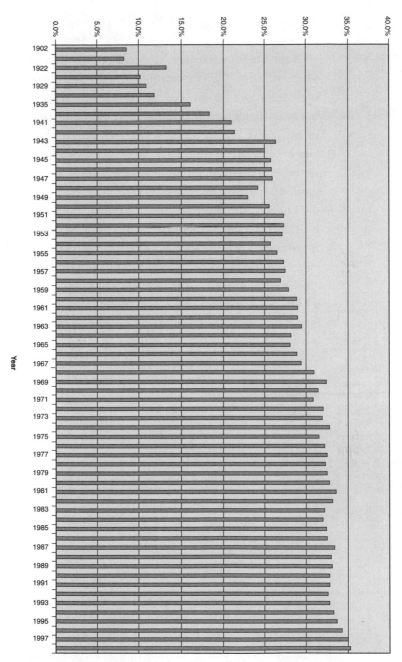

FIGURE 12.2: TAX AS % OF NET NATIONAL PRODUCT (NNP)

Illustrates the increase of taxes over time. **Note!**

burden was projected to be 35.9 percent of your income.

Your tax burden also depends upon the state where you live. This variation is due primarily to differences in per capita income among states, according to Patrick Fleenor, a Tax Foundation economist, in his "1997 Federal Tax Burden by State" report. Since taxes are levied as a percentage of income, states with high per capita income tend to have higher per capita federal tax collections.

This effect is further heightened by income bracket tax rates, which causes tax burdens to rise more than proportionally with income. Fleenor expected the average federal tax bill for fiscal year 1997 to range from a low of $3,683 in Mississippi to a high of $8,304 in Connecticut. See Table 12.2 for how many days you work to pay certain taxes.

Note! →
Most people think of taxes in terms of one big lump sum, but this table shows the average number of days it takes to pay different taxes.

TABLE 12.2: TAX FREEDOM DAY BY TYPE OF TAX (1998)

Average number of work days to foot the tax bill	Tax type
45	Personal income taxes (37 days of which will go to federal income taxes)
38	Payroll taxes
18	Sales and excise taxes (collected primarily at the state and local levels)
12	Property taxes
13	Corporate income taxes, which are ultimately passed on to consumers, employees, and shareholders
3	Miscellaneous taxes

Source: Tax Foundation

According to the Tax Foundation, the per capita federal tax burden has risen 57.5 percent since 1988. So when you're investing, you must consider three things:

1. As your salary increases, so does your tax burden. If your lifestyle changes to match your income, you must make up for this deficit in some way. Investing is one option, but there are risks involved.

2. Your investment must earn enough to cover the taxes you'll pay on capital gains and dividends to make it worthwhile.

3. It's wise to invest in tax-efficient mutual funds, and, sometimes, tax-exempt municipal bond funds, according to your financial needs and risk tolerance level.

But you must not let tax considerations be the sole determining factor when choosing your investments. The amount you are taxed is likely to change in the future.

Taxes and mutual funds

When you earn money, you have to pay taxes, even when it's your money earning money. There are two types of federal taxes you must pay on your investment earnings: capital gains taxes and income taxes on dividends.

By investing in mutual funds rather than stocks, you lose control of when you realize capital gains. That's the fund manager's decision. Each time the fund buys and sells shares, it's a taxable event. So when the fund sells shares at a profit, it realizes the capital gain and passes it along to you.

Likewise, when you sell shares you incur a taxable event and must pay taxes on any realized gains, except when your gains are realized in a tax-deferred investment or certain tax-exempt money market funds or tax-exempt bond funds. (Note: Some tax-exempt money market funds and

Bright Idea
As of May 1998, you can pay your taxes with a credit card, earning frequent flyer miles or money back. Credit card benefits and rates can be found at http://www. cardtrak.com and http://www. bankrate.com. (IRS surcharges apply.)

tax-exempt bond funds may be taxable at the state and local levels.)

Regardless of who's selling the shares, you or the fund manager, if the share is held for less than 12 months it'll be taxed as a short-term gain at your income tax bracket rate. When the share is held for more than 12 months, it's considered a long-term capital gain and it'll be taxed at 20 percent, unless you're in the 15 percent income tax bracket, in which case it will be taxed at 10 percent.

Dividends, on the other hand, like interest and short-term capital gains, are taxed as ordinary income.

Tax law

There are two types of capital gains, each taxed at different rates:

1. Long-term gains apply to assets held more than 12 months. They are taxed at a maximum rate of 20 percent.

2. Short-term gains for assets held 12 months or less are taxed at ordinary income tax rates.

Congress recently passed changes in the tax law. These changes cut the top long-term capital gains tax rate from 28 percent to 20 percent. This is especially helpful if you're holding shares that have increased in value substantially over the years. Should you decide to sell them, you'll save 8 percent in taxes. Plus, you'll pay that much less on realized gains from the funds long-term holdings. If you're in the 15 percent income bracket, you'll only have to pay 10 percent versus the earlier 15 percent capital gains tax rate.

Shares and other assets purchased after the year 2000 and held at least 5 years will be taxed at a maximum rate of 18 percent. If you're in the 15 percent tax bracket, your capital gains will be taxed at 8 percent.

These changes not only affect how much you'll have to fork over to the IRS in April, but they'll also have a significant impact on your investment returns if you reinvest your earnings, as shown in Table 12.3.

To see how the new rates would have impacted historical returns, T. Rowe Price computed the total after-tax return for growth stock funds, on average, over the 20-year period through 1996, based on actual fund performance, including annual fund distributions. The calculations were based on an initial investment of $10,000, an ordinary income tax rate of 28 percent, and liquidation of the account at the end of the 20-year period.

TABLE 12.3: IMPACT OF THE CAPITAL GAINS TAX CUT ON A GROWTH FUND INVESTMENT(AFTER-TAX VALUES OF AN INITIAL $10,000 INVESTMENT)

	Growth at a 28% Capital Gains Rate	Growth at a 20% Capital Gains Rate
5 Years	$17,187	$18,025
10 Years	$30,512	$33,071
15 Years	$55,217	$61,279
20 Years	$101,021	$114,162

* Results are based on the actual average annual performance of growth funds from January 1, 1977, to December 31, 1996. Values assume the accounts are liquidated at the end of each period. Ending values reflect a 28 percent income tax rate and the indicated capital gains rate on annual fund distributions and upon final sale of shares held in the account. To reflect the impact of differences in tax rates, values at the periods of less than 20 years assume that the average annual return for the full 20-year period was earned uniformly each year. Therefore, they do not reflect actual investment results or market fluctuation during those periods.

← **Note!** Illustration of how new tax rates would have impacted historical returns. Source: T. Rowe Price

According to the T. Rowe Price calculations, an investor would have netted slightly more than

$13,000 more in after-tax earnings for every $10,000 invested over this 20-year time period at the new, lower capital gains tax rate.

Keeping accurate records

You must keep meticulous records of your investments. In addition to making certain that the information on your statements is accurate, keeping good records can help you reduce your tax burden.

Keep every statement the mutual fund company sends to you. For tax purposes, you'll need to know the date of each transaction, the number of shares (this may be a fraction) purchased or sold, price per share, total price for the shares, and any fees or commissions paid for each transaction. Typically, most year-end statements from mutual fund companies will summarize the entire year's activity, so you may only need to keep one statement for each year. But in order to avoid double taxation you need to keep your own records, too. (See "Avoid double taxation" later in this chapter.)

Transactions occur when you buy, sell, or exchange shares. Each time you reinvest capital gains distributions and dividends, you're actually buying more shares. Since share prices fluctuate daily, the prices of these share will probably differ from the prices of the shares you purchased previously.

If you automatically reinvest dividends, you should consider that as sending a check to the fund, says Rande Spiegelman, manager of Investment Advisory Services for KPMG Peat Marwick, LLP. Essentially, you're purchasing more shares, and it raises your total cost basis.

A lot of people don't consider this when they're figuring gains, he says. So, they're taxed twice.

When you sell a fund, you pay again on the difference of the cost basis and the value of the fund when you sell it. For example, if you bought a fund for $10,000 and sold it at $20,000, you pay taxes on a $10,000 gain.

But if $2,000 comes from dividends, you've already paid an income tax on it, so you'll pay tax on this amount twice if you don't keep track of your reinvested dividends. You've increased your reported capital gain unnecessarily. You must keep tallies of your dividends so you don't pay taxes on them twice.

It's important to take note of share prices and the purchase dates. By doing so, when you sell shares in the future, you can strategize by price or by the length of time you've held the investment to take advantage of tax benefits. If you don't track your transactions, the IRS will assume the first shares you bought are the first you sell, and so on. It is referred to as FIFO (first in, first out.)

If you sell shares at a loss, you must report that as well. Losses can be used to offset gains. This strategy is discussed later in this chapter.

(Note: The fund company will send you a Form 1099-DIV, Dividends and Distributions, or a similar form. This tax statement will tell you capital gains and dividend distributions for the year. Sale proceeds will be sent on Form 1099B. You must report these on your income tax return.)

You must report your capital gain distributions on Schedule D (Form 1040) and mutual fund distributions on Schedule B (Form 1040) and Schedule D (Form 1040). You can use IRS publication 564 (Mutual Fund Distributions) to help you figure your taxable gains or deductible losses.

Calculating gains and losses

You must keep track of your capital gains and losses in order to evaluate your investment picks and keep

Bright Idea
When you begin to resent paying taxes, think of all the things you get for them: paved roads with traffic lights, public libraries, public schools, and more.

your taxes as low as possible. You can calculate gains and losses by comparing the amount you realize with the adjusted basis. Your cost basis is the amount of money you've invested in the fund, including fees and commissions as well as reinvested gains and dividends.

Amounts above the basis are considered gains, below are losses.

Timesaver
Use the IRS's
Web site (http://
www.irs.gov)
to download
publications.

When you buy or sell shares in a fund, you should receive a confirmation statement. When you buy shares it will show the purchase price you paid, often including any loads (commissions), and when you sell shares, it will show the selling price you received. These records will come in handy when it's time to figure out your basis in the fund.

Fees and commissions are not deductible, but you can usually add these purchase fees to the cost of the shares, increasing your basis. Redemption fees usually can be used as a reduction in the selling price.

The IRS gives this example from IRS Publication 564:

"You bought 100 shares of Fund A for $10 a share. You paid a $50 commission to the broker for the purchase. Your cost basis for each share is $10.50 ($1,050 ÷ 100)."

You must also keep tabs of shares purchased by reinvesting gains and dividends. You will need to know the date, amount, and number of full or fractional shares purchased. Furthermore, keep track of any adjustments to the basis of your mutual fund shares and the date when the adjustment occurs.

According to the IRS, the "amount of the distribution used to purchase each full or fractional share is the cost basis for that share."

Besides the FIFO method, the new IRS rules allow you to select from among three other methods of determining a gain from the sale of mutual fund shares:

- Average cost (single category)
- Average cost (double category)
- Specific shares

You must figure out which method is most advantageous for you with respect to taxes.

The FIFO method, as mentioned earlier, assumes the first shares you sell are the first shares you purchased. This method may not be advantageous tax-wise if the first shares you bought have substantial unrealized gains and subsequent ones show fewer gains or capital losses.

In order to use either average basis method for figuring cost basis, you must have purchased shares at different times and at different prices. If you decide to use this method, you must continue to use it for that fund.

Taxation WITH representation ain't so hot either.
—Gerald Barzan

Using the single-category average cost method, you determine the average cost of all shares (by adding up the total cost and dividing by the number of shares) owned each time you sell. Multiply the average cost by the number of shares sold to get your basis of the shares sold. The shares you sell are assumed to be the ones you bought first. This will determine your holding period, which determines whether you have a short- or long-term capital gain.

The IRS gives this example: "You bought the following shares in the LJP Mutual Fund: 100 shares in 1994 at $10 per share; 100 shares in 1995 at $12 per share; and 100 shares in 1996 at $26 per share. On May 16, 1997, you sold 150 shares. The basis of shares sold is $2,400, computed as follows:

1. Total cost ($1,000 + $1,200 + $2,600) = $4,800

2. Average basis per share ($4,800 ÷ 300) = $16.00

3. Basis of shares sold ($16.00 × 150) = $2,400."

There are drawbacks to using this method. If you've held some shares for 11 months, for example, and others 6 months, this method doesn't allow you to sell the ones you bought 6 months ago so you can wait 1 month and have long-term gains on the others. However, if you've held all shares for more than 12 months, then this method simplifies the math for you.

Although most mutual funds will compute this number, this method often fails to yield the best possible tax advantage, according to KPMG.

Using the double-category method, you must divide the shares in your account into two categories: short-term and long-term (more than 12 months) holdings. You can choose which shares you want to sell, but you must get a written confirmation from the fund or your financial planner that the ones you specified were the ones that were actually sold. Otherwise, the IRS assumes you are selling the long-term holdings.

There is a little more paperwork involved using this method because you must move shares from the short-term category to the long-term category after you have held them for more than 12 months.

The IRS defines holding periods from the day after you bought the shares. You should use that date—April 6, for instance—of each succeeding month (May 6, October 6, etc.) to calculate the number of months you've held those shares. You can include the day that you sold your shares as part of your holding time.

Using the specific shares method, you can sell whichever shares produce the best tax result. You must specify the share(s) to be sold and get the sale confirmed in writing by the fund or your financial planner, whoever is handling the transaction. You can figure a gain or loss by using the adjusted basis of those particular shares.

This method can be useful if, for instance, you've held two sets of shares, one for 11 months and one for 3 months. You may want to sell those you bought 3 months ago to allow the others to become taxable as long-term gains in another month. See Table 12.4 and Table 12.5.

TABLE 12.4

Date	Description	# of Shares	$/Share	$Total
01/02/95	Purchase	1,000	$10	$10,000
12/30/95	Reinvest	50	$12	$600
12/30/96	Reinvest	100	$15	$1,500
12/30/97	Reinvest	100	$18	$1,800
		1,250		$13,900

Average cost/share = $11.120 (13,900 ÷ 1,250)

Total current FMV @ $20/share = $25,000

Sell enough shares to raise $2,000 = 100 shares

← Note!
The Specific Share method (Tables 12.4 & 12.5) results in the lowest tax burden.

TABLE 12.5

Method	Cost Basis	Proceeds	Gain	LTCG @ 20%	STCG@ 39.6%
FIFO	$1,000	$2,000	$1,000	$200	
Average Cost	$1,112	$2,000	$888	$178	
Specific ID*	$1,500	$2,000	$500	$100	
Specific ID**	$1,800	$2,000	$200		$79

* 12/30/96 shares held > 12 months
** 12/30/97 shares held < 12 months

Surprisingly, in this case, the lowest tax burden results from the sale of shares held less than one year (short-term capital gain), even when taxed at the highest federal rate. The example assumes that the investor needs to raise $2,000 and cannot wait until December 31, 1998, to sell the highest cost shares at the long-term rate. Source: KPMG

Tax planning can equal substantial savings

You are taxed at two levels. One you have control over—that is, whether you hold on to your investments or actively trade them. The other, at the fund level, you don't, except to invest in a tax-efficient fund such as an index fund that doesn't have a rapid turnover in its portfolio, causing short-term gains.

To some degree, you have control over your adjusted gross income by the amount of deductions you take and by the capital gains you choose to realize by selling shares.

KPMG's Spiegelman suggests keeping adjusted gross income below a certain level. His general advice is to "defer income as long as possible." He adds that, "You never want to pay a tax today you can pay tomorrow."

Once you've made a decision to sell, though, it's time to see what makes the most sense from a tax position. It may pay to wait a matter of a few weeks. To decide, look at your tax situation and ask yourself these questions:

1. What is your adjusted gross income level? Will a gain push you into a higher tax bracket?

2. Do you have other gains you want to offset this year?

3. Are you getting a bonus in January? If so, you may want to take a loss next year to offset this gain.

If you sell at a loss and that loss exceeds your allowable net capital loss deduction, you may carry over the excess for as many years as it takes until it is used up.

But it is important to understand that you must make an investment plan that fits your long-term

> **"**
> The hardest thing to understand in the world is the income tax.
> —Albert Einstein
> **"**

investment goals and needs and meets your risk tolerance level before figuring how to benefit from tax laws because tax laws change. Although current tax laws benefit those invested in equities as opposed to income-producing investments such as bonds, it wasn't always that way.

One such example is the tax reform act that was passed in 1986. It raised the capital gains rate from 20 percent to 28 percent while lowering ordinary income tax rates. This made income-oriented investments more appealing. But had an investor made portfolio choices based on tax law, he or she would have missed out on the substantial annualized, after-tax gains of 10.4 percent in the stock market. Growth and income funds from 1986 to 1996 produced only a 9.6 percent after-tax average annualized return and taxable bond funds returned 4.7 percent.

According to Steve Norwitz, vice president of T. Rowe Price, investors "who revised their long-term strategies in reaction to the tax rate changes..., placing more emphasis on income-oriented investments and less on growth, would have significantly shortchanged themselves in the long run."

Tax laws can and do change. That's why you should use tax advantages only as a secondary consideration when making investment decisions. Your goals and risk tolerance should be your primary consideration. As many investment planners like to say, "Don't let the tax tail wag the investment dog."

That said, you can take advantage of some tax strategies, such as investing in tax-efficient funds and more.

Controlling costs

Timing can be everything when it comes to buying shares. At the end of the calendar year, funds usually

Moneysaver
You can offset
capital gains tax
and ordinary
income tax with
capital losses of
up to $3,000
per year.

distribute their capital gains and dividends, on which the shareholders must pay tax. If you can hold off buying until after the gains are distributed, you can save on your tax bill.

For example, you buy 1,000 shares at $10 a piece. Shortly after your purchase, the fund distributes a gain of 40 cents per share. The share price is adjusted downward by the same amount to make your total investment the same as before the distribution. You now have to pay taxes on $400, so even if you reinvest the gain, you've lost some of your investment to taxes. While you still have an investment worth $10,000, you have to pay $80 if it's a long-term capital gain and more if it's a short-term capital gain that the fund realized.

Invest in education IRAs

By investing in an education IRA, you can invest for your children's education and get a tax break. You can invest $500 per year for each child. Withdrawals are tax-free if used for qualified educational expenses.

In order to qualify for the education IRA, you must make $95,000 or less per year. If you're married, filing jointly, you must earn $150,000 or less annually.

Invest for your children

Tax laws give kids a break. If you invest in your child's name, the first $650 of investment income earned is tax-free. The next $650 is taxable at the child's tax rate, which is usually 15 percent.

But once the child's investment income exceeds $1,300, he or she is taxed at your tax rate. There are caveats, so check with an accountant.

Avoid double taxation

As mentioned above, you need to keep careful records of distributions to avoid being taxed twice on the same money. John Roberts, director of investment counseling services at Denver Investment Advisors, LLC, a money management firm in Denver, gives this example:

You invest $1,000 in a mutual fund and reinvest the capital gains and dividends. Over a 10-year period, the fund distributes a total of $100 in gains and dividends. Remember, you pay taxes on these distributions every year as added income. You sell your total investment at $1,500. At first glance it looks like you owe taxes on $500. But your capital gain is only $400. Most people pay taxes on the extra $100, too.

It's a double taxation, and it's one thing funds don't show in their statements so it's important to keep your own records. Roberts suggests figuring out your cost basis with every distribution. "It's time-consuming, but in the end it will save you a lot of time and money," he says. He suggests using a software program, but you can do it by hand, as well.

Avoid wash sales

Wash sales occur when you "sell mutual fund shares at a loss and within 30 days before or after the sale you buy...substantially identical property," according to IRS Publication 564. Losses from wash sales are not deductible.

But there is a way around this situation, according to Roberts.

Say you own a stock or shares in a fund that's losing money. You want to sell it to use the losses to off-set other gains. On the other hand, you still like the

Bright Idea
Go to the IRS's
Web site to find
answers to your
tax questions,
and print them
out. That way
you'll have it in
writing if there's
a dispute later.

investment, even though it's currently not doing well. If you sell shares and buy back identical stock within 30 days, you can't realize the loss.

In order to take advantage of the capital losses and at the same time stay invested, you can buy the same number of new shares that you want to sell and sell the old ones, those that show a loss, 32 days later, Roberts says. Your position, the number of shares in your portfolio, remains the same. And you can off-set any gains with those losses.

If you have a $100 gain and $100 loss you can net those two out, making your net capital gain zero. If your capital losses exceed your gains during a year, you can deduct up to $3,000 in capital losses pro-vided you have at least that much in taxable income. If you have more than $3,000 in capital losses that aren't offset by gains, you can carry that forward to offset future capital gains.

Spiegelman offers a different approach. He says you can swap similar mutual funds, realize your loss, never be out of the market for 30 days, and not get caught in the wash sale rule. Although you can't buy a virtual clone—that is, you can't buy the same fund in a different class (swapping a front load for a back load)—you can buy a fund in a similar area, like emerging markets, to keep your portfolio balanced.

You're not out of the market, he says. You've stayed in emerging markets. But if you had invested $10,000 and it was down $4,000, you could save sev-eral thousand dollars in taxes and buy into the mar-ket at a lower price.

Balancing act: Where to place what in your portfolio

You can also gain some control over taxable distrib-utions by buying funds that are tax efficient. Look at your after-tax returns when making buying decisions.

In addition, consider what you put in a taxable account versus your tax-deferred account. If your total portfolio asset allocation is 50 percent in fixed incomes and 50 in equities, Spiegelman suggests placing the 50 percent stocks in your personal account (as opposed to your retirement account). Your taxable distributions will be minimal if you pick tax-efficient funds and hold the investment for at least 12 months, taking advantage of the 20 percent capital gains tax rate. Place high-turnover funds and taxable bonds funds in your IRA.

If most or all of your portfolio is in tax-deferred retirement accounts, then he suggests buying funds that are best performers and concentrating on asset allocations.

Enlisting the aid of your computer

When it comes to taxes, using a software program like Intuit's TurboTax (MacIntax) or Kiplinger's Tax Cut can make tax time less taxing. But beware—you really need to know something about taxes to make these programs produce accurate tax returns. Since there's a lot of money at stake, you may want to have an accountant review your work.

Another warning: When you wait for the last minute to gather the receipts, inevitably things get left out. Keep track of your investments and daily expenditures using a software program like Intuit's Quicken. But if you're not organized, don't wait until April 15 to start the computations. You should let your completed return sit a day or two before mailing it, just in case you forgot a deduction.

In reality, most people wait to figure out their taxes until the last minute. If you find that the April

Moneysaver
Figuring taxes is complicated. Paying an accountant to review your work may save you money.

15th deadline is looming, file for an extension. It's better to take your time and consult a tax adviser than to rush and then file an amendment, increasing your chances of being audited. But, remember, you must include your payment when you file the extension or you will owe interest and penalties.

Tax relief on the Net

There's no need to wait on hold or stand in line at the IRS to ask a simple question (for which you may or may not get the correct answer, leaving you liable, anyway). The IRS's site (http://www.irs.gov) allows you to download forms and search for answers to both personal and business tax questions. At http://www.irs.ustreas.gov/prod/ind_info/index.html, you can find out about your rights as a taxpayer, get a list of qualified charities to which you can make tax-deductible contributions, find out about the latest tax changes, and more.

There are several useful sites in the private sector. T. Rowe Price has tax changes and tax strategies as well as a tax-efficiency calculator at their Internet site (http://www.troweprice.com). You can set up hypothetical portfolios of various combinations of stock funds and municipal funds. The calculations are based on your initial investment, tax bracket, and anticipated holding period as well as whether or not you expect to sell your shares at the end of the period.

Based on the information you enter, the calculator will generate tax figures, as well as risk and return, based on historical mutual fund data for the 20-year period ending December 31, 1997.

At http://www.strong-funds.com (Strong Funds), you can figure out if a regular IRA or Roth IRA is best for you. There's also a Roth conversion calcula-tor there. T. Rowe Price has a Roth conversion cal-culator at http://www.troweprice.com/retirement/troweretireIRAHome.html.

Wegner's Online Tax Encyclopedia at http://www.wegnercpas.com/encyclop/content.htm is a great place to get help on all the fine print. H&R Block has federal and state income tax forms, tips, and a refund calculator at http://www.hrblock.com/tax.

Bright Idea
Consult a tax adviser before making invest-ment decisions.

Just the facts

- You must work nearly four months to pay your tax bill.

- Tax implications should be a secondary, not a primary, consideration when creating your investment portfolio because tax rules change.

- You can avoid paying extra taxes by keeping good records.

- There's plenty of tax help on the Internet.

GET THE SCOOP ON...
Why you should consider more than returns ▪
Fees associated with fund investing ▪ Figuring
out what your investment is really earning ▪
How you can earn more

Figuring Out Your Tab

Chapter 13

N o doubt about it, taxes and fees eat up a
portion of your investment. As a savvy
investor, you can determine which funds
are most cost efficient.

In this chapter, you'll learn about some of the
different fee structures among funds, how to figure
out what your investment is really making, and how
to reduce the costs associated with investing in
mutual funds.

Taxes

Just as you must pay taxes on the income you earn
from working, you must pay taxes on the income
your investment earns. Until recently, the top capital gains tax rate was 28 percent. But now, if you
hold onto your investments at least 12 months and
only receive the gains after that holding period, the
tax rate is reduced to 20 percent, courtesy of
Congress. Congress also lowered to 10 percent those
gains that would have been taxed at the 15 percent
ordinary income rate. Dividends are still taxed at

your ordinary income tax rate. Remember, dividends and capital gains are taxable, even if reinvested.

Also, if you sell a bond at above face value, the profit realized is considered a capital gain.

(Note: if you're invested in a REIT or REIT fund, because of depreciation recapture, a 25 percent tax rate attributable to real estate depreciation.)

Timesaver
Use voice-activated software to enter your transactions.

Strategies to fix a broken investor

It's almost inevitable that at some time you're going to lose money in the stock market, perhaps due to the economy or a bad investment. This is especially true if you actively manage your portfolio, because the more you trade, the more risk you take.

If you find yourself facing that situation, you can employ some damage control tax strategies. These strategies can also work if you sell in a panic during a market crash or tumble.

If you decide to sell some shares at a loss, the loss can be used to offset any profits and therefore reduce your tax bill. You can use losses of up to $3,000 per year (or $1,500 a year if you're married and filing separately) to offset your gains in other funds. If you have no gains, or your losses exceed your gains, you can use those losses to offset your ordinary income, up to $3,000 per year. If you exceed the $3,000 annual limit, those losses can be carried over to future income tax returns. This strategy is especially useful if you have short-term capital gains, which are taxable at rates as high as 39.6 percent.

One of the downsides to investing in mutual funds is that you have no control over how often the fund manager turns over stocks in the portfolio.

Each time a stock is sold at a gain, you will incur a capital gains tax, which reduces your earning power over time because it will leave you with less to add to your principal investment. Fund managers are concerned with the overall performance of the fund, not on the tax implications trading has on shareholders.

So, returns aren't the only thing to consider when researching mutual funds. After taking taxes into consideration, the playing field is leveled out and you can compare funds' actual rates of return. To save on taxes, look for funds that pay out few dividends compared with their peers. Funds with lower turnover in their portfolio allow shareholders to defer paying taxes on the gains until they decide to sell the shares.

Moneysaver
Invest in a relatively new fund that is managed by someone with a known track record. This way there will be few unrealized gains to counteract its performance.

Timing is also a tax factor. If you receive dividends and capital gains from a mutual fund company, the share price will drop by the same amount as the distribution. For example, if the share price is $10 a share and the distribution totals $1 per share, the share price for the fund will drop to $9.

If you're buying into a fund near the end of a quarter or the end of the year, you should check to see if that fund is going to be distributing any gains because you will still be taxed on the full amount of the gains (even though you may only have the fund for a day or two). That tax will eat up some of your investment dollars. You'd be better off waiting until after the distribution to invest, buying shares at a lower price. Not only will you get a better price, this buying strategy will also help to cut your tax bill because then you won't owe taxes on the capital gains or the dividends.

Finding tax-efficient funds

Taxes can eat up a large part of your gain, decreasing your earning power over time. (See Table 13.1.) The trick, therefore, is to find tax-efficient stock funds. Craig Israelsen of the University of Missouri-Columbia has identified four factors that affect tax efficiency:

1. Funds with lower dividend yields have higher tax efficiency.

2. Funds with a low turnover rate have greater tax efficiency. (Why? You're not paying on a lot of capital gains. The investment can grow faster when gains are not realized.)

3. The manager's portfolio management strategies affect tax efficiency. For instance, if the manager buys a stock at three different prices, then sells the shares he's paid the least for first, you'll have higher capital gains and less tax efficiency.

4. Larger funds have more room to spread the tax burden. If there is a substantial growth of assets in the fund, the capital gains will be distributed among a larger asset base, so those taxes will be lower via dilution.

Note! ➡
You can make your investments work harder for you by investing in tax-efficient funds.

TABLE 13.1

A one-time $10,000 investment in a tax-efficient fund. The long-term capital gains total 0.5% of your investment. The short-term capital gains and dividends equal 3% of your investment. The fund earns 10% a year. (Note: Long-term capital gains are taxed at 20%, unless you are in the 15% bracket, where it's taxed at 10%. Short-term gains are taxed as ordinary income.)

Period	Amount Made	15% Tax Bracket	28% Tax Bracket	33% Tax Bracket
5 yrs	$16,105	$336	$631	$732
10 yrs	$25,937	$877	$1,648	$1,911
20 yrs	$67,275	$3,150	$5,922	$6,868
30 yrs	$174,494	$9,047	$17,008	$19,723

TABLE 13.2
A one-time $10,000 investment in a non-tax efficient fund that has a long-term capital gain totaling 5% of the investment and short-term capital gains and dividends equaling 4% of the investment. The fund earns 10% a year.

Period	Amount Made	15% Tax Bracket	28% Tax Bracket	33% Tax Bracket
5 yrs	$16,105	$739	$1,424	$1,558
10 yrs	$25,937	$1,929	$3,717	$4,068
20 yrs	$67,275	$6,931	$13,357	$14,617
30 yrs	$174,494	$19,906	$38,363	$41,982

Tax efficiency impacts a fund's overall performance, but you have to be careful. The most tax-efficient funds may have a large amount of unrealized capital gains that they may realize in a year of exceptionally active trading. Income funds tend to be less tax efficient. Dividends are taxed at your income tax rate, not at the long-term capital gains rate of 20 percent. High turnover funds aren't necessarily inefficient taxwise. It depends on whether or not the manager sells off poorly performing stocks, which may show losses or just small gains, while holding on to good performers and deferring those taxes.

> It's not enough to have good intelligence. The principal thing is to apply it well.
> —Descartes

Costs

By buying stocks through mutual funds as opposed to buying them directly, you're saving in fees. If you buy stocks, you have to pay a brokerage fee for each stock purchased, but you won't get professionals researching companies and industries and managing your portfolio for that fee.

No-load funds, as a general rule, have the fewest associated costs because you buy them directly from the fund, not through a broker or financial planner. In fact, financial planners usually don't make

mention of these funds because there is no provi-
sion built into them for a commission. Therefore,
financial advisers basically eliminate one-third of
available funds from their clients' portfolios.

More than two-thirds of all funds have a load
(commission), according to Israelsen. The load is
either front-end, deferred, or in the form of a
12b-1, a marketing fee.

Low-load funds typically have commission fees
up to 3.5 percent, while loaded funds can carry commissions as high as 8.5 percent, Israelsen says.

Bright Idea
Take turns with
your spouse log-
ging investment
transactions.
This will lighten
the paperwork
load for each
of you and
keep you both
abreast of your
investments.

But there are some financial planners who will
help you invest in no-load funds—for a price. They
charge a percent of the assets under management,
says Cindy Bohlen, a securities analyst and assistant
vice president of the Marshall Funds in Milwaukee.
If a planner is going to charge you 1 percent and
you invest $100,000, you'd have to pay him or her
$1,000, which is taken out of your investment. Fee-
based planners will also help you invest in no-load
funds. The fee is paid separately.

Loads/commissions

Remember that there are more than 10,000 mutual
funds, but some are duplicate portfolios. In fact, 30
to 40 percent could be taken out of the mutual fund
universe because of redundancy. There are about
6,500 unique mutual funds.

When we talk about the number of funds in existence, we tend to overstate the total because of these
fund clusters, Israelsen says. One fund can show up
three or four times in *Morningstar*, once as a front-
loaded fund, once as a back-loaded fund, and once
with a 12b-1 charge, for instance. The fund's portfolio and management remain the same. What
changes is the load structure—at what point the

commission is taken—and therefore the amount of the commission.

Funds are divided into classes. Different fund classes have loads structured in different ways. Class A is front-loaded, Class B is back-loaded, and Class C has a 12b-1 annual charge. There are additional classes as well. Israelsen says that Class A funds are best for long-term (10 or more years) investments and Class B for longer-term (i.e. longer than short-term) investments—after 6 years you usually won't have a load when you sell class B funds.

Although your investment has more earning power when you buy no-load funds, Israelsen says load fund representatives give personal attention, and that has some value.

But beware. Bill Stawski, founder of Cash University, a Grand Rapids, Michigan, investing program for children and parents (for more information on investing with your children, see Chapter 1), spent 6 years as a broker at Smith Barney. He says that one sales strategy used was promoting Class B shares, those with back-end loads. Brokers may tout them as having no commission, but you have to wait 5 years to sell that type of a fund to avoid paying the load. Stawski says that if you're looking at buying Class A or Class B funds within the same mutual fund family, it's better to pay the commission up front because with Class B shares you pay higher costs. The operating costs and management fees as well as the 12b-1 for these funds are higher than their counterparts, he says.

Management fees

Every fund has a management fee. The average annual management fee for stock mutual funds at the end of 1997, according to Israelsen, was

66
The noblest plea-sure is the joy of understanding.
—Leonardo da Vinci
99

1.5 percent, or $1.50 per $100 account value. The management fee for bond funds was about 1.10 percent, he says.

Large funds tend have lower management fees and internationals tend to have higher ones because of the additional work involved in researching and managing the portfolio. Index funds have lower management fees because they are not actively managed.

Note that some funds keep expenses low by waiving fees, but only for a specified period of time. Check the prospectus to see when the fees will be reinstated.

Watch Out!
Fees may not be apparent, and a salesperson may not tell you about them. Read the prospectus carefully to determine the fees.

There is some indication that there may be changes on the horizon in the ways that fees are charged. "Fee structures are beginning to change from a fixed percentage of assets to a more performance-based model," says Liz Davidson, CEO of Davidson Andrade, a hedge fund. "More and more funds are tying their performance to relevant market indices and charging customers, in part, based on how well they [the funds] perform relative to these indices." For instance, if the funds beat the S&P 500 index, they'll take 25 percent of the difference. Davidson says investors are tired of paying a fixed fee regardless of how a fund performs. This method of compensation gives fund managers an added incentive to achieve strong performance.

12b-1 fees

Some funds have an additional fee that is used for marketing purposes. Of the approximately 6,500 funds that charge this fee, the average is about .60 percent, or 60¢ per $100 for stock and bond funds, according to Israelsen. Sometimes it's used to pay a financial manager or someone handling the money (a broker or other distributor), Cindy Bohlen points out.

Bohlen says many salespeople try to hide the fact there's a fee, but all fees must be disclosed in the prospectus. Be aware and make sure the fees look fair, she said. In addition to the fees previously mentioned, there are other fees associated with buying shares of mutual funds, including the following:

- Contingency fees. This fee is collected by your financial planner if a certain predetermined event occurs. Your adviser may be rewarded by a higher percentage of your assets contingent on how well the fund performs; for example, if the fund returns 10 percent, your adviser may receive a 1 percent commission, and if it reaches 20 percent, your adviser may collect double or triple that amount. Financial planners also may have added incentives if they reach a certain sales level for a specific fund. Read your paperwork carefully.

- Annual maintenance fees. This fee is used to pay the fund manager(s).

- Redemption fees. Sometimes these are used as an incentive to get investors to stay in the fund for a minimum amount of time. This type of fee structure is especially damaging if you're an active trader.

- Transaction fees. Again, this type of fee structure is especially damaging if you trade actively.

- Additional fees. Some funds charge a fee for phone transactions.

Some funds actually have layers of fees. Called "wrap" accounts, you pay an annual fee of 1–1.5 percent of assets, and the brokerage firm manages the portfolio on your behalf, says Mark Riepe, vice president and head of Schwab Center for Investment Research. Layering fees include:

- Management fees to actual funds
- Fees paid to the wrap provider

Timesaver
Tend to your
record keeping
early in the
morning or late
at night, when
others are less
likely to disturb
you. That way,
you can get it
done faster, and
possibly more
accurately.

Most full-commission firms have variations of this theme. With thousands of mutual funds to choose from, some investors feel intimidated, Riepe says. This packaging method reduces that fund universe to six or seven funds, which can be used to fill their portfolio. "Of course, you pay for that service," he says.

So the question is, since someone's building and managing your portfolio, is that service worth that percentage?

"Most wrap accounts are lousy deals," headlines an article from *Forbes* online. Citing one fund in particular, reporters Thomas Easton and Julie Androshick conclude that you could lose as much as 5 percent of your investment per year in costs, which is more than four times the costs of an average no-load fund.

Figuring how much you're really making

Your annual salary is not the amount of money you take home at the end of the year; neither is a fund's total return the amount you get to keep.

Consider that, on average, the market returns about 10 percent historically. If you adjust for taxes at 28 percent, you have 7.2 percent left. Take off another 3 percent for inflation, and you're at 4.2 percent. If you have a no-load with a 1 percent management fee, you can expect to make 3.2 percent on your investment.

But if you choose a fund with any additional fees, you can begin to see that you will make very little on your investment and may even lose some of your principal to pay these fees during years when the market performs poorly.

However, with the bull market of the 1990s when investors were reaping upwards of 30 percent, they didn't spend much time considering fees. But realizing that the economy works in cycles will help you understand that the market will fluctuate accordingly, and shopping around for low management fees (1 percent and under) is a useful investment strategy if you want your money to work for you and not someone else.

Getting a clear picture

Sometimes it's easy to look at your investments at the end of the year and be rather pleased at what appears to be a strong market performance. But what you may forget to consider is that you added to your principal through automatic or lump sum investments. These additional investments distort the total return by increasing your portfolio's value, but the added principal adds to the gain as well. At what point during the year you made the investment also makes a difference. Likewise, the appearance of how well your investments performed may be decreased by any withdrawals you made. So the question is, how do you figure out what you really made?

The American Association of Individual Investors (AAII) has some answers. To figure out what your investment earned, you must determine the change in value from the end of one year to the end of the next year. Then you must add in any dividends or capital gains you received.

If you didn't make any additional investments or withdrawals throughout the year, the math is fairly

Bright Idea
Remember to always compare funds during the same time period.

Moneysaver
One way to save fees is to use one-stop shopping, a supermarket of funds. You'll avoid transaction fees when buying and selling mutual funds.

easy. Say you began the year with $100,000 and ended it with $110,000, and you made no additions to or withdrawals from your portfolio during that time and reinvested all your dividends. Divide $110,000, the end value, by $100,000. That equals 1.1. Subtract one, which leaves .1 and multiply that by 100. Your total return equals 10 percent.

For those of you who enjoy algebraic equations, it looks like this: $[(EV \div BV) - 1] \times 100 = R\ (\%)$, where EV = End Value, BV = Beginning Value, and R = the total annual return in the form of a percent.

But it's rarely that simple. You need to take cash flow into consideration, since, most likely, you're continuing to add to your principal investment throughout the year (except in the case of some retirement plans). That's why you must figure out the compounded return (internal rate of return), and the easiest way to do this is using computer software like Quicken.

If you don't have a computer or don't want to invest in the software, AAII suggests using the approximation method, which they say is reasonably accurate. The data for the equation can be found in your statement. It works best if you've only made periodic additions to or withdrawals from your principal investment that are no greater than 10 percent of your total portfolio.

"The return calculation compares ending values to beginning values and adjusts for net additions or withdrawals by subtracting 50 percent of net additions from the ending value and adding 50 percent to the beginning value," according to the AAII. "The 50 percent adjustment to both the beginning and ending values creates a midpoint average for the cash flows no matter when they were actually made."

This is the equation AAII uses:

Approximate Return Equation

$([(EV - 0.50(NA^*) \div (BV + 0.50(NA^*)] - 1.00) \times 100 = AR(\%)$ where EV = Ending Value, NA = Net Additions, BV = Beginning Value, and AR = Approximate Return in the form of a percent.

* Use net withdrawals, not zero, if total withdrawals are greater than total additions.

Ways to reduce costs

The best way to reduce costs is to invest in no-load funds. But that means you'll have to create and manage your own portfolio, do your own research on which funds will best meet your financial goals, assess your own risk tolerance, and hold tight when the market tests your tolerance. Doing this work on your own can save you bundles of money.

Cost can be further reduced because even among no-load funds, fees vary. You must shop around to get the best buy. By paying more than 1 percent for the management fee, you won't get any better research or better service. Even the funds with the lowest management fees give you diversification, professional investment, and liquidity. Investing in a well-managed fund with a 1 percent management fee versus a similar one with a 2 percent management fee can result in saving big bucks over time.

But if you do decide to invest in a loaded fund, get your money's worth. Your financial adviser should provide you with up-to-date research and solid investment advice.

Sometimes enough money talks. While financial planners are not liable or even able at some firms to reduce their fees, some can and probably will if you have exceptionally high assets.

Watch Out!
Double-check the data you enter into your computer when computing gains and losses. A transposed number or a keystroke made in error can throw off calculations.

Regardless of whether the fund carries a load or not, the type of fund you invest in can make a difference on your earnings. Index funds usually outperform actively managed funds, and most stocks found in actively managed funds are included in the indices. So if you're paying a 2 percent fee for the whole portfolio, but the fund is really only working the last 20 percent (80 percent are in the index, in this case), that's really a 10 percent fee, says Kacy Gott of Kochis Fitz investment planners.

This is where it makes sense to buy a concentrated fund, Gott says. Let the fund manager actively manage the entire portfolio. That's what you're paying for, he says.

Moneysaver
If you're in a fund that's not tax efficient, consider placing it in your retirement portfolio.

Just the facts

- You can reduce costs by investing in tax-efficient funds.

- There are a host of fees associated with investing in some mutual funds.

- You can calculate what you're actually earning after fees using mathematical formulas or, better yet, computer software.

- You can reduce costs by selecting your investments carefully.

Technology

GET THE SCOOP ON...
How the Internet is changing the way we
invest ▪ How the Internet is changing investment companies ▪ How hackers can get into
your computer ▪ How you can use the Internet
to become a better investor ▪ Where you can
find a wealth of information online ▪ The Year
2000 glitch—don't lose it all

PART VII

Using the Internet

Chapter 14

I magine a day without a computer. Fifteen years ago that would have been simple, but today, it's not so easy to envision. Computer technology has impacted our everyday lives—how we communicate, how we work, and how we play. It's also changed the way we manage our money, making this task much more efficient and reducing the possibility of making errors.

The Internet, specifically, has had a tremendous impact on investors. If you have a computer, you can go online, type in a few numbers, and see how much you'd have to save to reach your personal financial goals in 5 years, 10 years, and so on. You can research fund performance, get almost up-to-the-minute information on how the stock market is performing, and much more, all with the click of a mouse. The personal computer, especially coupled with the Internet, has empowered the individual investor, and by doing so, has forced the industry to change in order to compete for investment business.

This chapter will focus on how using the Internet can help you research your investment

Moneysaver
Go online to buy
or sell funds
when the mar-
ket's moving and
your broker's
phone is busy.

alternatives, calculate future earnings, track your portfolio, and move your money around electronically. This chapter will also explore the vulnerabilities of technology—in particular, how hackers can get your personal financial information (and how you can protect yourself against these attacks), and how the Year 2000 computer glitch may affect your investments and what actions you can take to protect your data.

The future of online investing

The Internet is providing you, the investor, with timely information that was previously only available to brokers, enabling you to make better decisions on your own. The number of people using the Internet to invest is growing, not in leaps and bounds, but slowly as more investors get online and feel safe making transactions there. This fact is reflected in the number of brokerages opening shop on the Web. If you surf the Net you'll find big names like Fidelity, Strong, T. Rowe Price, Schwab, and many more.

According to Forrester Research, there are already about 3 million online investing accounts. This independent research firm predicts that by 2002, online investing accounts will grow to 14.4 million, as shown in Figure 14.1. Assets managed online will reach $688 billion, a significant rise from a base of $120 billion in 1997, as shown in Figure 14.2.

Online mutual fund transactions now account for more than a quarter of all Schwab's mutual fund transactions, and that number is growing quickly.

Now that there's been this tremendous growth of the full service and discount brokerages online, it's forced several market changes which will ultimately benefit you, the online investor. Here's how:

FIGURE 14.1

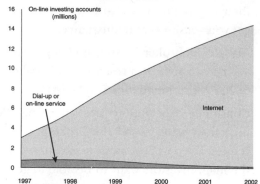

On-line investing accounts (millions)

	1997	1998	1999	2000	2001	2002
Internet	2.25	4.53	7.87	10.30	12.59	14.31
Dial-up or on-line service	0.71	0.78	0.55	0.27	0.14	0.07
Total	2.96	5.31	8.42	10.57	12.73	14.38

← Note!
The number of investments online is growing rapidly and is expected to multiply nearly seven times between 1997 and 2002 as more investors go online and as more brokerage firms offer online transactions. Source: Forrester Research

FIGURE 14.2

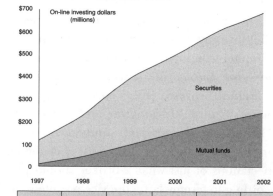

On-line investing dollars (millions)

	1997	1998	1999	2000	2001	2002
Securities	108	186	298	347	408	447
Mutual funds	12	47	99	149	201	241
Total	$120	$233	$397	$496	$609	$688

← Note!
The amount of assets managed online is expected to quintuple between 1997 and 2002. Source: Forrester Research

1. The Internet has brought about the creation of a new type of brokerage firm, one that weighs in somewhere between full service and discount do-it-yourselfers. They're referred to as mid-tier brokers.

2. The brokerages, in order to stand out from their competition, are offering more to you to get your business and allegiance.

3. The role of broker/adviser is changing now that you can do your own research and challenge his or her recommendations.

4. Consumer expectations are changing. People no longer want to call the brokerage house to request a report and wait for days to receive it in the mail. Investors want to be able to go online, at their convenience, and grab reports from the Web site. Consumers also expect to be able to log into their accounts online, rather than wait for a quarterly statement.

"
More than 20 percent of online households will invest electronically. By 2002, wired investors will manage 4.6 percent of total retail investment assets. Our definition of retail investment assets now includes fixed-income instruments along with equities and mutual funds—reflecting the growing diversity of investments being managed online.
—Forrester Research
"

In its "Online Investing Report," Jupiter, another independent research company, estimates that 44 percent of online households use the Internet to gather investment research. And, according to a survey Jupiter conducted, among online traders, the *Wall Street Journal* site attracts the most surfers researching investments. Next is Quote.com, Hoover's Online, Morningstar, and Quicken.com.

Being able to research mutual fund performance, fund managers, and more is changing the expectations of just what a broker should provide. According to Jeremy Jaffe, the vice president of electronic commerce at Liberty Financial Companies in Boston, it's lighting a fire under the brokers' feet.

Until recently, advisers were just the means to being able to complete a transaction. They'd also provide a reassuring pat on the back. But now they're feeling the pressure to give clearer advice, and they need to be sure it's sound because it can be confirmed or debunked quickly, Jaffe says.

Now, Jaffe says, advisers can help direct you to valuable sites on the Internet. More importantly, they can help you make sense of your findings. Enlisting their aid for that purpose alone could prove to be quite valuable. Consider the following:

British researchers, using two major search engines, Yahoo and Excite, searched the Web for medical advice on how to deal with fever in children. Children get sick often, and a fever is usually something parents can handle pretty easily.

But of the forty-one sites these researchers visited, only four adhered closely to the guidelines set forth in "Fever in Pediatric Practice," a standard medical work. Worse yet, a couple of sites suggested treatments that could place a child at high risk of a coma.

Surprisingly, thirty-two of these sites were commercial and nine were produced by health practitioners, clinics, academic institutions, and educational organizations. (This study was reported in the June 28, 1997, edition of the *British Medical Journal.*)

Although getting poor investment advice on the Web, or even acting upon it, wouldn't cause such dire consequences, it is clear from this study that not all sites are created equal and that the information they contain may or may not be valid. Anyone can set up shop on the Internet. Again, that's where the use of an adviser can come in handy.

Protecting yourself from hackers

Investors aren't the only ones surfing the Net— hackers consider it a recreational sport. Contrary to popular belief, most of them don't realize the havoc that they're causing; they think their pranks are harmless fun. But to the end user, they're annoying

Timesaver
Log on to the Internet at low use times to get from site to site faster than when there's a lot of traffic.

Moneysaver
Doing your own
research on the
Internet and
buying no-load
funds eliminates
the job of a
broker as well
as his or her
commission.

and costly in terms of time to diagnose and clean up after viruses and the like.

Just like in the real world, there are some criminals out there, and they are technologically sophisticated. These are the people you have to protect yourself from when you're using the Internet to gather data that would necessitate giving out personal information, invest, or perform other transactions.

Protecting yourself in the material world entails common sense:

- Don't broadcast how much cash you're carrying in your purse or wallet.

- Don't go to the automated teller machine alone late at night. In fact, don't go there late at night at all.

- Don't tell anyone your password for making phone transactions.

Protecting yourself in cyberspace also entails common sense, too.

Safety net

To protect yourself in the virtual world, you must first know what kinds of crimes are occurring there and what kinds can be expected to transpire in the not-too-distant future because of rapid technological advancements.

According to the International Computer Security Association (ICSA), there are several categories of risk to watch out for while you're surfing the Internet and visiting Web sites.

Exploitation of a user

This category is divided into two subcategories: swindles and privacy.

Swindles are sly switches. Say you're searching for information using keywords at a search engine and up comes a site called mutualfunds.com. You head over to check it out. It looks like a good site, with calculators and advice and research. But what you don't know is that the site has been set up by a bunch of teenagers in another country to try to get money by selling fake "funds."

You're being spoofed into believing this is a real company, says Peter Tippett, president of the ICSA. He gives this example to make his point: What do you think is at whitehouse.com? President Clinton? Let's hope not. It's a sex site (which was created long before the president began having troubles).

Another strategy these swindlers use to get you to visit their sites is misspelling a real site's address; as an example, they might use www.investmnts.com instead of www.investments.com. (The criminals are hoping you don't take time to proofread.) A third strategy these people use to misdirect you is changing the extension, or last part of the address. For example, if you want to see what the president has been working on, you can go to www.whitehouse.gov. Rather than .gov, a sex site uses .com as the extension. (Note: This is not to say that the owners of that sex site intended to use deceptive practices to get you to visit their site. It is used only as an example some swindlers use.)

Besides typing addresses carefully, you can stay safe on the Internet by only conducting business at sites that have a secure socket layer, or SSL.

An SSL authenticates the site and secures the information through encryption. The site will send a signed certificate to your computer verifying the authenticity of the site. Look for the certificate in your browser's drop-down menu.

Unofficially...
Bill Gates is a college dropout. But that didn't stop him from becoming the richest man in the world.

Watch Out!
If you're giving
out personal
information at a
Web site, be sure
it's secured with
a secure socket
layer, so you'll
know your infor-
mation is being
encrypted. Look
for a graphic
showing a key
turning or a lock
locking. Make
sure the site's
address changed
from http to
shttp.

Many Internet users are concerned about privacy. Privacy on the Internet just doesn't exist,
according to Tippett. But almost all good sites have
privacy policies posted telling you what they'll do
with the information you provide to them. For
example, they'll tell you if the data will be used for
internal use or if they plan to sell it.

Another privacy issue, but not necessarily a security issue, are cookies. Cookies are used by some
Web sites to make your next visit to the site run
smoother. Stored on your computer, this data tracks
where you go on the site and can include information you provide to the site, like your mutual fund
account number or credit card number. That way,
when you come back to the site, you don't have to
re-enter the data. Cookies become a security issue if
someone else uses your computer and visits those
same sites. They, too, will be able to access your
account. In cases where you've provided your credit
card number, subsequent users can make purchases
using your credit card.

But cookie files can be erased. Search your hard
drive for files with the word "cookie," highlight the
file names, and delete. Or, don't access sensitive
information or make transactions at your office.

Malicious hacking

When you're online, it is possible for a hacker to get
into your computer. However, it's unlikely because
your address changes through your Internet Service
Provider (ISP) everytime you go online. Therefore,
the hacker would have to guess your number out of
tens of thousands or even millions of addresses,
depending on your ISP and how many users it
serves. The hacker would also have to know when
you're going online, have hacking tools handy at

that time, and he'd have to know what addresses your ISP might give you and try to narrow down the list.

But if the hacker did get your address, you're easy prey. A hacker could take whatever he wants off your computer. But you'd probably notice he's there because your computer would slow down while he's accessing files in it.

Site attacks

It's more likely that a site containing your personal financial information (as opposed to your personal computer) gets hacked because Web sites have fixed addresses. Dr. Tippett estimates that mutual fund companies probably experience twenty to thirty attacks a day. But they work hard to protect your information.

Eavesdropping or "sniffing"

While you're at home typing personal financial information into a site, a hacker could eavesdrop on the conversation and grab the information. Theoretically, it's easy to do, and practically it's easy to do on networks. But if you're in the safety of your own home computer, there's really not much to worry about.

The number one online security worry is credit card number theft, according to Tippett, which he said should probably be number 10 because it virtually never happens. Here's why: When you send information over the Web, it makes a lot of jumps from computer to computer on the way to its destination Web site. Fiber cables, which carry your data, are fast and vast, so they're hard to listen in on. Plus, your information goes to the site in packets, maybe a thousand of them, which don't go down the same fiber. (The Internet is designed to automatically

Bright Idea
Phone the company to verify their Web address before attempting to give information.

route around slow moving data.) Commonly, information splits and takes different routes, meeting up at the destination.

To steal a credit card number or sensitive information, a hacker would have to plant a program looking for a credit card number or the files they're in at a specific site. Tippett says he feels comfortable using his credit card on the Internet, even more so than at a restaurant. But they're rarely stolen even there, he notes.

To effectively "sniff" your information while you're making a transaction, the hacker must be either at the brokerage's site or physically at your connection to the phone company outside your home.

Privacy, hacking, and denial of service

Chat rooms present three problems at once. Suppose you want to talk with other investors about mutual funds. You head over to a chat room. But that's one place where others, including hackers, can actually see your IP (internet protocol) address. (That's the one your ISP gives to you each time you log on.) A hacker with tools available can type in your IP address and send your computer information that makes it crash. It's called a denial of service attack. Although it's nothing more than an annoyance, a hacker also can enter your computer while you chat, taking what he wants. That could have much more serious repercussions.

Physical security

Physical access to private information is always a security issue, but it's not likely that a burglar will break into your home and steal the password to your online account. More likely, he'll take your tangible valuables. It's a bigger risk for the brokerage houses.

Malicious codes

Malicious codes are executable codes written specifically with malicious intent and launched from the Internet. Unlike viruses, which spread, "vandals" hit and run, often escaping unnoticed. They are not currently prevalent but are likely to be a problem in the future.

Here's how they could work: While you're at a site calculating your investment portfolio, you could be using a program that's running on a Java applet or by ActiveX controls. Whether purposeful or accidental, there's a theoretical risk that when a program runs on your computer it could do harm. If it's malicious, it could look for your password the next time you log on or commit some other type of malicious act.

A more likely risk is contracting viruses through an executable program on the site or being attacked by Trojan horses, a program that hides within another program's code until it's activated and then is used for destructive purposes.

Researching and trading online

Now that you know how to reduce your risks online, the question is: What can the Internet do for you? There are four primary services the Internet can provide:

- a variety of resources with which to conduct research on mutual funds

- the ability to trade funds

- the ability to check your portfolio, and access to calculators that can help you decide how much you'll need to save at various market returns

- rates of inflation in order to meet your financial goals

Watch Out!
Don't respond to e-mail investment solicitations. You don't really know who's on the other end.

Research

When considering which mutual funds you'd like to invest in, there are four main areas you can consider researching. (For more categories and more information on this topic read Chapter 7.) They are:

1. Performance in comparison to a standard, such as the S&P 500.

2. Number of shares in the fund that are outstanding. (If the fund is too large, it's difficult for them to find good stocks to buy and growth will probably slow at some point as a result.)

3. Fund manager's performance record, especially if there's been a recent change, because different managers have different styles. You can check his or her performance at previous jobs.

4. Fund comparisons, which can be illuminating. Compare your funds to similar ones—index funds to index funds, large-cap funds to large-cap funds.

Trading funds

You can buy, sell, and trade funds at some sites. Although the procedures and funds vary from site to site, you will have to have a password or PIN, along with your account number, to get in. Once you gain access to this secured area, you can get your account balance, purchase funds, switch investments among funds, and sell funds. For some 401(k) plans, you can change the percentage of how much of your paycheck deduction goes into each fund.

For example, Fidelity has a total of 3,400 funds you can buy and sell. More than 850 can be moved without paying a transaction fee to Fidelity (although you should check to see if you must pay one to another company).

Checking your portfolio

Using portfolio trackers, you can track your investments with that company 24 hours a day. Using other Web sites, you can track your entire portfolio, up to a certain number of funds. For instance, at Fidelity's site you can look up total current value, account balances, and holdings. You can also get current price quotes, review your account history, and monitor hypothetical portfolios so you can "try" them out before actually investing. At Vanguard's site you can monitor price movements, gains, and losses and get recent news on a security. Most of the brokerage sites have similar offerings.

Bright Idea
Open up a mutual fund for your children's savings and teach them early how to invest.

Calculating the possibilities

The calculators are designed to help you determine how much you need to save and at what interest rate in order to reach your financial goals by a specific age. Most are based on the following, although some do not contain as many details:

- Your current age
- The age at which you plan to retire
- Life expectancy
- Current annual income
- Expected annual raises
- Percent of your salary you want at retirement
- Expected annual Social Security benefit
- Annual pension income
- Other expected annual retirement income
- Retirement savings plans such as a 401(k)
- Your financial goals
- Future inflation, (your own guesstimate)
- Future annual average return on your retirement (another best guess)

Using the retirement calculator provided by *Money* magazine at www.moneymag.com, I'll show you four examples of how these programs work to help you reach your goals.

Example 1: You're 32 years old, single, and plan to retire at age 65. You're earning $30,000 a year, expect 4 percent annual raises and plan to live until you're 90 years old. You need 100 percent of your salary to live off of in retirement. You have $10,000 saved for retirement and your employer contributes nothing. You're figuring on a 4 percent annual rate of inflation and a 10 percent annual rate of return on your investments. According to the calculations, you'll run out of money at age 84. If inflation is higher or the market doesn't perform as well as you'd predicted, you'll run out sooner. But if you save 10 percent of your annual salary you'll have enough money and will be able to leave $465,655 to your heirs.

Example 2: You're 35 years old and your spouse is 38 years old. You both plan to retire at age 65 and you both expect to live until age 98. Together, you earn $70,000 a year and assume you will get annual raises of 3.5 percent. You want to retire on 70 percent of your current income. You don't expect any income from Social Security or pensions and have no trusts or annuities to reap further retirement income from, but you have $70,000 saved in your retirement funds already. You each put in 5 percent of your salary annually to this account. Your employer contributes nothing. You predict a 4 percent annual rate of inflation and 10 percent annual rate of return on your retirement investments. Based on these numbers you will run out of money at age 88. Now you know you'll have to save more to

reach your goals or make adjustments to your predictions on inflation rates or market performance.
Say you each save 10 percent of your income and
placed that in a 401(k). Not only would you outlive
your retirement, you'll be able to pass on $1,067,433
(in today's dollars) to your heirs.

Example 3: You're 46 and your spouse is 43, and
you both plan to retire when you're 60 years old.
One of you expects to live to age 90, the other to age
92. You earn $60,000 a year and your spouse earns
$70,000. You both expect 4 percent annual raises.
You want 80 percent of your combined salaries to
live off of in retirement. You expect to collect Social
Security but don't know how much. (You can let the
program estimate it.) Together your retirement
accounts are at $150,000 and you save a total of 15
percent of your income for retirement. Your
spouse's employer will match 5 percent of what he
puts in to his 401(k). You assume a 5 percent annual
inflation rate and a 12 percent average annual
return on your investments. According to the calculations, you will run out of money by the time you're
81 years old, so you need to make some adjustments. You choose to rebalance your portfolio by
investing in some more aggressive funds. The new
annual rate of return is 15 percent. Now you'll make
it with $7,130,257 left over for your kids.

Example 4: You're both 55 years old and plan to
retire together at age 65. You expect to live to age 95
and your spouse expects to live to age 92. You earn
$30,000 annually and your spouse earns $50,000 a
year. You're both banking on 3.5 percent annual
raises and plan to retire on 50 percent of your combined current income. You expect Social Security
payments and $20,000 annually from a pension.

Watch Out!
Web site calcula-
tors assume
you'll stay
invested at the
annual return
rate you predict.
It is unlikely
that the market
will return an
average of 15
percent for 50
years.

Together you've saved $50,000 for retirement. You each contribute 5 percent of your salaries to your 401(k) plans and so do your employers. You expect a 4 percent annual inflation rate and 10 percent annual return on your investments. According to the calculation, you'll outlive your retirement savings and have $995,510 to leave to your heirs.

The benefit to using this tool is that you can see the impact factors like inflation and market performance have on your investments over time.

A wealth of opportunity

The Internet provides a wealth of opportunity to research information on different mutual funds, investment strategies, and the economy. It also makes tracking your portfolio easier and keeps you abreast of the news.

Newspapers and magazines

For three years *Barron's* (www.barrons.com) has been posting quarterly reviews of mutual funds as well as ranking the top 100 mutual fund managers.

The online version of CNN's financial news is at www.cnnfn.com. In addition to financial news stories on all aspects of the industry, you can check out CNNfn/Lipper Analytical Services' report on recent performance and pricing information of more than 5,000 U.S. mutual funds.

Money magazine, located at www.moneymag. com, has the "Ultimate Guide to Mutual Funds," which includes information on hundreds of well-performing funds as well as other investment information. It also has a portfolio tracker, daily market performance graph, fund quotes that you can search by ticker or name, news search by keyword, and a retirement calculator.

The *Wall Street Journal's* interactive edition at www.wsj.com is fee-based after the two-week initial trial, but the *Journal* does have a solid reputation for reporting on the financial industry.

James Glassman's Sunday columns for the *Washington Post* (www.washingtonpost.com) often report on mutual funds. The articles are posted at this site for 2 weeks.

At Morningstar's site (www.morningstar.com), you can get unbiased performance information on 1700 mutual funds as well as other valuable information.

SmartMoney magazine's site (www.smartmoney. com) has a portfolio tracker that will monitor up to 10 mutual funds, a chart center that compares indicators, and articles.

Commercial sites

At www.quicken.com/investments, you can look up a mutual funds symbol if you don't know it, and see how the markets performed. Under mutual funds, the site has a fund finder, list of the top 25 funds, a question-and-answer page, Morningstar profiles, and Value Line profiles and ratings. Using the Morningstar page you can search for funds by ratings, from five starts down to one star. There are also articles on mutual fund performance and investment strategies. You can get fact sheets, prospectuses, and more from popular fund families. This is a very comprehensive site overall.

At Hoover's Online (www.hoovers.com), you can search for company information by industry, ticker symbol, location, and annual sales. It also has a lot of features if you're investing in individual stocks as well.

Timesaver
Keep all your investments and expenditures in a software program like Quicken. If you go to Quicken's site (and you have that software), you can update your portfolio's performance with a click of the mouse.

Wall Street Net at www.netresource.com/wsn/ is mostly a site for people who buy individual stocks, but it does have one feature that you'd probably be interested in. It has links to the three stock exchanges—NASDAQ, American Stock Exchange, NYSE Net (for the New York Stock Exchange). It also has links to international stock exchanges in London, Milan, Paris, Australia, Tokyo, and more.

At the NASDAQ site, which you can also get to by typing in www.nasdaq.com, you can see how the market did that day. You can enter up to 10 symbols for mutual funds (or stocks) to get quotes (share values) from all three exchanges. It gives the market close date (a quote for the end of the day), net change, if any, last distribution date for dividends, last dividend amount, capital gains (if any), beginning and ending net asset value, and an address and phone number to the fund. It also has a glossary of terms, of which the NASDAQ definition has a link listing the companies on this index. The site also has a portfolio tracking page.

On the "Investor Services" page, you can learn more about the different types of investments, learn about the structure of the market, and calculate projected investment gains.

The link to the American Stock Exchange can also be reached at www.amex.com. There you can also see how the three exchanges performed and go live to the AMEX trading floor. There's a page to the listed companies and a fast quote page that works for all three exchanges by symbol or name, but it gives less information than does the quick quote on the NASDAQ site.

The New York Stock Exchange link, which is also at www.nyse.com, has a page with market information, but only for that exchange.

A list of documents published or distributed by the United States Securities and Exchange Commission appears at www.moneypages.com/syndicate/stocks/sec/index.html, the Syndicate. They include the "SEC Guide to Investing Wisely (mutual funds)" and "Careful Investors Read Their Mail." This site also contains a comprehensive list of frequently asked questions about mutual funds and an extensive list of links to mutual funds sites and site information.

At Value Line (www.valueline.com), you'll find mutual fund manager ratings. It also has closing prices of mutual fund shares.

E*TRADE (www.etrade.com) offers mutual fund research and screening tools. You can find out about a fund's Morningstar rating, total return, and assets under management. There's also a portfolio tracker, current market information, and more. You can buy, sell, and exchange shares from more than 4,000 funds at that site.

At www.fool.com, the Motley Fools teach investors how to take control of their finances and give their views on beating the market with stocks.

The Year 2000 Information Center (www.year2000.com) is a good source of information for those interested in the year 2000 problem.

Cash University (www.cashuniversity.com), which helps parents teach children money management skills, is an educational, fun site for children.

You can find out about recent fund manager changes at www.fundalarm.com, a noncommercial Web site that's updated monthly.

Brokerage firms

The mutual fund company sites all have similar features including prospectuses, price of funds,

> **"**
> Every day I get up and look through the Forbes list of the richest people in America. If I'm not there, I go to work.
> —Robert Orben
> **"**

education information, planning for retirement, and information about their fund managers. Of course, since it's put out by the company, this information may be biased. Some sites have investment calculators.

Vanguard (www.vanguard.com) has stock market summaries, a learning center (which includes a "university" with 10 courses, four on retirement investing), a library, and a glossary with definitions of investment terms. The site also has a section on women and investing.

At The Young Investor Web site (www.younginvestor.com) you'll find a wealth of help to get your kids, and even you, interested in investing. This site by Liberty Financial lets you pick a guide from a wacky list of caricatures, complete with their own bios. It also has music if you want it.

Government and nonprofit sites

In addition to news, you'll find EDGAR at the Security and Exchange Commission's Web site at www.sec.gov. EDGAR is a searchable database of corporate information. You can also get investment assistance, which gives information on how to avoid fraud. This page tells you how to file complaints against your broker.

If you've got a complaint about the NASDAQ, contact the National Association of Securities Dealers (NASD) Regulation at www.nasdr.com. That arm of NASD oversees all brokers and the Nasdaq Stock Market.

You can learn how to protect yourself from securities fraud at www.nasaa.org. The North American Securities Administrators Association site also has e-mail addresses to report suspected Internet fraud.

Timesaver
Some sites have extensive links to others. Go to www.moneypages.com/syndicate/finance/broker.html and you'll find a comprehensive list of links to investment firms and securities information.

At www.mfea.com, sponsored by the nonprofit trade association Mutual Fund Education Alliance, you can create a customized portfolio tracker to track your mutual fund performances. The site has a database of more than 1,000 no-load mutual funds and links to leading no-load companies, educational information, including some specifically geared toward women, topics on children and investing, and an investment planning calculator.

The American Association of Individual Investors (AAII) has an educational Web site geared toward the individual investor at www.aaii.com. Some articles are accessible to surfers. Much more is available to members.

Y2K and investing—will you lose it all?

The Year 2000 computer glitch is getting a lot of press lately, as well it should. If left unfixed, it could wreak havoc.

Here's the problem: Computer systems are based on a faulty standard, the date format: MM/DD/YY. The format was originally designed to save on storage space because in the 1960s and 1970s memory was expensive. But this format makes it impossible for your computer to distinguish between the 20th and the 21st centuries. Because the year 2000 will be read 00, it is already causing calculation problems and is expected to cause more as the year 2000 approaches.

There is good news about this computer glitch. Of all the industries, the banking industry is the best prepared for the Year 2000 software problem, according to Capers Jones, chief scientist and vice president of Artemis Management Systems Inc., headquartered in Boulder, Colorado.

"

With over 58 million shareholders of record participating in markets experiencing nearly 200 billion shares being traded annually, it is critical that the computer systems upon which our securities market participants rely be prepared to deal with the challenges presented by the change in millennium.
—United States Security and Exchange Commission

"

That's because of all the industries, it would be the one hardest hit by this glitch, says Year 2000 speaker/consultant Peter de Jager.

But this is not to say there will be no problems. In its "Report to the Congress on the Readiness of the United States Securities Industry and Public Companies to Meet the Information Processing Challenges of the Year 2000," the SEC, in June 1997, said investment advisers and investment companies are required to disclose to clients and shareholders operational or financial obstacles presented by the Year 2000 problem.

Besides the Year 2000 glitch, there are other glitches that can occur in January 1999, and anytime in 1999, because of the fiscal year end and then again with the leap year, according to Jones.

Bright Idea
Check the Year 2000 compliance records of your mutual fund companies and the records of the stocks they invest in. Also, keep written statements of your accounts in case the records at the brokerage firms are lost or your accounts are miscalculated due to the glitch.

Although Y2K is mainly a software problem, the year 2000 dilemma can be hardware driven. Some computers can't be reset to January 1, 2000. To make sure you can get online or even use your financial software offline, take this test by de Jager:

"Set the date on your personal computer to December 31, 1999. Set the time to 23:58 hrs (11:58 PM) and then POWER OFF the computer. Wait at least 3 minutes and then turn the PC back on. Check the date and time. It should be a minute or two past midnight, on the morning of Saturday, January 1, 2000. (If it doesn't) the problem lies somewhere in your computer. If the system has the wrong date, then all your software has the wrong date."

This problem can be fixed with a software patch or by typing in the right date each time the computer is booted.

The Mac OS and Apple Macintosh computers and Mac software do not have problems with the

Year 2000. Problems may arise for those using their own date and time utility package.

Microsoft Windows NT and Windows 95 are okay until 2099. Besides inspecting the source code for customized programs, Microsoft recommends inspecting Windows-based systems that use a third party run-time library (that is, not Win32) and mainframe-based applications that are accessed from a PC.

At www.RighTime.com, there are hardware patch programs that can be downloaded and used free for personal users. There's also a free diagnostic file that will test hardware.

Just the facts

- Online calculators can show you how much you need to save under varying circumstances.
- Being aware of how hackers operate will keep you safer while you're online.
- Make sure the Web site you get information from is legitimate.
- Inflation rates and market returns can have significant impacts on your investment strategies.
- Keep all your paper records in case one of your mutual fund company has a Y2K computer glitch.

GET THE SCOOP ON...
What fraudulent tactics are most prevalent ▪
What red flags you should look for ▪ Why
investors fall prey on the Internet ▪ How to
protect yourself from deceptive practices

Protecting Yourself Against Investment Fraud

Chapter 15

Most fund salespeople, brokers, financial planners, and accountants are ethical and trustworthy. But, as in any business, there are those who are deceptive and unethical, and there are those who commit fraud.

The Internet has added a new medium for fraudulent behavior. While most of the fraudulent schemes online are similar to those offline, there are additional problems and security vulnerabilities.

In this chapter, you'll find out what types of deceptive practices and fraud are most prevalent, both offline and online. You'll also learn what red flags to look for and how you can avoid investing in scams or high-risk investments that benefit only those who sell them. And, you'll find out where you can get help if you've been taken.

" Fraud and deceptive practices

The unprecedented bull market of the past decade
has attracted many new, unsophisticated investors
who make easy prey for online and offline fraud.
State securities regulators warned that the bull market could be masking sales practice problems such
as unsuitable investments, high fees and excessive
commissions, and churning (excessive trading),
according to the North American Securities
Administrators Association (NASAA), which represents state and provincial securities regulators in the
U.S. and Canada. With the market returning 20 percent on some mutual funds, many investors aren't
paying close attention to commission rates and fees.
Churning pushes both of these higher.

Smart investing requires research. Some people
will spend more time investigating a washing
machine purchase than an investment.

For example, in 1997, Ohio alone received 223
complaints and opened 300 new enforcement matters. The state has pursued six to twelve criminal
cases during each of the last 4 years, according to
Thomas Geyer, commissioner of securities for the
State of Ohio.

There are two levels of fraud:

1. Improprieties by brokers. These sales practice
   violations are also referred to as front-office
   fraud.

2. Blatant fraud by "promoters." (Fraud occurs
   when a person acts with malicious intent.)

   Improprieties include:

   ▪ Unauthorized transactions

   ▪ Unsuitable recommendations

   ▪ Failure to execute a transaction

- Churning, i.e., excessive trading

Blatant fraud includes:

- Misrepresentation of facts
- Making promises that are impossible to fulfill
- Omission of material information
- Outright lies
- Misuse of offering proceeds

See the list below for the top 10 investment fraud issues that state regulators are dealing with today, according to the NASAA.

1. Affinity group fraud. Fraud is perpetrated on religious, ethnic and professional groups by members of these groups or persons claiming to want to assist these groups. Asian communities in Southern California, for example, have recently been targets of bogus investments in precious metals and foreign currencies.

2. Internet fraud. This includes market manipulation, insider trading and unlicensed broker and investment adviser activity on the Internet.

3. Abusive sales practices. Sales of securities to unsuitable investors, fraudulent offerings, and market manipulation, particularly in the micro-cap (that is, very small-cap) marketplace, are on the rise, according to state statistics.

4. Investment seminars. State regulators are monitoring the proliferation of investment seminars and financial planners, watching out for unlicensed activity, lack of disclosure of conflicts of interest, and hidden fees and commissions.

5. Telemarketing fraud. Nationwide, hundreds of "boiler rooms," or high-pressure telephone

Watch Out!
You can lose a lot of money if you place your trust in the wrong hands. Learn about fraudulent behavior and deceptive practices so you'll recognize it when you see it.

sales operations, peddle illegal or fraudulent investment products.

6. Deceptive marketing of municipal bonds. Risky bonds secured by over-valued real estate are being marketed as "safe" general obligation bonds.

7. Unregistered immigration investments. These are investments which allegedly would confer "alien immigration status" on foreign nationals seeking to immigrate to the United States. California recently acted against a Virginia company for offering such unregistered investments.

8. Illegal franchise offerings. Inadequate disclosure and fraud are connected with the offering of franchise investments, often through business opportunity and franchise shows.

9. High-tech products and services. Misleading or illegal offerings of high-tech investments target unsophisticated investors with promises of high profits and minimal risk in such areas as 900 numbers or the Internet.

10. Entertainment. Some scams offer opportunities for investments in movie deals and other entertainment products with promises of guaranteed profits that minimize or ignore risks.

Red flags

If you're not sure if you're dealing with an ethical financial planner or salesperson, there are several common indicators, or red flags, you can look or listen for:

- "Guaranteed return." There are no guarantees in investing.

- "Limited offer." This strategy is designed to give you a sense of urgency, so you'll sign on the dotted line before giving the investment thoughtful consideration.

- "Risk free." All investments carry risk.

- "High returns." Watch out for this promise, especially over the short term.

- Veil of secrecy. This strategy is designed to deter prospective investors from asking questions, making it easier for the scam artists to sell their "product."

- High-pressured sales tactics. If someone's selling a legitimate investment, he or she should have no reason to insult you or pressure you by saying, "You have to act now, I only have a few left."

"If there's someone who's pressuring you to make a decision right now, they're not in it for a long-term relationship," says Richard Babson, chairman and president of Babson-United Investment Advisors, Inc. Again, ask what's it in for them. Don't jump into anything. Take time to research your investment carefully. There have been opportunities you regret having missed, but others you're glad you missed, he says. Focus on the long-term, both for the investment and your relationship with your financial planner.

Ask about credentials. Scam artists often lie about their education, says Babson. He suggests calling the university they say they got a degree from. "Sometimes, (attending) a lecture (at) Harvard turns into an honorary doctorate," he says.

Other red flags include the following:

- Your financial planner recommends that you dramatically change your portfolio, for example,

Timesaver
When a salesperson calls to sell you a mutual fund or other investment you might be interested in, have him mail the information to you before spending a lot of time on the phone with him.

by moving from low-risk mutual funds to high-risk junk bonds or placing all or a large part of your investments in a single security. That move would likely benefit your planner more than you, while putting your money at a substantially greater risk.

▪ Your financial planner urges you to move your investment in a mutual fund to another fund that has similar investment objectives. This can be an unscrupulous method of generating sales commissions.

▪ Your financial planner brushes off an error in your account as clerical or otherwise. Ask a manager for a written explanation, and check to see if the problem was corrected in your next statement.

Work with a reputable company. Check with the Better Business Bureau and your county consumer complaints office to see if there have been unresolved complaints placed against the company, and check with the secretary of state in your state to see if the company is licensed. Babson notes that being registered with the Securities and Exchange Commission (SEC) doesn't mean the salesperson or financial planner has the SEC seal of approval. All it means is that they've passed an examination.

Always ask what's in it for the salesperson, Babson says. Brokers who are registered with the SEC and operate as certified financial planners or analysts have an ethical responsibility to declare what they get out of a sale. If they recommend a fund that gives a higher commission than another, they must disclose that, but only if you ask. If your broker is a crook, he will give you a sweet song that makes the investment sound attractive but won't give you a straight answer on his profit, Babson says.

If it sounds too good to be true, it usually is, Geyer says. The Ohio Department of Commerce, Division of Securities encourages *investigating* before *investing*.

If you use an accountant

Many people use an accountant to figure their taxes. If you do, you probably rely upon the accuracy of your accountant's financial reporting when making your investment decisions.

Noting that accountants play an important role in the financial reporting process, in September 1998, the SEC defined "improper professional conduct" as it pertains to accountants. An amendment to Rule 102(e) of the Commission's Rules of Practice clarifies when accountants engage in improper professional conduct:

1. Intentional or knowing conduct, including reckless conduct, that results in a violation of applicable professional standards; or

2. Negligent conduct, either a single instance of highly unreasonable conduct that results in a violation of applicable professional standards in circumstances in which an accountant knows, or should know, that heightened scrutiny is warranted, or repeated instances of unreasonable conduct, each resulting in a violation of applicable professional standards that indicate a lack of competence to practice before the Commission.

An accountant who engages in improper professional conduct can be censured, suspended, or barred from practice by the SEC.

Moneysaver
Make sure you're not overpaying on your investment. Check all the fees and commissions and compare them against similar investments in other companies and through other salespeople or financial planners.

There are other ways to deceive investors, says Kay R. Shirley, a registered investment adviser. Some no-load funds bury sales and marketing expenses under portfolio turnover transaction costs, leading people to believe that there are no marketing and sales expenses. Shirley suggests looking at the miscellaneous fees. If there are no fees listed there, check the portfolio turnover rate. If it's more than 100 percent, she thinks the money is coming out of those fees.

There's no rule saying that the salesperson has to define the turnover ratio, so anything can be hidden in the transaction fees, she says. A total expense ratio of 3.3, for instance, is double the industry average for growth and income funds. Anything greater than 1.43 is a red flag, Shirley says.

In a no-load fund, look for:

- A total expense ration of less than 1.4 percent
- A portfolio turnover of less than 100 percent

In addition, make sure there's not a 12b-1 fee for sales and marketing.

A few rules of thumb to remember:

- Never purchase an investment through a cold call, at least not if you're a novice or if you haven't invested before with that company.
- Don't give your bank account number(s), your mother's maiden name, or any PINs (personal identification numbers) or other security codes over the phone.
- When you get a sales pitch, request disclosure information. Ask about compliance with the securities law.
- Get written information about the investment and the broker. Take notes during the conversation so you have a record. Don't deal with

brokers who refuse to send you written information.

- Ask your state's securities regulator if the investment is registered, if the broker is licensed to do business in your state, if the state has received or knows of any complaints about the broker or the brokerage firm, and if either has a disciplinary history.

- Don't write a check to the sales representative. Make it out to the fund.

- Check to see if the address where you're asked to send the check differs from the address of the brokerage firm or that listed in the prospectus.

- Make sure your receive account statements each month or quarter, whichever is standard for that company. Such statements serve as your record of all transactions, so make sure all information contained in each statement is correct. Have any errors explained in writing and corrected immediately. Check the next statement to verify the change was made.

James B. Cloonan, president of the American Association of Individual Investors, gives these additional tips:

- Never make an investment based on a telephone call from someone you haven't met, even if the call is from a prominent brokerage firm.

- When you open a brokerage account, along with your forms send a letter to your financial adviser describing your financial situation, investment preferences, and your risk tolerance. Keep copies of everything. Send letters periodically thereafter.

Bright Idea
If you have elderly parents, relatives, or friends, teach them about deceptive and fraudulent practices and how to avoid them. The elderly are often prey to fraud.

- Keep a diary and record all conversations with investment professionals.

- Read confirmations and statements immediately after receiving them. If you see discrepancies, notify your broker by phone, followed by a letter.

- Approach promises and intimations of high returns with skepticism, even if they are provided by brokers or advisers you know.

- Don't invest in something you don't understand, especially if someone says, "It's too difficult to explain, but it's a good deal."

- Don't authorize a discretionary brokerage account. Use a no-load mutual fund or an investment adviser who's not paid on commissions if you want to have someone manage your money.

- Research investments before investing.

Denise Voigt Crawford, Securities Commissioner of the State of Texas and president of NASAA, offers a few simple tips to fight fraud and protect your money:

- Get the facts by checking up on your investment professional, his or her firm, and the product or service offered by calling the appropriate local, state, or federal regulator to see if they're licensed to sell in your state and what, if any, disciplinary record they've got.

- Hang up on aggressive cold callers and never allow yourself to be pressured into making an investment over the phone.

- Always read the prospectus and check references.

- If you don't understand the investment, don't invest in it. It may be that you don't understand it because it doesn't make any sense.

Ohio uses the acronym "THINK" before investing:

T—treating guarantees with skepticism

H—honing in on your objectives

I—investigating before you invest

N—not being pressured into investing

K—knowing how your investment funds will be used

Cold calling

It usually happens after a long day at work, just as you take your first bite into a hot dinner. But sometimes, cold call salespeople phone during the day or late in the evening. Although they're best known for selling long-distance phone service, sometimes these salespeople are selling investments.

While some of these callers are selling legitimate investments, others are more than just annoying; they're fraudulent. They often use tactics that should raise red flags. They may use pressure to sell you their product or the investment itself might be a scam.

You can stop cold calls. Legitimate cold callers must follow certain rules set forth by the SEC:

- If they are calling you at home, they must phone between 8:00 a.m. and 9:00 p.m. But they can call you anytime at work, and the time restrictions don't apply if you're already a customer of the firm or if you've given them permission to call you at other times.

Watch Out!
Stay in control of your money. Don't sign away your rights to approve each investment move your financial planner makes on your behalf.

- They must identify themselves and the nature of their call. Specifically, they must tell you their name, the name of their firm, address, and telephone number, and they must note that they are calling to sell you an investment.

- At your request, they must add your name to their "Do Not Call" list. (However, you must use those exact words in order for them not to get around the letter of the law.)

- They are barred from threatening you in any way, trying to intimidate you, using offensive language, or calling you repeatedly in an effort to annoy, abuse, or harass you.

- Before taking money directly from your bank account, brokers must get your permission in writing.

- They must tell you the truth about the investment.

Unscrupulous salespeople use certain tactics. Cold call red flags include:

- High-pressure sales tactics. The salesperson will have retorts to every objection you make, if you can get a word in edgewise.

- A sense of urgency. You will be encouraged to buy now or you might lose the opportunity. Remember, researching your investment is of paramount importance.

- Appealing to your self-esteem by telling you not to be stupid.

- An offer of spectacular profits or "guaranteed" returns.

Don't expect a dishonest broker to take or return any of your phone calls if you're trying to sell the investment you bought from him or her.

"
He who tampers with the currency robs labor of its bread.
—Daniel Webster
"

Three-call technique

Another cold call tactic is the "three-call" technique. During the first call, the salesperson builds up your trust by touting the firm's "strengths." He will say he'll call you back if something "hot" comes along. During the second call, the "set up," he will tell you about some sure-fire deal. In the third call, "the close," he lays on the sales pressure.

If you have doubt about the validity of the investment, try asking the salesperson about the level of risk and how appropriate the investment is to your financial plan. Most likely, rather than a direct, honest answer, you'll get more on the investment's high returns. Heed this red flag. It couldn't be waving any faster.

Bait-and-switch technique

With this technique, the broker sells you a good investment. After gaining your trust, he tries to sell you high risk investments. Likely scenario: commissions for him, losses for you.

Cyber-security

The Internet presents the same problems and more. It's not like a private letter, it's more like a postcard, says Babson. "The more interesting the picture, the more people will read it," he says.

Furthermore, anybody can say anything on the Internet. You can't trust everything you hear on the Net, especially in chat rooms and on bulletin boards. Although it's not legal to try to manipulate stock prices, some people talk up or talk down stocks so that they'll sway investors.

Verify all you hear with the offline world. "Always watch out for the 'hot' tip," Babson says.

Security provided by each Web site, your Internet security provider, and by the architecture

Bright Idea
Visit the Securities and Exchange Commission's Web site (www.sec.gov) and other Internet sites that discuss fraud before responding to any sales solicitation.

of the Internet reduces the chances of fraud, mostly by reducing the opportunities for hackers. But it does not eliminate it.

Transactions in cyberspace

Watch Out!
Don't buy into an investment just because your friend or family member is selling it. Some people get involved in scams unwittingly. Check it out as you would any other investment.

More and more mutual funds are allowing their customers to track their portfolios and make transactions online. If you decide to invest using the Internet, you'll enter the site through a browser, such as Netscape Navigator or Internet Explorer. Through the browser, you'll click on the icon for trading or transferring mutual funds. The site will send a message saying you're entering an encrypted area, and you'll begin an SSL (secure sockets layer) encrypted session. Typically, sites that deal with money have firewalls in place to prevent outside hackers from getting into their servers. In general, it's safe to buy over the Net; relatively speaking, it's safer than making a transaction over a cellular or wireless phone, although these phones are also now more secure.

Cyber-safety check

Before providing sensitive information to a Web site, look for three things:

1. A privacy statement disclosing how the information will be used and how the site is secured.

2. The ability to cancel a transaction that contains sensitive information.

3. A message that you're entering an encrypted session. If you're sending sensitive information, it should be under an SSL.

   The SSL is necessary because the information you provide—your account number, for instance—may not go directly to that site's server. It may hop into and out of many computers (servers) along the way.

Using an SSL-encrypted session guarantees that your information can be read only by an authorized user at the specified address of the Web server. Both Microsoft Internet Explorer and Netscape Navigator support SSL.

To determine if you have an SSL-enabled session, there is a lock icon in Microsoft Internet Explorer that appears closed if the SSL is enabled. In Netscape Navigator, the icon is a key. If the key is broken, the SSL is not activated. Most sites support SSL-encrypted sessions.

Another way to tell if the Web site is secure is to look for the International Computer Security Association (ICSA) seal. The ICSA provides guidelines, a remote test (a vulnerability analysis), an on-site inspection, and two random spot checks to companies that enlist their aid.

You might also ask your financial planner or fund what security provisions they have online.

Protecting yourself against fraud on the Internet

The Internet is a double-edged sword, Geyer says. It provides both unprecedented access to fund information, and at the same time provides another arena for scam artists to operate.

In this relatively new medium, scam artists can set up shop simply by creating a Web page that looks like that of a professionally managed, legitimate fund company. Another way scammers attract surfers to their site is to use an address that either closely resembles a legitimate site by using, for instance, .org instead of .com as an extension or by using an address similar to a legitimate company but with a common typographical error. For example, instead of "bigfund.com" they might use "bigfudn.com" or "bgifund.com."

Many people believe that all Internet sites are legitimate. "Nothing could be further from the truth," Geyer says.

So, if a Web site looks credible, how do you tell if it's a scam? The same red flags apply to online scams as offline scams. In addition, most legitimate funds will send you a pile of marketing materials upon receiving an e-mail or phone request. If you don't receive these materials, or if the materials don't look professional, that could be a sign that the company is not legitimate.

But professional-looking literature is not difficult or expensive to create nowadays with desktop publishing programs. Get the disclosure statement, prospectus, and other marketing materials. Then call the toll-free 800 number and double-check.

The Ohio Department of Commerce, Division of Securities, offers these tips to fight cyber-fraud:

- Verify that the fund (or other investment opportunity) and the person promoting it is licensed by your state's department of commerce division of securities. The NASAA Web site (http://www.NASAA.org) has links to other states' departments of commerce.

- Don't expect to get rich quick.

- Don't assume your Internet provider polices bulletin boards or chat rooms.

- Don't buy fund shares strictly on the basis of online hype.

- Don't take advice from people who hide their identity (which is exactly what a screen name does).

- Don't assume the salesperson has done his homework (such as visited all of the companies in which the fund invests), even if he or she says so.

- Beware of conflicts of interest. A growing number of stock analysts get paid in cash or stocks in exchange for endorsements. While some disclose this information, others don't.

- Don't post personal information online, including your name, address, or phone number. Aside from the obvious risks this poses (it takes less than one minute to get a map and driving directions to your house from some sites and CDs), the Ohio Department of Commerce, Division of Securities says that you could be harassed online. You could also be placed on a "suckers list," which is used by con-artists for e-mail, mail delivered by the U.S. Postal Service, or boiler-room telemarketing.

In addition to the scammers, there are also hackers who can gain access to your account information if you send it by e-mail or if you give it to a site that is not secure or has a security hole.

Besides the signs of fraud and deception offline (i.e. in the real, non-virtual, world), be wary of salespeople who hide their true identity. Don't believe everything you read on the Internet. It's easier to post messages and set up a professional-looking Web page than it is to send solicitations by regular mail or advertise in a newspaper or magazine. Plus, it's free.

The SEC suggests downloading and printing a hard copy of any online solicitation that you are considering. Note the Internet address (URL) and the date and time that you saw the offer. Keep this information filed on a hard copy as well as a disk.

The SEC also suggests the following:

- If you want to invest in a fund company or other security online, first check with a financial adviser, your broker, or attorney.

- Find out from the online promoter where the firm is incorporated. Call that state's secretary of state to verify the information is true and ask for an annual report.

- Ask a librarian for information about the company, such as a payment analysis, credit report, lawsuits, liens, or judgments.

Getting help

If you think you've been the victim of fraud or deceptive practices, there are several places where you can report it.

1. Write to your sales representative's manager or the firm's compliance officer and ask for a written explanation.

2. Contact the SEC's Office of Investor Education and Assistance (U.S. Securities and Exchange Commission, Office of Investor Education and Assistance, Mail Stop 2–13, 450 Fifth Street, NW, Washington, D.C. 20549; phone: (202) 942-7040; fax: (202) 942-9634; e-mail: help@sec.gov). After receiving a complaint, one of their specialists will contact the firm, company, or individual that is the subject of the complaint. If the problem is not resolved, the SEC will tell you about your legal options. In addition, that office provides research and answers to your questions. The SEC will tell you if a broker or investment

Timesaver
Call the Security and Exchange Commission to find out about a company or investment before investing. You may find out the company has a bad track record and save yourself a lot of clean-up time (not to mention grief and money).

professional is licensed and if a company is registered with the SEC. The SEC also offers publications and holds periodic investors' town
meetings around the country.

3. Contact your state's securities regulator. The
North American Securities Administrators
Association (Toll-free: (888)846-2722; Internet
address: www.nasaa.org) will help you locate the
address and phone number for your state's
office.

Crooks hunt. How do you make sure that you're
not their prey? "Keep a firm hand on your wallet,"
Babson says.

Just the facts

- Don't trust that a stranger has your best interest
  at heart—investigate before investing.

- There are many red flags that indicate that
  you're dealing with a less than honest salesperson.

- The Internet provides a new medium for criminals, but the types of scams and tactics they use
  are similar to those used offline.

- On the Internet, everyone uses screen names,
  so you never know whom you are actually talking to.

Glossary

Automatic Reinvestment   Most mutual funds allow you to automatically reinvest income dividends and capital gain distributions. By reinvesting, you're buying additional shares and thereby dollar cost averaging.

Back-End Load   This is the sales commission charged when you sell shares from a back-loaded fund. This fee, used as a sales commission, usually phases out after 5 years.

Bid or Sell Price   The price a mutual fund pays to buy back shares. This price is the current net asset value minus any redemption fees or back-end loads.

Bond Fund   This type of mutual fund has a portfolio primarily made up of corporate, municipal, or federal government bonds. Bond funds are considered income funds because they often pay out dividends. Many of these funds are tax-free.

Bond Rating   Both Standard & Poor's and Moody's Investor Services evaluate the probability of a bond issuer defaulting by analyzing the financial stability of the issuer. Bonds are rated from AAA or Aaa, the top rating, to D, which means the issuer is currently

327

in default. Bonds with a BBB or Baa rating or below are considered high risk. Read the prospectus to find out the ratings of bonds in the portfolio and those that may be considered for purchase.

Capital Gain Distributions   When a fund sells a stock at a profit, it passes the profit along to shareholders in the form of capital gains. These gains are usually realized annually at the end of the year and are subject to short-term (held 12 months or less) or long-term (held more than 12 months) taxes.

Capital Growth   This occurs when the value of the mutual fund's securities increase in value. The result is a rise in the net asset value of the mutual fund shares.

Diversification   Spreading an investment among a variety of securities to reduce risk.

Dollar Cost Averaging   Investing a fixed sum at regular intervals. This investment technique has two advantages: you don't have to time the market to invest at market lows and it makes it easier to stomach investments made at market highs.

Exchange Privilege   Also known as conversion privilege, it allows you to transfer investments from one fund to another. Some brokers and fund families charge for these transactions.

Ex-Dividend Date   In order to receive dividends, you must own shares by this date, which is usually 4 days before the record date, or the date of distribution. On the ex-dividend date, the fund's net asset value is lowered by an amount equal to the dividend and/or capital gains distribution. This date is indicated by an "X" after the fund's name in publications that list closing net Asset Values.

Expense Ratio   The ratio of total expenses, which include management fees, 12(b)-1 charges (if any), the cost of shareholder mailings, and other administrative expenses, to net assets of the fund. You can find the E/R in the fund's prospectus.

401(k) Plan Many employers offer this type of retirement plan. Often, the employer matches all or part of your contribution, making this an especially good investment tool. In addition to salary reduction, depending on the company, contributions can be made by a "cash election" profit-sharing or stock bonus plan.

Front-End Load This is the sales fee taken from your investment and used to pay a sales commission.

Global Fund Also known as a world fund, this type of mutual fund invests in both U.S. and foreign securities.

Growth Fund The objective of this type of fund is long-term growth of capital. The portfolio is mostly stock.

Income Dividend Some mutual funds distribute interest and dividends, which are taxed as income.

Income Fund The objective of this type of mutual fund is to seek current income rather than capital growth.

Index Fund This type of fund seeks to mirror a broad-based index, most often the Standard & Poor's 500-stock index. Because it is not actively managed, there is usually a low management fee.

Individual Retirement Account (IRA) This is a personal, tax-sheltered retirement account that you can invest in if you meet certain requirements. Contributions are tax-deductible for some, depending on circumstances. Earnings in these plans can grow tax-deferred or, in the case of the Roth IRA, tax-free.

International Fund These mutual fund portfolios are made of foreign securities and carry more risk than domestic funds because of the difficulty in researching companies outside the United States and political volatility.

Investment Objective   Fund managers set financial goals, such as long-term growth or current income.

Keogh Plan   This is a tax-deferred retirement account. You can set one up if you're a self-employed individual or own a partnership business.

Load   About one-third of all mutual funds carry a load, or sales commission. Some loaded funds can carry commissions as high as 8.5 percent of the fund's offering price.

Low-Load Fund   Low-load funds typically have commission fees up to 3.5 percent.

Management Fee   This is the fee paid to the fund's portfolio manager(s). It usually ranges from .5–1 percent of the fund's asset value.

Money Market Fund   These low-risk funds pay money market interest rates. They typically invest in safe, liquid securities like bank certificates of deposit and U.S. government securities.

Municipal Bond Fund   These mutual funds provide tax-free income to their investors by investing in tax-exempt bonds issued by states, cities, and other local governments.

Mutual Fund   This is an open-end investment company that invests the pooled money of many people in a variety of securities.

Net Asset Value per Share   This is the current market value of a mutual fund share. It's calculated daily by adding together the fund's total assets, deducting liabilities, and dividing the difference by the number of outstanding shares.

No-Load Fund   This is a commission-free mutual fund that sells its shares at net asset value.

Offering Price This is the current net asset value per share plus any sales charges.

Payable Date This is the date on which distributions are paid to shareholders who don't want them reinvested.

Prospectus This publication gives a wealth of information about the mutual fund, the fund manager's objectives, loads (if any), and much more. It must contain certain information as required by the Securities and Exchange Commission.

Record Date Often the business day before the ex-dividend date, this date determines the shareholders, who then on record receive the fund's income dividend and/or net capital gains distribution that year.

Redemption Fee Some funds charge a redemption fee for redeeming shares.

Redemption Price Usually the current net asset value per share, this is the price at which a mutual fund's shares are redeemed by the fund.

Reinvestment Date Also known as the payable date, this is the date dividends and/or capital gains are reinvested.

Sector Fund This type of mutual fund invests in a specific industry, like health care or technology.

Short-term Municipal Bond Fund This is a mutual fund that invests in municipal bonds that have maturities of 2 years or less.

Simplified Employee Pension A simplified employee pension, or SEP for short, allows you to make contributions to your own plan, if you're self-employed, and your employees' plans. You can make contributions if you're the boss of a S-corporation or a C-corporation, as well.

Specialty Fund   This type of mutual fund invests in securities of a specific industry or group of industries or special types of securities.

Total Return   This is a measure of a mutual fund's performance. The total return includes yield—that is, dividends—interest, capital gains, if any, and changes in share price. It is calculated over a specified period of time. You can calculate total return by multiplying the number of shares you own by the net asset value per share. Then subtract your original investment from the result and divide that difference by the original investment, and multiply it by 100. (For example, if your shares are valued at $10,000 and your original investment was $5,000, divide $10,000 by $5,000, which equals 0.5. Multiply that by 100, and your portfolio increased, or had a total return of, 50 percent.) This equation assumes you are reinvesting capital gains and interest and dividends.

Trade Date   This is the date your shares were bought or sold.

Turnover Rate   This rate, measured in a percent, indicates the percent of the portfolio that is changed each year. A higher turnover rate is often associated with higher investment expenses because you'll owe short-term capital gains on any distributed profits. Funds with high turnover rates are usually aggressively managed, which means they carry a higher risk. Conservative funds have lower turnover rates, and consequently lower risk, because the manager is investing for the long term.

12(b)-1   This is a marketing fee used to cover some or all of the costs associated with advertising, sales literature, and dealer incentives. These charges are included in the total expense ratio figures, which are disclosed in the prospectus.

Yield   Usually expressed as a percentage of market price over a specified period of time, the yield is the interest or dividends prior to any gain or loss in the price per share.

Internet Resource Directory

Newspapers and magazines

Barron's (www.barrons.com) ranks the top 100 mutual fund managers and reviews mutual funds quarterly.

An online version of CNN's financial news can be found at www.cnnfn.com. The site has a CNNfn/Lipper Analytical Services' report on recent performance and pricing information on more than 5,000 U.S. mutual funds.

Money Magazine (www.moneymag.com) has the "Ultimate Guide to Mutual Funds" and other financial information.

The *Wall Street Journal* has an interactive edition at www.wsj.com. A subscription is required after the two-week initial trial.

James Glassman's Sunday columns for the *Washington Post* (www.washingtonpost.com) often include reports on mutual funds. The articles are posted at this site for two weeks.

At Morningstar's site (www.morningstar.com), you can get unbiased performance information on 1,700 mutual funds.

SmartMoney magazine's site (www.smartmoney.com) has a portfolio tracker that will monitor up to 10 mutual funds, a chart center that compares indicators, and articles.

Commercial

Quicken's site at www.quicken.com/investments contains information on mutual funds.

Hoover's Online (www.hoovers.com) has company information by industry, ticker symbol, location, and annual sales.

Wall Street Net at www.netresource.com/wsn/ has links to the three domestic stock exchanges—NASDAQ, American Stock Exchange, and NYSE Net (for the New York Stock Exchange).

Value Line (www.valueline.com) has mutual fund manager ratings.

E*TRADE (www.etrade.com) has mutual fund research and screening tools.

Motley Fools (www.fool.com) teaches investors how to take control of their finances.

There's a site at www.fundalarm.com that contains information on recent fund manager changes.

Year 2K

The Year 2000 Information Center (www.year2000.com) is a good source of information for those interested in the Year 2000 problem.

Investment clubs

To learn how to start an investment club, contact the National Association of Investors Corporation (NAIC) at (248)583-6242, or write to them at P.O.

Box 220, Royal Oak, MI 48068. The NAIC Web site is www.better-investing.org/index.html.

Kids

Money Camps, Inc. (www.moneycamps.com) offers financial literacy programs for children and for women along with recreation and camaraderie. For more information, write to Money Camps, Inc., 4102 Washington Rd., West Palm Beach, FL 33405. You can also reach them by phone at (888)837-9446 or fax at (561)838-9442.

The Young Investor Web site (www.younginvestor. com) is designed to get kids interested in investing.

Cash University (www.cashuniversity.com) helps parents teach children money management skills.

Investment companies

Vanguard (www.vanguard.com)

T. Rowe Price (www.troweprice.com)

Fidelity (www.fidelity.com)

Strong (www.strong-funds.com)

Charles Schwab (www.schwab.com)

Capital Growth Management Funds (www. cgmfunds.com)

Franklin-Templeton (www.franklin-templeton.com)

Invesco Funds Group, Inc. (www.invesco.com)

Janus Funds (www.janus.com)

Kemper Funds (www.kemper.com)

PBHG Funds (www.pbhgfunds.com)

Scudder Funds (www.funds.scudder.com)

Government and nonprofit sites

The nonprofit trade association Mutual Fund Education Alliance sponsors a Web site at www.mfea.com, where you can create a customized portfolio tracker. The site has a database of more than 1,000 no-load mutual funds and Web site links, educational information, investing topics for children and women, and an investment planning calculator.

The American Association of Individual Investors (AAII) has an educational Web site at www.aaii.com geared toward the individual investor. Some articles are accessible to surfers, but much more is available to members. For more information, contact the AAII at 625 N. Michigan Ave., Chicago, IL 60611. You can reach AAII by phone at (800)428-2244 or (312)280-0170 or by fax at (312)280-9883.

The North American Securities Administrators Association (NASAA) (www.nasaa.org) helps protect investors. Their Web site has links to state security commissioners' sites. For more information, contact NASAA at 10 G Street, NE, Suite 710, Washington, D.C. 20002. The phone number is (202)737-0900 and the fax is (202)783-3571.

If you've been the victim of fraud or want to file a complaint against your broker, contact the Securities and Exchange Commission. Their Web site (www.sec.gov) has a searchable database of corporate information. You can also get investment assistance there. For more information, write the SEC at Office of Investor Education and Assistance, Mail Stop 2–13, 450 Fifth Street, NW, Washington, D.C., 20549, or call (202) 942-7040. The fax number is (202)942-9634. The e-mail address is help@sec.gov.

Recommended Reading
List

Dr. Tightwad's Money-Smart Kids
Janet Bodnar
Price: $15.00
Paperback—280 pages 2nd edition (1997)
Kiplinger Books
ISBN: 081292889X

Mom, Can I Have That?: Dr. Tightwad Answers Your Kids' Questions About Money
Janet Bodnar
Price: $13.00
Paperback—208 pages (1996)
Kiplinger Books
ISBN: 0812927540

Cyberspace and the Law: Your Rights and Duties in the On-Line World
Edward A. Cavazos and Gavino Morin
Price: $21.50
Paperback—220 pages (1994)
MIT Press
ISBN: 0262531232

Consumer Reports Mutual Funds Book; Minimize Risk, Maximize Returns
Greg Daughtery
Price: $22.95
Hardcover (1994)
Consumer Reports Books
ISBN: 0890437238

Web Security and Commerce
Simson Garfinkel and Gene Spafford
Price: $32.95
Paperback—483 pages (1997)
O'Reilly & Assoc.
ISBN: 1565922691

The Complete Idiot's Guide to Making Money on Wall Street
Christy Heady
Price: $18.95
Paperback—423 pages (1994)
Alpha Books
ISBN: 1567615090

Get a Financial Life: Personal Finance in Your Twenties and Thirties
Beth Kobliner
Price: $12.00
Paperback—283 pages (1996)
Fireside
ISBN: 0684812134

Get a Financial Life: Personal Finance in Your Twenties and Thirties
Beth Kobliner
Price: $12.00
Audio Cassette Cassette edition (1997)
Simon & Schuster (Audio)
ISBN: 0671575570

The Complete Idiot's Guide to Making Money With Mutual Funds
Alan Lavine, Gail Liberman, Jonathan D. Pond
Price: $18.95
Paperback—361 pages 2nd edition (1998)
Alpha Books
ISBN: 0028624130

A Random Walk Down Wall Street: Including a Life-Cycle Guide to Personal Investing
Burton Gordon Malkiel
Price: $15.95
Paperback 6th edition (1996)
W.W. Norton & Company
ISBN: 0393315290

Overcoming Overspending: A Winning Plan for Spenders and Their Partners
Olivia Mellan; Sherrie Christie (Contributor)
Price: $12.95
Paperback—216 pages (1997)
Walker & Co
ISBN: 0802774954

Money Harmony—Resolving Money Conflicts in Your Life and Relationship
Olivia Mellan and Warren Farrell
Price: $9.95
Paperback Reprint edition (1995)
Walker & Co
ISBN: 0802774563

The 9 Steps to Financial Freedom
Suze Orman
Price: $23.00
Hardcover—278 pages (1997)
Crown Pub
ISBN: 0517707918

NetLaw: Your Rights in the Online World
Lance J. Rose
Price: $19.95
Paperback—372 pages (1994)
Osborne/McGraw-Hill
ISBN: 0078820774

The Millionaire Next Door: The Surprising Secrets of America's Wealthy
Thomas J. Stanley, William D. Danko
Price: $14.00
Paperback—272 pages (1998)
Pocket Books
ISBN: 0671015206

The Vanguard Guide to Investing During Retirement: Managing Your Assets in Retirement
Vanguard Investment Group
Price: $17.95
Paperback—306 pages 2nd edition (1997)
McGraw-Hill
ISBN: 0070668922

A

Account agreement, 207–8
Accountants, 263
  fraud and, 313–17
Adjusted gross income, 258
  Roth IRAs and, 97–98
Advisers. *See* Financial advisers;
  Mutual fund managers
Affordability of mutual funds, 47
Age, investment strategies by,
  73–90
  20 and under, 73–74
  20-30, 74–82
  30-40, 82–85
  40-50, 85–87
  50-60, 87–89
  60 and over, 88–90
Aggressive growth funds, 134,
  157, 161–62
American Association of
  Individual Investors
  (AAII), 141–42, 277–79,
  303, 338
American Association of Retired
  Persons (AARP), 55–56
American Stock Exchange, 300
Analysts, stock predictions and,
  145–46
Androshick, Julie, 276
Annual reports, 136
Annual return, average, 137–38
Apple Macintosh computers,
  Year 2000 and, 304–5
Approximation method, 278–79
Asset allocation funds, 51, 174
Asset-based commissions, 205
Asset classes, 48–50
  risk and, 127–28
Attitudes toward retirement,
  22–24
Automatic investments, 60, 162
Automatic reinvestment, 222,
  327
  taxes and, 252–53
Average, 11–13
  method for computing,
  11–12
Average cost methods, 255–56

Average return, 7–8, 137–38
Averaging, dollar cost, 6, 114,
  222–24, 328

B

Babson, Richard, 311, 312–13,
  319
Back-end loads, 273, 327
Back-loaded funds, 273, 327
Bait-and-switch technique, 319
Bajkowski, John, 234–36, 239
Balanced funds, 158, 162. *See
  also* Asset allocation funds
Barra Growth, 162–63
Barra Value, 162–63
Barron's, 298, 335
Benefits of investing, 1–41
Better Business Bureau, 312
Bid price, 327
Black Monday (October 19,
  1987), 131
Blatant fraud, 308–9
Bodner, Janet, 36–38
Bohlen, Cindy, 46–47, 48, 52,
  53–54, 275
"Bond chasers," 186
Bond funds, 70–71, 178–87, 327
  advantages of, 180–81
  bonds versus, 179–81
  buying, 185–87
  disadvantages of, 181
  interest rates and, 183
  risk and, 119, 120–22,
    129–30, 178–79, 183–84
  stock funds versus, 181,
    182–83, 185–86
  types of, 50–51, 178, 184–85
  yield and, 181–82
Bond funds managers, 182, 183
Bond ratings, 184, 186, 327–28
Bonds, 178–83
  bond funds versus, 179–81
  buying, 185–87
Books, recommended, 339–42
Bradley, Susan, 40, 56
Brokerage firms, online, 301–2,
  337

343

National Commission on
  Retirement Policy, 28
Natural resources funds, 170
Nemec, Carol, 75, 219,
  232–33
Net assets, 146–47
  value per share, 212, 330
Newspapers, online, 298–99,
  335–36
New York Stock Exchange, 300
No-load funds, 135, 146–48,
  271–72, 273, 279, 330
Nondeductible IRAs, 99–100
Nonprofit Web sites, 302–3,
  337–38
North American Securities
  Administrators
  Association (NASAA),
  302, 308, 309, 325, 338
Norwitz, Steve, 108–9, 259

O

Objectives, investment, 69–70,
  153, 330
Offering price, 331
One-stop shopping, 208–11, 278
Online investing, 284–87
  hackers and, 287–88
  researching and trading,
    293–98
  security concerns, 288–93,
    319–24
Online portfolio trackers, 63,
  69, 212–13, 295
Online resource directory,
  298–305, 335–38
Online Tax Encyclopedia, 265
Overcoming Overspending
  (Mellan), 14–17
Overspenders, 16–17

P

Payable date, 331
Payden, Joan, 135–37
Payment methods, to financial
  advisers, 204–6
PBHG Funds, 337

Pensions, 31, 32
Personality of financial advisers,
  203
Personality types
  investing styles and, 14–17
  retirement funding and,
    22–25
Physical security, online, 292
Planners, retirement funding
  and, 23
Political turmoil, as risk, 117,
  123
Portfolio, 133–53
  criteria for, 134–37
  fund performance and,
    137–38
  prospectus, 149–53
  research and, 134–37
  risk, 117, 123–24
  tax planning and, 262–63
  tracking, 211–14
    online, 63, 69, 212–13,
      295
  turnover rate and, 139–41
Prepayment risk, 183–84
Preservation of capital, 69–70
Privacy on the Internet, 290
Producer Price Index, 237
Professional management,
  46–47, 141–44
Prospectus, 149–53, 331
  buying and selling shares,
    152
  expenses, 150–51
  financial highlights,
    151–52
  investment objective, 153
  investment policies and
    practices, 152–53
  management, 152
Purchasing mutual funds. *See*
  Buying mutual funds
Purchasing power, inflation
  and, 10

Q

Quicken, 212–13, 286
Quote.com, 286